CRUSADE FOR FREEDOM

CRUSADE FOR FREEDOM

Women of the Antislavery Movement

By ALMA LUTZ

BEACON PRESS : BOSTON

Library of Congress catalog card number: 68–12841

Published simultaneously in Canada by Saunders of Toronto, Ltd.

Beacon Press books are published
under the auspices
of the Unitarian Universalist Association

Printed in the United States of America

ACKNOWLEDGMENTS

I am grateful to the many librarians who helped me locate letters of antislavery women – especially to John Alden of the Rare Book Division of the Boston Public Library, which has an outstanding Antislavery Collection; to Miss Reid and Miss Cassidy of the Worcester Historical Society; to Margaret S. Grierson of the Sophia Smith Collection, Smith College; to the staffs of the American Antiquarian Society, Worcester, Massachusetts, and the Arthur and Elizabeth Schlesinger Library, Radcliffe College; and to Frederick B. Tolles, Director of the Friends' Historical Library, Swarthmore College, for the loan, through the Boston Athenaeum, of a photostatic copy of *A Brief Sketch of the Life and Labors of Elizabeth Heyrick*. I am also indebted to the following library staffs: the Boston Athenaeum; the Clements Library, Ann Arbor, Michigan; Columbia University Library; the Friends' Historical Library, Swarthmore College; Connecticut College Library; Cornell University Library; Library of Congress; Michigan Historical Collection, University of Michigan; and the Vassar College Library.

CONTENTS

PREFACE

Women made an outstanding contribution to the abolition of Negro slavery, and at a time when the participation of women in public reform movements was frowned upon. The names of a few of them are mentioned in histories of the antislavery movement, but in general their important work has been overlooked. Fortunately, however, they have left an inspiring record in their personal letters which have been preserved in a few libraries and historical societies. This book tells their story.

We are reminded of these women today as we see history repeating itself in race and color prejudice and in the too prevalent phrases, "white backlash" and "black power." As Lucy Stone explained in 1863, "Slavery is let down in the hearts of the people of this country deeper than they themselves know."

The antislavery women, believing wholeheartedly in the American dream of equal rights for all, helped create public sentiment for the Thirteenth, Fourteenth, and Fifteenth Amendments to the Federal Constitution and their successors have finally implemented the Fourteenth and Fifteenth Amendments by means of the Civil Rights Act. Laws, however, although setting the standard for justice, do not immediately eradicate traditional prejudice and antagonism. In the words of Abby Kelley Foster, "It is only by labor, incessant labor, in season and out of season, that we can create such a public sentiment as we need."

Such a public sentiment can be achieved today only by a better understanding of the troubled history of race relations in this country and by rededication to the ideal of equal rights for all citizens.

ALMA LUTZ

Boston
May 1967

When the true history of the antislavery cause shall be written, woman will occupy a large space in its pages; for the cause of the slave has been peculiarly woman's cause. Her heart and her conscience have supplied in large degree its motive and mainspring. Her skill, industry, patience and perseverance have been wonderfully manifest in every trial hour. Not only did her feet run on "willing errands," and her fingers do the work which in large degree supplied the sinews of war, but her deep moral convictions, and her tender human sensibilities, found convincing and persuasive expression by her pen and her voice.

FREDERICK DOUGLASS——*Life and Times of Frederick Douglass*

CRUSADE FOR FREEDOM

CHAPTER I

Voices Crying in the Wilderness

Elizabeth Margaret Chandler's thoughts were far from Philadelphia. They were on the wide stormy Atlantic, on a slave ship carrying a cargo of frightened Africans in chains. She relived with them the anguish they felt when, torn from their families, they were herded into the crowded hold. She sensed the desperation of their proud chief as he contemplated slavery. As always when deeply moved, she turned to poetry. She wrote:

> The slave ship was winding her course o'er the ocean . . .
> Though heavy with guilt was the freight that she bore . . .
> And ceaseless the groans of the wretches ascended
> That from friends and from country forever she tore. . . .[1]

Through six verses she continued, until the proud chief, unable to face the future, burst his bonds and plunged into the sea.

Pleased with her poem as she read it over, she gave it a title, "The Slave Ship," signed it Emily, and sent it to the new magazine, *The Casket,* published in Philadelphia, which offered prizes for poetry. For some time Elizabeth Chandler had been writing poems and sending them to newspapers without her signature, for she was an earnest Quaker and tried to guard against vanity and the pride of authorship. Although this was the first poem she had written about Negro slavery, the subject had weighed on her conscience, and the sermon of a Quaker minister inspired "The Slave Ship."

Elizabeth Margaret Chandler was born of Quaker parents in Centre Delaware, December 24, 1807. When she was a year old her mother died, and her father, Thomas Chandler, a prosperous farmer and physician, took her and her two young brothers to Philadelphia to live with their grandmother, Elizabeth Evans, a devout Quaker. He continued the practice of medicine in Philadelphia until his death eight years later, when Elizabeth Evans assumed the entire responsibility of the Chandler children. Elizabeth Chandler attended the Friends' School. Here her sympathy for the slave was aroused and she listened eagerly to discussions of slavery at home and among her teachers.

Very early, the Pennsylvania Quakers had responded to the antislavery sentiments of George Fox, who had warned of the spiritual danger of the master-slave relationship. In 1688 the Germantown Friends had issued the first antislavery document in America, a protest against slavery presented at their monthly meeting. Later the Quaker minister, John Woolman, and Anthony Benezet, the schoolmaster, exerted such influence against slavery among Quakers through their speaking and writing that in 1776 the Philadelphia Yearly Meeting disowned members who refused to free their slaves.[2] Elizabeth Chandler revered both Woolman and Benezet and her tribute to them was a poem.

There were slaves in all the colonies when the Declaration of Independence was issued. Vermont, adopting a constitution in 1777, provided for the abolition of slavery. Massachusetts soon followed in 1780, through a provision in its constitution which declared that all men are by nature free, and New Hampshire followed her example in 1784. Pennsylvania initiated gradual emancipation in 1780, as did Connecticut and Rhode Island in 1784.[3]

The National Constitutional Convention of 1787, however, failed to face the issue of slavery. The importance of avoiding controversy and holding the colonies together prevented free and full discussion of the subject. As John Jay Chapman so aptly expressed it,[4] "slavery was a sleeping serpent" under the table at the Constitutional Convention. Petitions from Quakers in several states, urging the abolition of the slave trade, were presented to the first Congress, but the committee appointed to inquire into the powers of Congress reported that the Congress could not interfere with slavery in the States and that slaveholders were entitled to legislation providing for the return of fugitive slaves. In 1793 the first fugitive slave law was enacted, but in 1794 slave trade with foreign countries was prohibited and in 1808 the importation of slaves was banned. Nevertheless, smuggling was frequent.

Public opinion regarding slavery was generally apathetic. Only among Quakers was there a gradual but definite movement against it. In the South as well as in the North, many recognized slavery as an evil, but at the same time felt nothing could be done about it. To quiet their consciences, some joined the Colonization Society, founded in 1816, which advocated the colonizing of free Negroes in Africa.

As new states were admitted to the Union, a balance-of-power struggle developed which was temporarily solved by admitting states in pairs, a free state with a slave state. The admission of Missouri as a slave state precipitated a bitter contest. Although Maine was paired with Missouri, the debate continued with increasing bitterness, rousing the whole country and ending finally in 1820 in the Missouri Compromise, by which Missouri was admitted as a slave state but slavery was forever prohibited in the remainder of the Louisiana Purchase north of the thirty-sixth degree, thirtieth parallel. Sensing the significance of this debate, Thomas Jefferson, writing from Monticello, declared, "This momentous question, like a firebell in the night, awakened and filled me with terror. I considered it at once the knell of the Union."

At the time of the Missouri Compromise agitation, Elizabeth Margaret Chandler was thirteen years old. She listened eagerly to the serious discussion of the subject at home. With her grandmother and aunts, she attended the women's meetings of the Friends, where the education of free Negroes and the use of free produce were discussed. Here the warning of the Long Island Quaker, Elias Hicks, was heeded and repeated – that those who used sugar, rice, molasses, and cotton produced by slave labor shared the guilt of the slaveholder. The use of free products appealed strongly to these women as a peaceable method of protest against slavery and they held up the zeal of the women of the Revolution who refused to drink tea taxed by the British as an example to be followed. Among them was the Quaker minister, Lucretia Mott, who was an inspiration to them all.

A few of them were in touch with antislavery Quakers in England and had heard of their success in abolishing the slave trade and their continuing efforts to abolish slavery in the Dominions. One of these English Quakers, Elizabeth Heyrick, came vividly into their lives through her pamphlet, reprinted in Philadelphia in 1824, which advocated immediate, not gradual, emancipation as the "shortest, safest, and most effectual means of getting rid of West Indian slavery." She gave them much to think about, for they had favored gradual emancipation and colonization in Africa. It gave them courage to find a woman writing on the subject and her ideas spanning the Atlantic. From an antislavery paper which circulated among them, *The Genius of Universal Emancipation,* published by still another Quaker, Benjamin Lundy,

Elizabeth Margaret Chandler

they soon learned that Elizabeth Heyrick's proposal of immediate emancipation had won the support of Wilberforce and other leading British abolitionists. Benjamin Lundy now published her *Immediate, Not Gradual Emancipation* in his paper, giving it wider circulation. Regarded as too radical in Philadelphia and among abolitionists elsewhere in the United States at this time, her ideas nevertheless left their mark and were soon to revolutionize the American antislavery movement.

All this made a deep impression on young Elizabeth Chandler and started her on her way to becoming one of the earliest American antislavery poets. "The Slave Ship," which she sent to *The Casket* in January, 1826, was awarded third prize, and was copied in Benjamin Lundy's paper, the *Genius of Universal Emancipation*. When Benjamin Lundy learned from Elizabeth Chandler's friends in Philadelphia that she had written "The Slave Ship," he at once asked to meet her and suggested that from then on she send her antislavery poems to the *Genius*. In this way he widened her influence just as he had widened that of Elizabeth Heyrick, for "The Slave Ship" was followed by "The Slave's Appeal," "The Recaptured Slave," and many other poems. On July 4, 1827, an article of hers in the *Genius* pointed out the contrast between the principles stated in the Declaration of Independence and the acts of the government of the United States in relation to slavery. Impressed by her clear thinking on the subject of slavery and her ability to express her views forcibly and well, Lundy asked her to take charge of a ladies' department which he wished to add to the *Genius of Universal Emancipation* and she accepted. Only one other woman, Sarah J. Hale, had entered the field of journalism, and Mrs. Hale's *Ladies' Magazine*, issued in 1828, was not a crusading journal, but was very ladylike, and intent on encouraging women to remain in their proper sphere.

The more Elizabeth Chandler heard about Benjamin Lundy, the more she admired his dedication to the cause and his courage. Benjamin Lundy, born in New Jersey, had gone to Virginia as a boy to learn the saddlers' trade. Moving on to Ohio where he worked as a saddler, he continued to be so aroused by the slave trade that he organized an antislavery society which he called the Union Humane Society and began sending articles to an antislavery paper there. His own publishing venture started in Ohio in 1821 when, with a dollar and only six subscribers, he issued the *Genius of Universal Emancipation*. He drew subscribers from abolition societies which were being formed in the border states. Traveling far and wide on foot to preach his message of gradual emancipation and colonization and to get subscribers for the *Genius,* he often carried his press on his back so that he could bring out his paper wherever he might be. In 1824 he moved to Baltimore, where the influence of the *Genius* reached beyond the abolitionists in the border states to the antislavery Quakers in Philadelphia, among them James and Lucretia Mott. It became known in Boston and in Bennington, Vermont, where it roused the interest of a young editor, William Lloyd Garrison, whom Lundy persuaded to come to Baltimore to help him edit the *Genius*. Garrison joined the staff of the *Genius* in 1829, the same year in which Elizabeth Chandler took charge of the *Ladies' Repository*.

In the *Genius* of September 2, 1829, when Lundy announced his partnership with William Lloyd Garrison, he also stated, "I have obtained the aid of an amiable and highly talented female writer, who will have the principal direction of a ladies' department to be devoted . . . to 'philanthropy and literature.' Though she does not permit her name to appear . . . as an editor, I most cordially recommend her invaluable and praiseworthy performance to the friendly attention not only of philanthropists of her own sex, but to every advocate of justice and humanity and every admirer of literary merit."

Elizabeth Chandler did not move to Baltimore to edit the ladies' department, but handled the work from Philadelphia. She was now twenty-two years old, a young woman of pleasing appearance, with dark friendly eyes and a happy expression, dark hair piled high on her head. By this time her grandmother had died and she and her brother, Thomas, made their home with their aunt, Ruth Evans, to whom they were devoted. Work for the *Genius* took most of her time, but she read widely and attended meetings of the Ladies' Free Produce Society. With a group of liberal Quakers, including James and Lucretia Mott, who felt impelled to rededicate themselves to the principles of George Fox, William Penn, and the early Quakers, she had separated from the orthodox Friends and become a member of Philadelphia's Hicksite Society.

The *Genius,* with its high mission, challenged her to give it her very best. In 1829 it was a weekly paper of eight pages, nine by thirteen inches, running four columns to a page. The cut of an eagle soared above the title and underneath were the familiar words from the Declaration of Independence announcing that "all men are created equal and endowed by their Creator with certain inalienable rights. . . ." Elizabeth Chandler not only conducted the ladies' department, but it was almost entirely written by her, filling from two to three columns of every issue with poetry and essays. She introduced it with "An Appeal to the Ladies of the United States," taking for granted that the great majority of women acknowledged the injustice of the slave system and that few were deaf to the cry of suffering. "We wish to impress you," she wrote, "with a firm steady conviction of the manifest injustice and pernicious effects attendant on slavery, and with a deep sense of your own responsibility in either directly or indirectly lending it your encouragement." To those who looked upon slavery as a necessary evil and absolved themselves from responsibility by persuading themselves that the slaves were happy, she pointed out the stark facts. To those who protested that she should appeal to men rather than to women to eradicate the evil, she retorted, "You deceive yourselves, American women! Your power is sufficient for its extinction. . . . We would have you exert your influence by instilling into the minds of your offspring a deep-felt sense of their duty as men and Christians to break the fetters of the oppressed." She pointed out to them that by buying the products of slave labor they gave their support to the slave system and she urged them to buy only the products of free labor and by their patronage to make them fashionable. "Will you stand boldly and nobly forth in the face of the world," she asked, "and declare that American women will never be tamely made the instruments of oppression."

When she was criticized by more conservative women for encouraging "females" to step out of their sphere by becoming public advocates of abolition, she replied that she had no wish to see her sex transformed into a race of politicians, but could not see how pleading for the suffering slave could be regarded as unfeminine or at variance with right principles. Women, she contended, did not advocate the emancipation of slaves for political reasons, but because slavery was "an outrage against humanity and morality and religion, because it is criminal, . . . and because a great number of her own sex are among its victims."

"It is because we highly prize . . . the domestic privileges of our sex," she continued, "that we would have them extended to those who are less fortunate than ourselves . . . We would have the name of *Woman* a security for the rights of the sex. These rights are withheld from the female slave: and as we value and would demand them for ourselves, must we not ask them for her?"[5]

She was definitely in the vanguard of the woman's rights group in the antislavery movement, claiming, as a matter of course, her right as a woman to alleviate suffering and to correct injustice.

Both Lundy and Garrison kept in touch with the antislavery movement in Great Britain and its efforts for emancipation in the West Indies, and published reports contrasting the encouraging activity of the British with the apathy of Americans. Likewise, Elizabeth Chandler, in the Ladies' Repository, called attention to the Ladies' Antislavery Societies in Great Britain, hoping always to arouse her American sisters to similar zeal. She also published extracts of Elizabeth Heyrick's *Letters on Colonial Slavery*.

In a series of letters, "To the Ladies of Baltimore," she appealed to the women of the South, pointing out to them the horrors of the domestic slave trade which forcibly separated husbands and wives, parents and children. She told them of the New Orleans slave market, of the cruel crowding of slaves in the holds of ships transporting them from Baltimore to New Orleans. "It is a dark and fearful wickedness to make merchandise of men," she warned them, and appealed to them to use their influence against it, suggesting that they form associations to spread knowledge of what could be done. She urged them to teach the slaves among them religion and morality. In a sense, she was as courageous, as bold, and as devastating in her indictment of slavery as was William Lloyd Garrison.[6]

Both Lundy and Garrison valued highly her work for the *Genius,* her industry, intelligence, and dedication. They especially noted the wide appeal of her poems. Her essays did not always deal with slavery and the need of emancipation. She also pleaded for women's education, as was natural for a Quaker. She was convinced that the preservation of democratic government depended upon a well-informed, educated, alert people. She made a special plea for women to serve as teachers, observing that there was no fault or lack in the female mind, but a need for more and better education for women.

Early in 1830 misfortune disrupted the *Genius* for a few months and it ceased publication as a weekly, continuing as a monthly, in more compact form, at one dollar a year. The gentle, soft-spoken Lundy had brought a firebrand to the *Genius* in William Lloyd Garrison, whose vehement, harsh language and advocacy of immediate emancipation in his editorials alienated subscribers, until their numbers, never sufficient, fell off alarmingly. Upon learning that Francis Todd of Newburyport, Massachusetts, had transported a cargo of slaves in chains from Baltimore to the slave market in New Orleans, Garrison rebuked him in the *Genius,* calling him and his captain, "highway robbers and murderers . . ." fit for the "lowest depths of perdition."[7] Todd countered with a libel suit against the editors, with the result that Garrison was declared guilty and fined. Unable to pay the fine, Garrison spent the next two months in the Baltimore jail until the wealthy New York merchant and abolitionist, Arthur Tappan, heard of his predicament and sent Lundy the money to pay Garrison's fine and obtain his release, adding as well $100 to help the *Genius* continue publication. Lundy and Garrison dissolved their partnership amicably and Garrison returned to Boston. Lundy carried on alone, cheered by the steady help of the editor of the ladies' department who remained undismayed during the upheaval.

During the summer of 1830, however, even Elizabeth Chandler made herself less available by moving to the Territory of Michigan with her aunt and her brother, Thomas, who, like so many young men, wanted to try his fortune in the West. They settled near the village of Tecumseh, about sixty miles southwest of Detroit. So committed was Elizabeth to her work for the *Genius* and the antislavery cause that she carried on her editorial duties from Michigan with renewed devotion. The journey West, the new scenes, the semi-wilderness in which they settled were filled with interest for her which shone through her writing. There were Quakers in the Raisin River settlement where the Chandlers located, and as several in the group were friends of Benjamin Lundy, this at once established a bond between them.

The land which Thomas Chandler had purchased was situated on the Raisin River and here he built a log cabin for the family. Elizabeth named it Hazelbank. They had brought their most cherished possessions with them and soon their log cabin was a comfortable home, with a portrait of their antislavery hero and friend, Dr. Benjamin Rush, hung on the wall. "The front of our house," wrote Elizabeth to her aunt, Jane Howell, in Philadelphia, "looks quite pretty with the vine that creeps around the door and one of the windows. Every morning it gives us a fresh and luxuriant blow of morning glories which remain in bloom the whole day."[8]

She was often lonesome for her Philadelphia friends, but they corresponded with her faithfully and kept her up-to-date on antislavery news. The Chandlers were great readers and they missed the books so readily available in Philadelphia. This was soon remedied when the Raisin River Quakers formed the Adrian Library Association, each family buying shares. Newspapers from Philadelphia, New York, and Boston were generously circulated by the few families subscribing to them. Occasionally a Quaker from Mount Pleasant, Ohio, delivered a course of lectures in the schoolhouse on chemistry, astronomy, and natural philosophy, and Elizabeth commented to a Philadelphia friend, "The character of the people here is decidedly intelligent, and that in no trifling degree. . . . Bumpkins are very rare and the young people are growing up respectable and intelligent."

In spite of all the hard work involved in establishing a home on the frontier, Elizabeth Chandler found time to carry on her work for the *Genius* and for reading and enjoying the beauties of nature which inspired many poems. She had always been interested in the Indians, who had been dispossessed by the white man of their lands. Here on the frontier, her thoughts turned more often to them and her concern for their problems was expressed in "The Appeal of the Choctaw" and other poems.

To friends in the East who feared that in her new home, far from an active group of abolitionists, she might forget the sufferings of the slave, she replied in character with her poem, "O Tell Me Not, I Shall Forget." To her aunt in Philadelphia, she wrote, "I have chosen my lot, and *am satisfied* with it. I believe that I am in my place and that we did well in coming here."[9]

Benjamin Lundy was particularly concerned because she had settled in such a remote place, far from the centers of antislavery activity. He corresponded with her frequently. "My valued friend," he wrote her in March, 1831, "if thee but knew of half the good thee is doing in the holy cause to which thee has so nobly devoted thy attention for a few years, I am sure thee would see the propriety of placing thyself in a situation where thee might have every advantage that the most extensive and early information of passing events would give thee. . . . I have seen many of thy articles copied into more than 20 papers – some of them introduced in terms of high commendation. But if it must be so – if thee cannot see thy way clear to take up thy residence where thee could benefit by the advantages above mentioned, rest assured that I shall use every effort to furnish thee with whatever thee may request, or that I may consider needful to thee." Then he added, "It rejoices me to find thee so ardent in the good cause."[10]

Before he left on a long, difficult journey to Texas and Mexico, where he hoped to settle free Negroes, he told her who would print the *Genius* in his absence and where to send her packet of articles and poems. He also sent her books, pamphlets, and magazines to keep her informed and asked William Lloyd Garrison to mail her his *Liberator* regularly. Not only had she heard of the publication of the *Liberator*, January 1, 1831, from her Philadelphia friends, but the first issue had come to southern Michigan to some of the Quaker settlers, and she, wholly in sympathy with Garrison's militancy, and his call for immediate emancipation, rejoiced that another antislavery paper was circulating. In fact she was soon having a small part in the *Liberator*. So impressed had Garrison been by her work for the *Genius*, that when the *Liberator* was in its second year he announced the introduction of a ladies' department, believing it would "give a new impetus to the cause of emancipation."[11] Then he proceeded to make use of Elizabeth Chandler to introduce the *Liberator's* ladies' department by reprinting from the *Genius* her stirring appeal to women, *Our Own Sex*. He continued to reprint from the *Genius* many of her poems, her *Letters on Slavery to Isabel,* and many of her challenging appeals for the interest of women and for the purchase of Free Produce. In a sense, she conducted the ladies' department of the *Liberator* through 1832, as well as that of the *Genius.*

In the *Genius,* she continued to prod women to feel a responsibility for and to take a more active part in antislavery work, repeatedly holding up as examples the Female Antislavery Societies in Great Britain. She noted with satisfaction the formation of Female Antislavery Societies in New England, adding "Such associations ought long since have been established in every State and Territory in the Union. It appears to us that the Females in this land are without excuse for their heartless indifference to the miserable conditions of so many of their countrymen." She called attention again and again to the importance of buying Free Produce and told of the Ladies Free Produce Society in Philadelphia and the Association for Promoting the Manufacture of Free Cotton. Her poems, "Slave Produce," "The Sugar Plum," and "Oh Press Me Not To Taste Again," dealing with the use of slavery-tainted sweets, were very popular among abolitionists. Many of her poems were sung as hymns at antislavery meetings, and reprinted in other papers.

In the spring of 1832, Benjamin Lundy wrote her praising her work, adding, "Thee is beginning to see the fruits of thy labors. Already the effusions of thy muse have attracted the attention of thousands. O suffer not that harp to rust, nor hang it on the Willow tree."[12]

That same spring, after a journey to the Wilberforce Negro settlement in Ontario, Canada, Lundy stopped for a visit with the Chandlers and renewed his acquaintance with several of the Quakers in the community, stimulating antislavery sentiment there to such an extent that within a few months Elizabeth Chandler and Laura Haviland, a Quaker from New York, organized the first antislavery society in Michigan among the Raisin River Valley Quakers in their log meetinghouse.

Following the progress of the antislavery movement in the East through the columns of the *Genius* and the *Liberator,* Elizabeth Chandler learned of Prudence Crandall's courageous decision to enroll a Negro student in her academy for young ladies in Canterbury, Connecticut. Commenting in her column under the heading, "The Canterbury Persecution," she wrote, "We have no acquaintance with Prudence Crandall, but our sympathies are warmly interested for her . . . . The spirit which existed in Connecticut in the days of Cotton Mather and witchcraft seems to have revived again in the town of Canterbury. . . ."[13] She herself was moved to write a poem, "To Prudence Crandall."

She commented as well in the *Genius* and with praise on the publication of the leaflet, *An Appeal in Favor of That Class of Americans Called Africans* by a Boston author, Lydia Maria Child. Even more important was the good news that Great Britain had abolished slavery in her colonies in August, 1833, that abolitionists had gathered in Philadelphia to organize the American Antislavery Society, that Lucretia Mott's voice had been heeded in that convention exclusively of men, and that immediately afterward a Philadelphia Female Antislavery Society had been formed.

When she read in 1834 that Female Antislavery Societies had also been organized in Boston and New York, Providence, Rhode Island, and Portland, Maine, and Amesbury, Massachusetts, she declared, "There is a spirit abroad that we hope may never again slumber till the work of emancipation is fully accomplished." She now began to feel that her efforts in the *Genius* were bearing fruit and had no regrets that she had sacrificed literary reputation to antislavery poetry and propaganda. "Our cause is a righteous one and worth every effort," she wrote a friend. "There are times when I feel as if I could go unflinching to the stake or the rack, if I might by that means advance it."[14]

She emphasized in the *Genius* the importance of supporting the right method of emancipation, pointing out the fallacies of colonization and gradual emancipation, both of which she called unsound in principle. The Colonization Society, she added, was not an antislavery society, although many believed it to be and mistakenly supported its activities. She had been completely won over by William Lloyd Garrison's exposé of the American Colonization Society, *Thoughts on African Colonization,* published in 1832. On this subject, she had moved far beyond her colleague and employer, Benjamin Lundy.

Unfortunately, however, these were her last battle cries; in the spring of 1834, she was suddenly taken ill with a fever which resulted in her death within the year, on November 2, 1834, when she was only twenty-seven years old. She was buried on the farm near a grove of trees that she loved.

In the *Liberator* of November 29, 1834, under the heading "Death of a Meritorious Female Abolitionist," William Lloyd Garrison paid tribute to her memory in these words: "There is not a female in the United States who has labored so assiduously, or written so copiously in the cause of the oppressed, or who has such claims upon the gratitude and admiration of the colored people of this country and their advocates, as this departed Friend." Later he rated her "worthy to be associated with Elizabeth Heyrick of England" and "to be known and honored as the first American woman who devoted her time and talents to the cause of the slave." Visiting her grave in Michigan twenty years later, he wrote a sonnet to her memory which closed with these lines:

I consecrate anew, beside thy grave,
My life to bring redemption to the slave.[15]

Benjamin Lundy was traveling in Mexico at the time of Elizabeth Chandler's death and did not hear the tragic news until nine months later. Then he immediately wrote Thomas Chandler, "The loss is irreparable . . . While thee has lost thine only one, I too am thus deprived of the dearest sister I had upon earth. Never indeed will the vacuum be filled."[16]

He tried to fill the vacuum by writing her *Memoirs* and assembling her poems and essays with the help of their mutual Philadelphia friends. At this time he wrote Thomas Chandler, "I shall never be able fully to discharge the obligation which I am under to the family, for the inestimable, valuable labors of our dear departed sister in conducting my periodical work. '[17] He wrote a tribute to her in the *Genius*, November, 1835, and in 1836, in Philadelphia, he published her *Memoirs, Poetical Works and Essays Philanthropic,* in a small leather-bound volume. He sent out a prospectus before leaving on another journey to Mexico, hoping to sell the book by subscription, for, as he wrote Thomas Chandler, "The book-sellers are afraid to touch the unpopular subject of slavery. Many of our friends are very anxious for its publication. . . . I have no doubt it will meet with a large patronage."[18] It was hailed by Maria Weston Chapman of the Boston Female Antislavery Society as "one of the gratifying circumstances of the year."[19] It did "meet with a large patronage," so much so that in 1853 Thomas Chandler considered bringing out another edition, writing William Lloyd Garrison, "The work has been sought after and read and has performed silently and unobtrusively its mission among many who would not have been reached by any other instrumentality."[20] Her work lived on as well in her poems, which continued to be sung with fervor as hymns at meetings of Female Antislavery Societies.

CHAPTER II

William Lloyd Garrison Calls Out the Women

Meanwhile, the ladies' department of the *Liberator,* headed by a woodcut of a kneeling slave, with the caption, "Am I not a Woman and a Sister?" carried on Elizabeth Chandler's work and stirred women to action as Garrison had hoped it would. His confidence in the help women would bring had been strengthened by a letter from women in Philadelphia, who not only had sent him a small sum for the support of the *Liberator* but had assured him that "every female amongst us feels the cause you are engaged in as her own."

He issued his own challenge to women in the *Liberator,* early in 1832: "The cause of bleeding humanity is always legitimately the cause of women. Without her powerful assistance, its progress must be slow, difficult, imperfect. A million females in this country are recognized and held as property – or used for the gratification of the lust or avarice or convenience of unprincipled speculators. . . . Have these no claim upon the sympathies – prayers – charities – exertions of our white countrywomen? When woman's heart is bleeding, shall woman's voice be hushed?"[1]

The women of Salem quickly responded by forming a Female Antislavery Society and adopting this resolution at their meeting on February 22, 1832: "Resolved, that as we believe the Boston *Liberator* to have been the means of enlightening the minds of many in regard to the dangerous scheme of African colonization, and also removing the monster, prejudice, from the minds of many in regard to the free people of color . . . we are determined to support it and all antislavery publications."[2]

Twelve women of Boston responded on October 14, 1832, by organizing the Boston Female Antislavery Society. Fired with enthusiasm for the cause and wanting a part in it, they would gladly have joined their husbands and brothers who early that year had formed the New England Antislavery Society, but as this would have been considered highly improper, they were bold enough to take the slightly less improper step of forming their own organization. Like the New England Antislavery Society, they too renounced the conservative approaches to abolition such as gradual emancipation and colonization and declared for the militant doctrine of immediate emancipation, which had been advocated so successfully to abolitionists in Great Britain by Elizabeth Heyrick, and was now pointing the way in America as well.

The Boston Female Antislavery Society chose as their first president, Charlotte Phelps, the wife of a Congregational clergyman, Amos A. Phelps. Other members were Maria Weston Chapman, her sisters, Caroline, Anne, and Deborah Weston, their aunt, Ann Greene Chapman, and Mary S. Parker. At their weekly meetings, held in their homes, they offered prayers for the slaves; they circulated petitions which they sent to their Congressman, John Quincy Adams, asking for the abolition of slavery and the slave trade in the District of Columbia; and they distributed the *Liberator,* in this way increasing its circulation and spreading the gospel it preached. By inviting Negroes to their meetings, they at once aroused criticism, and soon they were labeled fanatics and denounced for stepping out of woman's sphere. Maria Weston Chapman almost immediately became their leader, "the real soul of the

Boston Female Antislavery Society,"[3] as Garrison expressed it.

Maria Weston Chapman, born in Weymouth, Massachusetts, July 25, 1806, had spent much of her girlhood in England with the family of her uncle, Joshua Bates, a partner in the London banking firm, Baring Brothers. Here she was educated in an environment of wealth and social position, acquiring poise and the social graces, and learning to speak French fluently. Her keen inquiring mind and independent spirit soon demanded a less restricted field and she returned to Weymouth in 1829. She was a beautiful, radiant young woman, with blue eyes and brown curls, tall and imposing. She taught school in Boston until her marriage in 1830 to Henry Grafton Chapman, a young, prosperous, Boston merchant. Both her husband and her father-in-law, Henry Chapman, were among the very few Boston businessmen who had antislavery sympathies and could tolerate William Lloyd Garrison. Her interest was at once aroused and both she and her husband became increasingly ardent abolitionists, in spite of objections by their pastor, William Ellery Channing. Although Channing looked upon slavery as evil, he abhorred the controversy stirred up by abolitionists and particularly disapproved of the vehement language of William Lloyd Garrison.

In fact, Garrison was speedily becoming public enemy Number One, not only in the South, but in Northern financial and manufacturing circles. With no financial backing, he had courageously issued his paper, the *Liberator,* January 1, 1831, demanding immediate emancipation and declaring, "I do not wish to think, or speak, or write, with moderation. . . . I am in earnest – I will not equivocate – I will not excuse – I will not retreat a single inch – *and I will be heard.*"[4]

"He was young, unknown, and poor," recalled Maria Weston Chapman in *Right and Wrong in Boston,* "but he had the best of all qualifications for his work, an entire devotedness to the principles of liberty which he had espoused. . . . He was enabled by his ability as a writer, his skill as a practical mechanic, and his laborious self-denial, to issue the first number of a periodical without having obtained a single subscriber. To him and to the principles he advocated, the important thing was to find readers; which the power evinced in his little sheet enabled him to do. Its name was characteristic. . . . He called it *The Liberator*. Any other name would have but feebly expressed the depth and affirmative nature of its principles."[5]

His courage, sincerity, and zeal drew to him devoted supporters, among them the Boston lawyers, Samuel E. Sewall, Ellis Gray Loring, and David Lee Child; the Boston merchant Henry Chapman, and his son; the New York merchants, Arthur and Lewis Tappan; a Quaker hat manufacturer from Providence, Arnold Buffum; a Connecticut wool dealer, George Benson; a Unitarian clergyman, Samuel J. May; and Oliver Johnson, an editor. When Samuel J. May, always a devoted friend, remonstrated with him because of his harsh language he replied, "Brother May, I have need to be *all on fire,* for I have mountains of ice about me to melt."[6] His fire continued to melt the ice, bringing into the fold the popular novelist, Lydia Maria Child.

Lydia Maria Child was born in Medford, Massachusetts, February 11, 1802, and was educated there at the academy. She wrote her first novel when she was twenty-two years old and soon after began editing one of the first children's magazines, the *Juvenile Miscellany*. While living in Watertown in the home of her brother, a Unitarian minister, she met a young lawyer, David Lee Child, whom she married in 1828. They lived in Boston, where she continued her writing and editing and was given the special privilege of using the

Athenaeum, Boston's famous library, restricted to men. At this time, she was rated by the *North American Review* as one of the country's most important authors.

Although sympathetic to abolition, which she often discussed with her husband, who was one of the founders of the New England Antislavery Society, she was not a charter member of the Boston Female Antislavery Society, for her real interest was literature. Then one day she met her husband's friend, William Lloyd Garrison, commenting later, "I little thought then that the whole pattern of my life would be changed by that introduction. . . . He got hold of the strings of my conscience and pulled me into reforms. It is no use to imagine what might have been if I had never met him. Old dreams vanished, old associations departed, and all things became new."[7] The result was the publication in Boston in 1833 of a small but powerful book, *An Appeal in Favor of That Class of Americans Called Africans*. Clear, moderate in tone, compact, and convincing, it won many converts as it outlined the history of slavery in the United States, showed its effect on slave and slaveholder, and considered various remedies.

It was hailed by abolitionists. The fact that a popular author had taken her stand for abolition had great publicity value. It shocked conservative Boston, where feeling against abolitionists ran high. Depending upon the South for raw materials and for the sale of their products, New England manufacturers and their bankers decried antislavery agitation, which they feared would upset the status quo. Accusing abolitionists of stirring up strife which injured business, they exerted strong pressure against them. Mrs. Child's *Appeal* could not be tolerated. At once her card to the Athenaeum was canceled, as were subscriptions to her children's magazine, *Juvenile Miscellany*. Sales of her previously popular books decreased, and her reputation as an author rapidly declined. She had expected ridicule and censure but hardly the pressures that were now exerted against her. Hoping that her previous popularity as an author would give her *Appeal* a hearing, she had pleaded with her readers in her *Preface* not to put down the book as soon as they had glanced at its title. "If I have the most trifling claims on your good will . . ." she continued, "read it for my sake. Read it, if merely to find fresh occasion to sneer at the vulgarity of the cause. Read it, from sheer curiosity to see what a woman . . . will say on such a subject. Read it on any terms, and my purpose will be gained."

Her "purpose was gained," for her *Appeal* was widely read, rousing both men and women, and it brought her letters of gratitude from free Negroes. It converted to the cause three young men who became leaders in the antislavery movement – Wendell Phillips, Thomas Wentworth Higginson, and Charles Sumner. In later years, when Wendell Phillips was at the height of his influence, she loved to recall "how a very small mouse helped gnaw open a net that held a great lion."[8] Her *Appeal* impressed other prominent Bostonians as well, impelling Dr. John A. Palfrey of the Harvard Divinity School to free his slaves and convincing William Ellery Channing that he could no longer be silent on the subject. It convinced Mrs. Child herself that she could not remain aloof from antislavery activities and she joined the Boston Female Antislavery Society.

Like Elizabeth Margaret Chandler, Lydia Maria Child sacrificed literary fame by speaking out boldly for the abolition of slavery. "No woman in this country," declared her friend and fellow abolitionist, John Greenleaf Whittier, "has sacrificed so much for principle as Mrs. Child. She gave promise in early life of great literary ability, but when she espoused the cause of the Abolitionists, she found no market for her books and essays. . . ."[9]

* * *

The *Liberator* now carried its message of immediate emancipation to Prudence Crandall, who had established a most successful academy for young ladies in Canterbury, Connecticut. Brought up a Quaker, Prudence Crandall had always regarded slavery as a sin theoretically but had never come in contact with its results or associated with active abolitionists. Now, as she read a copy of the *Liberator,* loaned to her by a young Negro maid who worked in her household, she was deeply moved. Turning to her Bible for direction and comfort, she read in Ecclesiastes 4:1, "So I returned, and considered all the oppressions that are done under the sun: and behold the tears of such as were oppressed, and they had no comforter; and on the side of their oppressors there was power; but they had no comforter." Reading and rereading these words, she felt that she had been called to bring comfort to Negro slaves and would be shown the way.

Born in 1803, in Hope Valley, Connecticut, near Providence, Rhode Island, Prudence Crandall attended the Friends' School in Providence. When she was ten years old her father moved the family to a farm near Canterbury, Connecticut, but she continued as a pupil at the Friends' School and later taught in Plainfield, Connecticut.

Canterbury, six miles from the county seat, Brooklyn, Connecticut, was a quiet town surrounded by low hills. Stage coaches drove into the village daily on the turnpike, for business was good in its small factories, which produced cotton and woolen goods, leather, and carriages. Its wealthy citizens had beautiful homes, marked off by white picket fences and shaded by stately elms. An enterprising community, with a library and a temperance society, it had lacked a female seminary until a group of Canterbury citizens, hearing of Prudence Crandall's successful school in Plainfield, asked her to open a school so that their daughters might have education beyond the district school. They arranged for her to purchase the Elisha Paine house on the village green in which to establish the Canterbury Female Boarding School. It was a large attractive house, low-pitched and hip-roofed, with two-story pilasters at the entrance, and it was opposite the new house built by one of Canterbury's leading citizens, Andrew T. Judson, a successful lawyer active in State politics.

Prudence Crandall was 27 years old when she opened her school in 1831, enrolling young ladies from the first families of Canterbury and the neighboring towns. She looked very young to assume such a task, with her boyish bobbed hair, blue eyes, and winning smile, but she proved to be a teacher of exceptional ability, and parents were well pleased with her. Her sister, Almira, was her able assistant. In the midst of this feeling of general satisfaction, Prudence Crandall was faced with a difficult decision when Sarah Harris, the daughter of a free Negro living on a farm near Canterbury, asked if she might attend the school as a day pupil so that she might learn enough to teach colored children. Sarah, a neat, good-looking, well-mannered girl, had attended the district school with many of Miss Crandall's pupils and was a member of the Canterbury church. Her father was able and ready to pay her tuition. The only argument against her admission was her color. Prudence Crandall hesitated, telling Sarah to return for an answer. Then as she analyzed her hesitancy, it became clear to her that she would have admitted Sarah at once, had she herself not had a slight prejudice against color. As the desire for the success of her school wrestled with her conscience, she turned again to Ecclesiastes

Prudence Crandall

4:1 and realized that she was being shown the way to help destroy this cruel prejudice. She enrolled Sarah in her school. The pupils did not object, for Sarah had sat beside them in the district school, but soon there was a protest from the wife of the Episcopal clergyman, who demanded that the "nigger" be dismissed. Other parents speedily joined their protests to hers, and no appeals for justice or tolerance had any effect. The parents made it clear that if Sarah Harris were not dismissed they would withdraw their daughters from the school.

Now an even more difficult decision confronted Prudence Crandall. A profitable, respectable career opened before her, if she would conform. She had put all her savings into the school and had borrowed to finance it. Should she follow the easy road of conformity or serve the people of color? Thinking the problem through, she came to this conclusion: "I saw that the prejudice of the whites against color was deep and inveterate. In my humble opinion it was the strongest, if not the only chain that bound those heavy burdens on the wretched slaves. . . . I contemplated for a while the manner in which I might best serve the people of color. As wealth was not mine, I saw no other means of benefiting them, than by imparting to those of my own sex that were anxious to learn, all the instruction I might be able to give. . . ."[10]

She refused to turn Sarah out of her school and, as opposition increased and students were withdrawn, she began to make plans to open her school to colored girls only, turning to William Lloyd Garrison for advice, in January, 1833.

"I am to you, Sir, I presume, an entire stranger," she wrote him, "and you are indeed so to me, save through the medium of public print."[11] Then she told him about her school and asked his opinion regarding a change from white to colored pupils, whether he thought that twenty or twenty-five "young ladies of color" could be found who would care to enroll in her school at $25 a quarter. She urged him not to make her plans public, as first she would come to Boston to discuss them with him.

In February, 1833, she took the stagecoach to Boston, where she had an encouraging interview with him. He assured her she could find colored pupils eager to enroll in her school, and at his suggestion, she conferred with one of his colleagues in Brooklyn, Connecticut, George W. Benson, and with the Rev. Simeon S. Jocelyn, known for his work among the colored people of New Haven. Both encouraged her. Next, she discussed the matter with one of the Board of Visitors of her school, Captain Daniel Packer, a prosperous manufacturer, who regarded her project as praiseworthy, but feared the outcome. She continued to talk with abolitionists in Providence and New York about the possibilities of enrolling colored pupils and, assured that Negroes would welcome the opportunity to attend her school, she made a definite decision to break with the past. She dismissed the white pupils who still remained in her school and, in an advertisement in the *Liberator,* March 2, 1833, she thanked those who had previously patronized her school and announced that on the first Monday in April, her school in Canterbury would be open to "Young Ladies and Little Misses of Color," to teach them reading, writing, arithmetic, grammar, geography, history, philosophy, chemistry, astronomy, drawing, painting, "music on the piano," and French. The terms – including board, washing, and tuition – were $25 per quarter in advance. As references, she gave not only her friends among the abolitionists, such as Arthur Tappan, Arnold Buffum, and Samuel J. May, but also the wealthy Negro, James Forten, of Philadelphia, and five Negro clergymen in New York. William Lloyd Garrison assured the readers of the *Liberator* that "An interview with Miss Crandall has satisfied us that she richly deserves the patronage and confidence of the people of color; and we doubt not they will give her both."[12]

These announcements roused the fury of the citizens of Canterbury, who considered the establishment of such a school a breach of faith on her part. They did their best to dissuade her, calling on her again and again, hoping to win her over by their arguments. They were determined to block the opening of a school for Negroes. None had as yet been tolerated in the North.

The citizens of Canterbury continued to urge her to give up her plans, but she refused, convinced that it was her duty to open a school for colored girls. When they offered to buy her house for what she had paid for it, she expressed her willingness to move her school to a location where it would attract less attention. Then they pointed out the dangers which were sure to develop out of the education of Negroes, such as intermarriage of whites and Negroes. This led her to remind them, "Moses had a black wife." Horrified by this remark, they were more determined than ever to keep her from carrying out her plans, and called a town meeting for March 9, 1833, to act on the matter.

Her courage won her friends at once among abolitionists, with Arthur Tappan, Arnold Buffum, and the young liberal Unitarian clergyman, Samuel J. May, of Brooklyn, Connecticut, offering their help. At her request, Samuel J. May came to counsel with her, bringing with him George W. Benson. They found the fury and excitement of Canterbury citizens far beyond their expectations. In fact, as soon as they entered the town they were warned that any of Miss Crandall's friends risked injury. From Prudence Crandall herself they learned that she had been insulted and threatened, that many false rumors about her and her school had been circulated, that her father had been threatened and had begged her to give up her school. In spite of all this, she was determined to live up to her principles, whatever the consequences.

As it would have been highly improper for a woman to speak for herself at a town meeting, Samuel J. May consented to represent her, and on the day of the meeting he was on hand with George Benson and, to his surprise and delight, found Arnold Buffum already there. Arnold Buffum at that time was the principal lecturer of the New England Antislavery Society. Prudence Crandall gave these three men a letter of introduction to the moderator of the town meeting, asking that they be heard as her attorneys and promising that she would be bound by any agreement they might make. Again she expressed her willingness to sell her house to the citizens of Canterbury and to locate her school in a less conspicuous part of the town.

The church where the town meeting was held was filled to capacity. Judge Adams proposed a resolution protesting the establishment of a colored school and appointing a committee of selectmen to confer with Miss Crandall to point out to her the injurious effects on the community of such a school and to persuade her to abandon it. Then Andrew T. Judson, one of the State's leading politicians, who occupied the house next to the school, declared vehemently that to have "a school of nigger girls" so near him was unbearable. He readily aroused the emotions of the crowd as he led them to believe that the town faced dire calamity because of Prudence Crandall and her antislavery conspirators, who would make Connecticut the Liberia of America. When Mr. May and Mr. Buffum asked to be heard, they were accused of trying to interfere in the town's affairs, and the audience threatened to attack them should they express their opinions.

After a roaring vote of approval of a motion condemning the school and pledging opposition, the moderator announced adjournment. Making use of the momentary lull, Samuel J. May jumped up on a seat and shouted, "Men of Canterbury! I have a word for you! Hear me!" Hurriedly and briefly he stated Prudence Crandall's case. Then, as Arnold Buffum tried to take over, the crowd was ordered out and the doors were closed, but outside on the green both men talked with those willing to listen.

While this was going on, William Lloyd Garrison in Boston was writing to George Benson commending him for his defense of Prudence Crandall. "Miss Crandall must be sustained at all hazards," he wrote. "If we suffer the school to be put down in Canterbury, other places will partake of the panic, and also prevent its introduction in their vicinity. We may as well 'first as last' meet their proscriptive spirit and conquer it. We – i.e., all true friends of the cause – must make this a common concern. . . . In Boston we are all excited at the Canterbury affair. . . ."[13]

Under the headline, "Heathenism Outdone," the *Liberator* reported the Canterbury town meeting. So biting were Garrison's comments that George Benson warned him to tread more lightly and Prudence Crandall wrote him, "Permit me to entreat you to handle the prejudices of the people of Canterbury with all the mildness possible, as everything severe tends merely to heighten the flame of malignity amongst them. . . . Mr. May and many others of your warmhearted friends feel very much on this subject, and it is our opinion that you and the cause will gain many friends in this town and vicinity if you treat the matter with perfect mildness."

This, however, did not prove to be the case, for Andrew T. Judson soon threatened to invoke the old pauper and vagrancy laws as a means of discouraging the enrollment of Negroes in the school. He also made it clear that he intended to get a law passed by the Connecticut Legislature, forbidding the establishment of a school for Negroes in any part of Connecticut. At the same time, he did his best to persuade Samuel J. May to abandon his support of Prudence Crandall, for the two men had been friends in the past and he hoped to capitalize on their friendship. Samuel J. May, however, was as convinced as Prudence Crandall that Negroes had a right to an education and he wrote a series of letters to the *Liberator,* addressed to "A. T. Judson and Others in Canterbury, Remonstrating with Them on Their Unjust and Unjustifiable Procedure, Relative to Miss Crandall and Her School for Colored Females." These letters were also published as a pamphlet and widely distributed.

Meanwhile, Prudence Crandall, carrying out her plans quietly and with determination, opened her school early in April to "young ladies and misses of color" from Philadelphia, New York, Providence, and Boston. At once Canterbury retaliated. The stores refused to sell her supplies. Rotten eggs and stones were thrown at her doorway, manure was dumped in her well, and she was obliged to depend upon her father and a sympathetic Quaker for food and water. Soon they were forbidden to visit her and were threatened with violence. Boys followed her pupils whenever they ventured out, jeering and tooting horns. The stage refused to transport the day pupils, but a Negro in the vicinity volunteered to drive them from their homes to the school.

"My soul is sick with every day's report of wrong and outrage with which Canterbury is filled," she wrote William Lloyd Garrison, "and were it not for the confidence I have in the hand of Omnipotence, I should fall like a fading leaf before the northern blast."[14]

Yet she and her pupils carried on courageously, even holding special exercises at the school at which her pupils sang these verses which she had composed for the occasion:

Sometimes when we have walked the streets
Saluted we have been
By guns, and drums, and cowbells too
And horns of polished tin

With warnings, threats, and words severe,
They visit us at times,
And gladly would they send us off
To Afric's burning climes.[15]

Canterbury's next move against the school was to invoke Connecticut's obsolete vagrancy law, which provided that selectmen of a town might ask any person not an inhabitant of the state to leave, to pay a fine of $1.67 a week while remaining, and after ten days to be whipped on the naked body not exceeding ten stripes. A warrant was served on one of Prudence Crandall's pupils, Eliza Ann Hammond of Providence, Rhode Island, in spite of the fact that Samuel J. May had given the treasurer of Canterbury a $10,000 bond, signed by a prominent citizen of Brooklyn, Connecticut, to protect the town from the vagrancy of any of the pupils. Neither Eliza Ann nor any of the other pupils were intimidated by this action, as the Canterbury citizens had hoped. In fact, Eliza Ann even asked that the sentence be carried out, but the citizens of Canterbury did not care to go that far.

Prudence Crandall wrote to Mr. Jocelyn at this time, "The thought of such opposition as has been raised in the minds of the people of Canterbury and the adjoining towns never once entered into my mind while contemplating the change I am now endeavoring to effect in my school. Very true, I thought many of the high-minded worldly men would oppose the plan, but that Christians would act so unwisely and conduct in a manner so outrageously was a thought distant from my view. I have put my hand to the plough and I will never, no never look back. . . . If this school is crushed by inhuman laws, another I suppose cannot be obtained, certainly one for white scholars can never be taught by me. As for myself I think I shall fare well enough – I have sufficient property in my hands to pay my debts – to work I am not ashamed and to beg I do not fear the necessity."[16]

Petitions were then circulated and presented to the legislature pointing out the evil consequences of bringing people of color into the state, especially for the purpose of disseminating doctrines opposed to the colonization of Negroes, and asking the legislature to enact laws to forbid it. Finally, through the influence of Andrew T. Judson, a law was passed by the Connecticut Legislature which provided that "no person should set up a school or educational institution for the instruction of colored persons who were not inhabitants of the State, nor instruct in such a school, nor harbor or board any colored person instructed in such a school without the consent in writing . . . of a majority of the civil authority and selectmen in the town in which such a school is situated under penalty of a fine of $100 for the first offense. . . ." Bells were rung and cannon fired in Canterbury when word came that this law had been passed.

As the press carried news of the Black Law and Prudence Crandall's determination to continue her school for Negroes, public hostility against Negroes and their white antislavery friends attracted national attention for the first time. The *Liberator,* as was expected, commented scathingly, using its largest headlines, with the result that William Lloyd Garrison was threatened with libel suits and arrest. However, he managed to elude the sheriff before sailing to England from

New York on an antislavery mission, although he stopped over in Brooklyn, Connecticut, to visit the Benson family and spoke in Samuel J. May's church. Prudence Crandall, hearing that Garrison was to be in Brooklyn, drove over from Canterbury with her sister, Almira, to talk with him. She made such a favorable impression upon him that he wrote to Isaac Knapp, the co-publisher of the *Liberator,* "She is a wonderful woman, as undaunted as if she had the whole world on her side,"[17] and he recommended that, in his absence, the *Liberator* give her good work favorable notice and encouragement.

Soon there was plenty to report in the *Liberator,* for on June 27, 1833, Prudence Crandall was arrested for breaking the Black Law, and arraigned before the justice of the peace, who ordered her to trial before the county court in August, and to prison in the county seat, Brooklyn, Connecticut. Her friends did not at once come forward with bail, for they had previously discussed with her the possibility of her arrest, and she had agreed with them that her temporary imprisonment might well rouse public opinion against the infamous Black Law as nothing else would. The only cell available was the one which had been occupied by a recently executed murderer, but Samuel J. May had put a clean bed and bedding from his own home into the cell, making it as comfortable as possible for her. Meeting her when she arrived at the jail with the sheriff, he assured her that should she want to change her mind, he would furnish bail for her, but she replied, "Oh no, I am only afraid they will not put me in jail."[18] In fact, the sheriff, embarrassed by his task, delayed, hoping bail would eventually be furnished, but it was not, and finally he turned Prudence Crandall over to the jailer, who led her into the cell where she spent the night. The next morning her friends were on hand with the necessary bail, and she returned to her school as newspapers carried word of her imprisonment to all parts of the country.

Realizing the expense of the legal contest in which she would soon be involved, Arthur Tappan offered to finance it and asked Samuel J. May to employ the ablest lawyers to defend her. Finding that newspapers were misrepresenting her and her school if they mentioned them at all, he also proposed to finance a paper to publish the facts. Coming to Canterbury to see for himself just how matters stood, he rented a printing shop, recently closed, and employed as editor, a young law student, Charles C. Burliegh. The first issue of his paper, *The Unionist,* appeared on July 25, 1833. After a few months, his brother, William, helped him with the paper, and taught as well in Prudence Crandall's school, for with her trial imminent, someone was needed to assist her loyal sister, Almira.

On August 23, Prudence Crandall was tried before Judge Eaton of the county court in Brooklyn, Connecticut, for the crime of keeping a boarding school for colored girls who were not inhabitants of the state. During the trial she was a guest of Samuel J. May, while the hospitable Benson home welcomed her pupils who were summoned to testify. As she sat calmly through the long ordeal, she was comforted by the fact that her good friend, Samuel J. May, was by her side, and that George Benson was there reporting for the *Liberator* and Charles Burliegh for the *Unionist*. She watched the audience with interest, hoping for tolerance and justice. The prosecuting attorney was the ringleader of her Canterbury opponents, Andrew T. Judson, with whose point of view she was thoroughly familiar. Maintaining that education was available to Negroes in the state, he justified the new law on the grounds that towns must have control of the schools in their jurisdictions. He declared that since only free white males were citizens under the state constitution, Negroes could not claim citizenship. Then he added that the public safety of the state and the preservation of its true interests required this law. Otherwise the Southern states might emancipate their slaves and send them all to Connecticut instead of Liberia.

She was proud of the three able lawyers who defended her – Calvin Goddard, Henry Strong, and W. W. Ellsworth – as they questioned the constitutionality of the Black Law and refuted the prosecuting attorney's claim that only white males were citizens.

To her dismay, however, the judge, in his charge to the jury, advised that the Black Law was constitutional. The jury voted seven for conviction and five for acquittal and, after three attempts to reach agreement, was discharged.

The trial behind her, Prudence Crandall had no respite from persecution, as unfriendly groups gathered about her house, throwing rotten eggs and stones and breaking windows. In the meantime, the *Unionist* was printing the facts about this persecution and distributing a full report of the trial, so that great sympathy for Prudence Crandall was aroused among abolitionists, and more friends were won for the cause.

As the case had not been settled to the satisfaction of the citizens of Canterbury, further charges were brought against her, and in October, 1833, she was tried in the State Supreme Court in Brooklyn, Connecticut, before Chief Justice David Daggett, who was known to be not only hostile to Negroes and an advocate of the Black Law, but a defender of slavery as well. Again her counsel maintained that the Black Law was unconstitutional, but Chief Justice Daggett, advising the jury that the Black Law was constitutional, charged them to convict. "It would be a perversion of terms . . ." he declared, "to say slaves, free blacks, or Indians were citizens within the meaning of that term as used in the Constitution."[19] The jury rendered a verdict of guilty and in so doing gave the United States Supreme Court a precedent for the Dred Scott decision in 1857. Immediately the case was appealed to the Supreme Court of Errors, which, in July, 1834, set aside the decision on the grounds of insufficient information, but did not reverse it, nor did it render a decision on the constitutionality of the Black Law or on the citizenship of colored persons.

A Report of the Arguments of Counsel in the Case of Prudence Crandall v. *State of Connecticut* was immediately published as a pamphlet by William Lloyd Garrison and his partner Isaac Knapp, in spite of their precarious financial situation, because, as Garrison expressed it, "a trial so important . . . involving such momentous consequences to a large portion of our countrymen — implicating so deeply the character of this great nation — ought not to go unpublished, and shall not, while we have the necessary materials for printing it."[20]

In the opinion of the historian, Professor Dwight L. Dumond, of the University of Michigan, the Prudence Crandall case was one of our most important cases in the history of the antislavery movement. It restated and argued in court questions which had been debated in Congress prior to the Missouri Compromise. Its basic issue was the biological inequality and inferiority of the Negro. It publicized the differences between the advocates of colonization and antislavery groups, between the prejudices of the people and the great truths of the Declaration of Independence.

During this legal contest, Prudence Crandall was cheered by the many letters of gratitude and praise which she received from abolitionists in Canada, England, and Scotland, as well as the United States. One from Scotland told her of a silver plate to be sent to her by the Women's Antislavery Society of Glasgow, "in testimony of their high admiration" and "affectionate respect." Her pupils as well, received letters and gifts from the Women's Antislavery Societies of Liverpool and Edinburgh.

Visiting Boston in the spring of 1834, she was warmly welcomed and entertained by members of the Female Antislavery Society. Her portrait was painted by Francis Alexander and steel engravings of the portrait were sold at antislavery fairs. Lydia Maria Child took a special interest in her, including in her antislavery miscellany, *Oasis,* a reproduction of the Alexander portrait[21] as well as Samuel J. May's account of her school for colored pupils and her trial. In addition, the New England Antislavery Society adopted a resolution declaring that "Miss Prudence and Miss Almira Crandall merit the warmest approbation of all friends of the colored race for their persevering and untiring exertion to educate colored females under a most bitter and unchristian persecution."

No further court action followed, but the citizens of Canterbury took the matter into their own hands. Late one night they set fire to Prudence Crandall's house. Smelling smoke, she located the fire and was able to extinguish it before it did serious damage, but, to her dismay, it was blamed by the townspeople on a free Negro who had recently repaired her clocks. He was arrested and tried, but was acquitted.

During her first trial, Prudence Crandall, surveying the audience, had noticed a young man and his daughter sitting beside her good friend, Levi Kneeland, the Baptist minister from a nearby town, who had always welcomed her and her pupils to his church. At the close of the trial, Mr. Kneeland introduced Calvin Philleo to her and she learned that he was a Baptist minister from Ithaca, New York, and a widower.

They became better acquainted as he drove her back to Canterbury. Much attracted to each other, they corresponded frequently after he returned to Ithaca. They were married in September, 1834, hopeful that they could carry on the school together – if not in Canterbury, elsewhere. They went to Philadelphia to discuss with Lucretia Mott and members of the Philadelphia Female Antislavery Society the advisability of opening a school for colored girls there. Lucretia Mott reported, "Prudence Crandall and her husband have passed a week in our city since their marriage. They previously visited New York and Boston with a view to decide in which of these places they should open a school for colored girls, having determined no longer to conflict with the iniquitous law of Connecticut – Esther Moore was much pleased with the prospect – she and myself called with Prudence on about 50 families of our most reputable colored people, and engaged a sufficient number to warrant her beginning here – but there was so much opposition to the attempt, at this time, by a few of our *prudent* abolitionists, that she was induced to return to Canterbury and wait until after our elections, when it is probable they will all remove here – It appears by the papers that fresh insults awaited them there."[22]

Returning home, Prudence and Calvin Philleo were undisturbed for a few days. Then suddenly one night the shattering of glass awakened them and they saw a large mob outside, armed with iron bars and heavy clubs, smashing window panes, ripping out window sashes and doors, and breaking up furniture. As they looked over what was left of the house, they were appalled as they considered the expense of the necessary repairs. With the threat of further vandalism hanging over them, it was more than they felt they could undertake, and they also questioned the advisability of keeping pupils in the school under continued fear and tension.

Samuel J. May had driven over immediately to offer his helf and they discussed future plans with him. Calvin Philleo in sisted that the school be given up and the house sold. Re luctantly Prudence consented and even more reluctantly Samuel J. May agreed, commenting later "I felt ashamed of Canterbury, ashamed of Connecticut, ashamed of my country, ashamed of my color."[23]

After putting a For Sale sign on the house, Calvin and Prudence Philleo left Canterbury for Ithaca, New York, mov- ing later to northern Illinois. There is no record of further militant abolition activity on their part, except that Prudence continued to teach Negro girls and boys. Her efforts for the education of Negroes in Connecticut bore fruit, as several of her Negro pupils in Canterbury became teachers and active abolitionists.

Neither persecution, nor disappointment, nor a conserva- tive husband, nor the traditional role of a clergyman's wife were able to close Prudence Crandall's active mind nor curb her liberal ideas. When interviewed in 1886 in Elk Falls, Kansas, where she had moved with her brother after the death of her husband, she said, "My whole life has been one of opposition. I never could find anyone to agree with me. Even my husband opposed me, more than anyone. He would not let me read the books that he himself read, but I did read them. I read all sides, and searched for the truth whether it was in science, religion or humanity."[24]

In 1885, at the suggestion of and with the help of friends in the Connecticut Legislature, she asked that the record of her conviction in 1834 be wiped out and that she receive compensation for the destruction of her property. Writing her friend, John L. Smith, she said, "My plea will be for justice. When a State has falsely imprisoned an innocent citi- zen and passed unconstitutional laws by which they are harassed and property destroyed, it is right they should compensate the abused. . . . I feel it is a duty I owe to myself and also the State to ask for redress for such slander and abuse as I received at their hand."[25]

Regarding the compensation, she added, "I wish to make no exorbitant demands. . . . I shall never plead poverty – for with industry and the economy that I daily practice, I have enough to lay me honorably in the grave – I would be glad to enjoy a few of the luxuries of life, such as taking the cars occasionally, visiting old friends and colored people, scattered in many parts of the State, whose cause has always been close to my heart. . . . Owning a horse and buggy to take me where I wish to go and not walk or be dependent on some good friend is what I much desire."

Justice was done in 1886 when the Connecticut Legislature erased the record of her conviction and granted her an annuity of $1,400. This was accomplished through the influence of a group of prominent Connecticut citizens, including Mark Twain and Andrew T. Judson's nephew. Mark Twain had also wanted to buy her Canterbury house and present it to her, but this she refused, writing that she was happy and well in her "little pioneer house of three rooms."[26] When word of the action of the Connecticut Legislature reached her, she expressed her gratitude for the "change that has been wrought in the views and feelings of the mass of the people" and contrasted it with the ringing of the bells when the Black Law was passed fifty-three years before in 1833.

This courageous woman, who faced mob violence before Garrison or any of the antislavery lecturers, blazed the trail for women in the antislavery movement.

CHAPTER III

Women Take Hold

When abolitionists met in Philadelphia, in December, 1833, to organize the American Antislavery Society, a warm welcome awaited them in the home of James and Lucretia Mott.

Slavery had weighed on the conscience of Lucretia Mott ever since her Nantucket childhood, when in her school books she had read about the cruelty of the slave trade and had seen pictures of slave ships. Born of Quaker parents in Nantucket, January 3, 1793, and brought up among Quakers who had early taken a stand against slavery, her concern was a natural outgrowth of her environment, as was her independence of thought and action. Her father, Thomas Coffin, was a whaler and a trader who owned his own ship until it was lost in a dispute with Spaniards on the west coast of South America about 1795. Soon after, the Coffin family left their comfortable home in Nantucket for Boston. When Lucretia was 13 years old, she was sent to a Friends' Boarding School, Nine Partners, in Dutchess County, New York, where, after two years, she became a teacher. Here she met a most congenial fellow-teacher, James Mott, from Long Island. In the meantime, her family moved to Philadelphia and she joined them there. James Mott soon followed her, and they were married in 1811. Lucretia's father, then a successful commission merchant, took James Mott into his business. After the death of Thomas Coffin, in 1815, James Mott established his own commission business. By this time, there were three children in

James and Lucretia Mott

the family, but in spite of her household duties Lucretia managed to find time for serious reading and a systematic study of the Bible. For years she kept Mary Wollstonecraft's *Vindication of the Rights of Women* close at hand on the center table.

Both James and Lucretia Mott were dedicated Quakers, and occasionally Lucretia offered a prayer in meeting. The quality of these prayers and her way of life were so highly valued that within a few years she was designated a minister of the Society of Friends. Traveling through Pennsylvania, Maryland, and Virginia to speak at Friends' Meetings, she saw slavery at first hand. This strengthened her antislavery sentiments, as did the Quaker minister, Elias Hicks, who took a definite stand against slavery and the use of slave products. It was not, however, until she left the Orthodox Friends in 1827 to join the Hicksite group that she made the decision to take part in the great work of freeing the slaves, even though this ran counter to the traditional activities of women. She spoke on the evils of slavery at Friends' Meetings and became a member of Philadelphia's Free Produce Society. By 1830, both she and her husband were convinced that he must no longer buy and sell cotton raised by slave labor, and, at considerable financial loss, he turned instead to trading in wool.

During these years of developing antislavery sentiment, they had subscribed to Benjamin Lundy's paper, the *Genius of Universal Emancipation,* and had welcomed Lundy to their home. They had read with interest and approval Elizabeth Heyrick's pamphlet, *Immediate, Not Gradual Emancipation,* and when William Lloyd Garrison visited them after his imprisonment in Baltimore, they were ready to support him in his drive for immediate emancipation, which he soon carried on through his paper, the *Liberator*.

The convention of abolitionists from all parts of the country meeting in Philadelphia, in December, 1833, not only gave James and Lucretia Mott the opportunity to renew friendships and widen their circle of antislavery friends, but it brought comforting assurance that the good work was going forward. James Mott, as a matter of course, attended the convention, but Lucretia, although longing to be there, well knew that women were never included in such meetings. However, on the second day of the convention, she and some of her friends received an invitation to attend as "spectators and listeners." Hurrying with eagerness to Adelphi Hall, Lucretia Mott, Esther Moore, Lydia White, and Sydney Ann Lee were cordially received and ushered into reserved seats. They were impressed as they watched and listened. The wealthy, deeply religious Tappan brothers, Lewis and Arthur, from New York, were there, and William Lloyd Garrison, just returned from an antislavery mission in England; also the young poet, John Greenleaf Whittier, the Unitarian clergyman, Samuel J. May, and Beriah Green of Oneida Institute. The Quaker hat manufacturer from Providence, Rhode Island, Arnold Buffum, was there, also young men from all walks of life – some teachers, some theological students and clergymen, and a few free Negroes (among them young, handsome Robert Purvis). All were men with dreams of a better world, and these dreams had been encouraged and stimulated by Great Britain's abolition of slavery in the West Indies a few months earlier. Most of these men had in the past supported the Colonization Society with its policy of gradual emancipation and colonization in Liberia, but now they recognized the importance of calling for immediate emancipation.

Considerable excitement and antagonism had been aroused in Philadelphia by this gathering of ardent abolitionists, and, to prevent disturbances, police were stationed at the door of Adelphi Hall, and abolitionists were warned not to hold evening sessions. This obvious disapproval made it difficult to find a prominent Philadelphian willing to preside at the convention, and when it was announced that two influential Quakers, Thomas Wister and Robert Vaux, had felt it prudent to refuse an invitation to preside, disappointment, apprehension, and caution swept through the gathering. Instantly Lucretia Mott came to the rescue, although it was against all rules of propriety for a woman to speak in an assembly of men. Accustomed to speak in Meeting when the Spirit moved her, she was now moved to declare, "Right principles are stronger than great names."[1] Then this handsome woman, in gray, with Quaker bonnet and white kerchief, courageously continued in a clear, pleasant voice, "If our principles are right, why should we be cowards? Why should we wait for those who never have had the courage to maintain the inalienable rights of the slave." This broke the mesmeric state, and she was greeted with approving shouts of "Go on!"

One of their own number, Beriah Green, was then pressed into service as president, and the meeting continued. Discussing and approving a Declaration of Sentiments and a constitution, they were so absorbed that although they were in session from ten in the morning until dark, they took no time out for dinner, and, as Samuel J. May reported, "Baskets of crackers and pitchers of cold water furnished all the bodily refreshment we needed."[2]

During the discussion of the use of the products of slave labor, Lucretia Mott again made history for women by taking part. This was a subject to which she had given a great deal of thought, but, not wishing to appear too bold, she hesitated after she had said a few words, until President

Beriah Green encouraged her with, "Go on, Ma'am, we shall all be glad to hear you," and several men in the audience shouted, "Go on, go on!" Samuel J. May commented later on her impressive and effective speech. She also made several valuable suggestions during the discussion of the Declaration of Sentiments, and a young man in the audience, J. Miller McKim, who had never before heard a woman speak in a public meeting, reported that she spoke "so modestly, in such sweet tones, and yet . . . so decisively that no one could fail to be pleased."

However, when the time came for signing the Declaration, neither Lucretia Mott nor any of the other women, who had been listening to its noble sentiments with pride and admiration, were asked to sign, nor did they expect to be asked. "I do not think it occurred to any one of us," reminisced Lucretia Mott, "that there would be a propriety in our signing the document."[3]

In spite of this omission, the women felt very much a part of the convention because Lucretia Mott's spontaneous remarks had been so well received. As they listened on the third day to the reading of the Resolutions, they were grateful for further recognition, "the thanks of the Convention" to "our female friends for the deep interest they have manifested in the cause of antislavery during the long and fatiguing sessions." They were encouraged by these statements in the resolutions that followed; that "the cause of abolition eminently deserves the countenance and support of American women;" that "the ladies antislavery societies" already in existence were "the harbinger of a brighter day;" and that "all ladies of the land" were "respectfully and earnestly invited" to organize antislavery societies in "every State, County, and Town in the Union."[4] There was notice, too, of Prudence Crandall's courageous stand in Canterbury, Connecticut, and the Convention's assurance of its "approval, sympathy and help." The women had definitely made an impression. Yet when the American Antislavery Society was organized to carry out the purposes of the convention, women were not invited to become members, although its constitution specified that any person not a slaveholder, who had paid dues qualified as a voting member.

Not offended by this omission and not expecting to be included, Philadelphia women wishing to form their own society were in a quandary as to how to proceed, for they had had no experience in organizations that were not completely under the direction of their church. "I had no idea of the meaning of preambles, and resolutions, and votings," Lucretia Mott confessed. "Women had never been in any assemblies of the kind. I attended only one convention . . . before that; and that was the first time in my life I had ever heard a vote taken, being accustomed to our Quaker way of getting the prevailing sentiment of the meeting . . . There was not a woman capable of taking the chair and organizing that meeting, and we had to call on James McCrummel, a colored man, to give us aid in the work."[5]

With his help, the Philadelphia Female Antislavery Society was organized in December, 1833, enrolling about sixty women, among whom were several free Negroes – Sarah Douglass, the school teacher; Hattie Purvis, the wife of Robert Purvis; and the daughters of James Forten – all the intellectual and cultural equals of the white members. Lucretia Mott soon became the natural leader of this active group, whose members also included Esther Moore, its first president; Mary Grew, for many years its secretary; Sarah Pugh; and Lydia White, whose Free Produce Store had become well known as far afield as New England and the

Middle West. They distributed antislavery tracts and Garrison's *Liberator,* circulated petitions for the abolition of slavery in the District of Columbia, raised money for the American Antislavery Society, of which they were an auxiliary, took a definite stand on the use of free produce, and looked after the general welfare and education of free Negroes in the city, sponsoring Sarah Douglass' school for Negro children. They regarded the circulation of petitions as particularly important, for the American Antislavery Society had pledged itself "to influence Congress to abolish slavery in the District of Columbia." This meant sending petitions to their friend, John Quincy Adams, who could be depended upon to present them to Congress, no matter what the opposition. In this way women indirectly had a part in bringing the antislavery issue before Congress and influencing public opinion. By 1834, Female Antislavery Societies had been organized not only in Philadelphia and Boston, but in New York and Providence, Lynn and Salem, Concord, New Hampshire, and Ohio. So active was the Philadelphia Female Antislavery Society that Lydia Maria Child, after visiting in Philadelphia, wrote Maria Weston Chapman that it might be profitable for the Boston Society to study its program.

* * *

The women of Boston, however, soon had the opportunity to test their metal. They saw antagonism toward abolitionists increasing, not only in the South, but also in New York in the summer of 1834, during which houses and two churches in the Negro section were destroyed and Lewis Tappan's house was looted. Lydia Maria Child, then in New York, wrote her Boston friends "I have not ventured into the city, nor does one of us dare to go to church today, so great is the excitement here. . . . 'Tis like the times of the French Revolution, when no man dared trust his neighbors. Private assassins from New Orleans are lurking at the corners of the streets to stab Arthur Tappan. . . . There are 7,000 Southerners now in the city. . . . Violence, in some form, seems to be generally expected."[6]

While this news saddened the antislavery women of Boston, it did not intimidate them. They were ready to follow in the footsteps of Prudence Crandall, whose courage they respected and honored. It cheered them to read of the Lane Seminary students in Ohio who, forbidden to form antislavery societies or to debate the subject, withdrew from the Seminary, some of them to become antislavery lecturers.

With the arrival in Boston of George Thompson, the English abolitionist and friend of Garrison, there was a strong revival of antagonism, so much so that his life was continually in danger. His trip to America had been financed by the antislavery "Ladies" of Scotland in the hope of furthering the cause, for he was an effective speaker and had played an important role in freeing the slaves in the British West Indies. He began lecturing at once throughout New England, often to hostile audiences. In the spring of 1835 he spoke for the Boston Female Antislavery Society to a large audience that more than filled Bennett Street Church. Tall, imposing, and eloquent, he made a most favorable impression, winning many converts. So disturbed were the businessmen and the socially elite of Boston over this antislavery "agitation" and the interference in their affairs of a foreign agent, as they labeled George Thompson, that they held a protest meeting in August in Faneuil Hall, which had recently been refused the abolitionists for their convention. At this protest meeting, abolitionists were charged with madness, treason, insurrections, and bloodshed, and Mayor Lyman, who presided, warned them of the danger of holding further meetings. In reply, Garrison spoke out boldly in the *Liberator,* declaring that Faneuil Hall, once the "Cradle of Liberty" had become "the Refuge of Slavery." The antislavery women of Boston heartily agreed, and well aware of the mob violence which would probably be directed against them, they went ahead with their plans to hold their annual meeting on October 14, 1835, with an address by George Thompson. Denied the use of four halls, they finally secured Congress Hall, or thought they had, and published a notice of their meeting in the newspapers. They sent notices as well to the churches to be read before their services. The press lost no time in expressing disapproval and indignation over the presence in the city of that "notorious incendiary" and "foreign emissary," George Thompson. Letters to the editor ran like this, "Has it come to this, that the women of our country – not content with their proper sphere, the domestic fireside – must hold public meetings to encourage the efforts of a foreign emissary to destroy our peace?"[7]

As a result, permission to use Congress Hall was withdrawn. Because public opinion had been so aroused and rioting and violence seemed certain, the women decided not to endanger the life of George Thompson by asking him to address them. At first they announced postponement of their meeting but, as they counseled together, they came to the conclusion that they should not be intimidated, that it was their duty to uphold free speech. They decided to hold their annual meeting a week later, on October 21, in the small lecture hall next to the office of the Massachusetts Antislavery Society at 46 Washington Street, and sent an announcement of it to the Boston *Courier.*

This immediately alerted the opposition to distribute handbills which read:

THOMPSON, THE ABOLITIONIST

> That infamous foreign scoundrel, Thompson, will hold forth this afternoon, at the Liberator Office, No. 46 Washington Street. The present is a fair opportunity for the friends of the Union to *smoke Thompson out!* It will be a contest between the abolitionists and the friends of the Union. A purse of $100 has been raised by a number of patriotic citizens to reward the individual who shall first lay violent hands on Thompson so that he may be brought to the tar kettle before dark. Friends of the Union, be vigilant![8]

It was not a pleasant prospect that confronted the twenty-five women as they started out for their meeting early on the afternoon of October 21, 1835. Some of their friends begged them to stay away from certain danger, but they went on their way, sending word, however, to Mayor Lyman, that there were indications their meeting would be attacked. On Washington Street, they found a restless crowd of Boston aristocrats and businessmen milling about.

Pushing their way through the crowd, the women reached 46 Washington Street and climbed two flights of stairs to the hall without incident, but immediately the passage was blocked, keeping out all late-comers. The mob did not try to enter the hall, but remained outside, stamping and shouting for George Thompson. When Garrison arrived to address the women, the crowd shouted, "That's Garrison." Fearing for his safety, the women urged him to leave, and, realizing that his presence might well endanger them, he slipped into the Antislavery Office, as it was impossible to leave the building by the main stairway which was packed solidly with shouting men.

The women tried to carry on their meeting above the roar of the crowd on the stairs and in the street. Mary S

Parker presided. Fists banged on the door as she read from the Bible and led the women in prayer. While the secretary was reading her report, Mayor Lyman entered and ordered them all to go home. When they remonstrated with him, he impatiently asked, "Ladies, do you wish to see a scene of bloodshed and confusion? If you do not, go home."[9]

To this Mrs. Chapman retorted, "Mr. Lyman, your personal friends are the instigators of this mob. Have you ever used your personal influence with them?"

"I know no personal friends," he replied. "I am merely an official. Indeed, ladies, you must retire. It is dangerous to remain."

"If this is the last bulwark of freedom," Mrs. Chapman declared, "we may as well die here as anywhere."

Then Mary S. Parker asked, "Can we pass out safely?"

"If you will go now, I will protect you," the Mayor replied, "but cannot unless you do."

Yielding finally, they voted to adjourn and marched out, two by two, each with a Negro friend.

"When we emerged into the open daylight," reported Mrs. Chapman, "there went up a roar of rage and contempt. . . . As far as we could look either way the crowd extended – evidently of the so-called wealthy and respectable. . . . We saw the faces of those we had, until now, thought our friends – men whom we never before met without giving the hand in friendly salutation. . . ."

As they walked rapidly to the home of Mrs. Chapman a few blocks away, twenty or more women who had been kept out of the hall joined them. Arriving safely, they continued their business, first giving thanks to God for His protection. Soon they were interrupted by an excited, breathless friend bringing word that Garrison had been seized by the mob and dragged through the streets.

"We could only find relief and composure . . . in fervent prayers for his life,"[10] reported Mrs. Chapman. They did not regret holding the meeting, although now more than ever they realized what the consequences might be, but regarded it "a righteous deed for the slave, for freedom of assembly and free speech."

Mrs. Chapman had no word of Garrison until after dark, when her brother, Warren, came to report that Garrison had been rescued by a truckman, who had carried him in his arms through the mob to the City Hall, where the Mayor had ordered him transferred to the city jail for safety. Then, as Deborah Weston recorded in her diary, "We . . . began to fear for the property, particularly the antislavery rooms and some for Maria's house, for the cry had been raised among the mob, 'To West Street, Chapman's.' "[11]

That evening, the justice of the peace and the sheriff called at the Chapmans, urging them to send George Thompson away, if he were with them. Then four newspaper reporters came, and, according to Deborah Weston, "Maria gave them their dues all around."

Criticism of the women who had taken part in the meeting of the Boston Female Antislavery Society now came thick and fast from the press and the public in general. The women were condemned and not the mob. Yet, a few newspapers with no abolitionist sympathies took their stand for free speech and order, as did several young men who had observed the rioting, among them John Greenleaf Whittier, then a member of the Massachusetts Legislature, and Wendell Phillips, just beginning his practice of law. Dr. Henry L. Bowditch, disgusted with the laxness of city officials, who appeared to him more anxious to suppress the abolitionists than the mob, resolved then and there to become an abolitionist, and the next morning he subscribed to the *Liberator*. Dr.

Charles Follen, German scholar and Harvard Professor, spoke out in favor of the activities of Female Antislavery Societies, declaring, "I maintain that with regard to the antislavery cause, men and women have the same duties and the same rights. . . . Men have at all times inclined to allow women peculiar privileges, while withholding from them essential rights. . . . I look upon the formation of Ladies' Antislavery Societies as an event of the highest interest, not only for its direct beneficial bearing on the cause of emancipation, but still more as an indication of the moral growth of society."[12]

Dr. Follen's comments were a great satisfaction to Maria Weston Chapman, who maintained that she and her colleagues were only following the example of the brave women of the Revolution who never shrank from any duty because it was a new and painful one.[13]

One of the women unable to get into the hall at 46 Washington Street on October 21 was Helen Benson Garrison, Garrison's wife of a year. Helen Benson had been brought up in a family of abolitionists, the youngest daughter of Garrison's good friend, George Benson, a wool merchant of Providence, Rhode Island, who, after his retirement, lived in Brooklyn, Connecticut. He had been a member of one of this country's earliest abolitionist societies and a friend of Benjamin Lundy. Both of Helen Benson's brothers, George and Henry, were active in the antislavery movement. She first met Garrison in April, 1833, at the African Church in Providence, after he had spoken to a grateful congregation of Negroes just before leaving for England on an antislavery mission. He impressed her even more than she expected, and she stayed on after the service to hear him talk. The next day she met him again at her brother's store. This time it was Garrison who was attracted, by her "sweet countenance and pleasant conversation." Later, he confessed, "If it was not 'love at first sight' on my part, it was something very like it."[14]

Helen Benson was then twenty-three years old and the picture of health, with rosy cheeks, blue eyes, and brown hair. Her "exceeding prettiness"[15] impressed her friend Elizabeth Buffum Chace. Full of fun, thoughtful and kind, always self-controlled, and deeply religious, her family called her "peace and plenty." Yet she was often sensitive and distrustful of her own ability.

After his return from England, Garrison wrote her, suggesting that she form a Female Antislavery Society in Providence, but she replied that she had too little influence, showing clearly that she preferred to stay in the background. Eager to see and to talk with her, he soon visited the Benson farm, Friendship Valley, and repeated his visits frequently. He found her more and more important to him, and soon they were planning their marriage. She, however, could not understand why a man of genius would propose to her, while he was troubled by his precarious financial situation. The *Liberator* had always been a financial liability. As publisher, he continually faced a deficit and his salary as editor was only $700 a year. When he talked this over with Helen, showing her how little they had to live on, her response was, "Bread and butter agree with me perfectly."[16] Both recognized that his life was continually in danger. Not only was the hatred of proslavery factions directed against him, but the Georgia Legislature had offered a $5,000 reward for him. While none of these circumstances dissuaded her, it was nevertheless hard for her to leave her safe, happy, and quiet home for the uncertainties bound to be the lot of the wife of a hated but determined reformer. They were married on September 4, 1834, by their good friend, Samuel J. May.

Their first home they called Freedom Cottage. It was a

small house with a beautiful grove beside it, back of the mansion of Mayor Joseph H. Chadwick in Roxbury, three miles from Boston. Because it was isolated and a mile from the omnibus, Helen Garrison was often anxious when her husband came home from work after midnight. For a time, Isaac Knapp, the co-publisher of the *Liberator,* and his wife, lived with them, as did George Thompson and his family, when they first arrived from England. After seven months, the Garrisons moved to a house on Brighton Street, taking over Thompson's lease when it seemed wiser for him to move further away from the hatred and threats of Boston. Here they awakened one morning to find a nine-foot gallows erected in front of their home, carrying the sign, "By order of Judge Lynch." Incidents such as these repeatedly faced Helen Garrison.

She had been concerned for her husband's safety when he left home for the meeting of the Boston Female Antislavery Society, which he was to address as a substitute for George Thompson. Even so she did not plead with him to stay away, but instead left for the meeting herself, shortly after, eager to become one of the women taking their stand for freedom of assembly and free speech. Reaching Washington Street, she found an unfriendly mob blocking the entrance to the hall. A friend, John E. Fuller, seeing her there, came to her assistance and finally persuaded her to go home with him. She stayed with his family that night while her husband was being dragged through the streets by the mob. When this news reached her, she stoically remarked, "I do not believe my husband will be untrue to his principles." To her great relief, word soon reached them that he had been rescued from the mob by Mayor Lyman, who had put him in jail to keep him safe. The next day, when he was released the sheriff urged him to leave the city until the excitement had subsided, and drove him to Canton, where Mrs. Garrison joined him to take the train to Providence. From there they went to the Benson home in Brooklyn, Connecticut, where he remained a few weeks, but she stayed on several months, until after her first child was born. Her bravery, her confidence in her husband and his work for the cause, and her unfaltering cooperation were her contributions to the antislavery movement. Never an active public advocate of abolition, she nevertheless played an important role, though an indirect one. "I did not marry her," Garrison wrote his brother-in-law, "expecting that she would assume a prominent station in the antislavery cause, but for domestic quietude and happiness."[17] This she gave him in full measure. She not only steadied and encouraged him, but made his friends feel welcome at any time, and she became their friend as well, as her wide correspondence indicates.

* * *

Boston's treatment of its Female Antislavery Society so roused the indignation of the wealthy merchant Francis Jackson that he offered his home on Hollis Street for a continuation of their interrupted annual meeting. An ardent abolitionist, he admired the spirit of these women. Gratefully, they accepted his offer and announced the meeting for November 19, 1835.

In spite of threats, there was no disturbance, except the shouts of a few boys on the street, and the 130 women who gathered in Francis Jackson's home were particularly honored to have with them not only Mrs. George Thompson, but Harriet Martineau and her companion, Miss Jeffrey, who were making an extended tour of the United States, later described in *Society in America*.

At this time, Harriet Martineau and Miss Jeffrey were

guests in the home of Professor Henry Ware in Cambridge. Calling on them there, Dr. Follen asked Miss Martineau if she would consider attending an abolition meeting. She assured him that she would, and added that, having attended Colonization meetings and others which might throw light on the subject of slavery, she was anxious to hear what the abolitionists had to say. Then Dr. Follen told her of the meeting to be held at the Jackson home, but warned her that she might be in danger, as a mob probably would be on hand to break it up. This, however, did not intimidate her and later when, through Ellis Gray Loring, she received an invitation from the Boston Female Antislavery Society, she accepted, although Dr. Ware continually warned her that she would be mobbed.

On the day of the meeting, Mr. Loring called for her and Miss Jeffrey, taking them first to his home for dinner. As Harriet Martineau tells the story in her *Autobiography,* "We found Mrs. Chapman and one of her sisters at Mr. Loring's house and the Rev. Samuel J. May. During dinner, the conversation was chiefly on the Southern slave-holders, whose part was taken by Miss J. and myself, so far as to plead the involuntariness of their position, and the extreme perplexity of their case. . . . Immediately after dinner . . . when I was putting on my shawl upstairs, Mrs. Chapman came to me, bonnet in hand, to say, "You know we are threatened with a mob again today; but I do not myself much apprehend it. It must not surprise us, but my hopes are stronger than my fears."[18]

Mrs. Chapman made a lasting impression on her. "I hear now . . . ," she later recalled, "the silvery tones of her who was to be the friend of the rest of my life. I still see the exquisite beauty which took me by surprise that day: — the aspect meant by nature to be soft and winning only, but that day (and ever since) so vivified by courage, and so strengthened by upright conviction, as to appear the very embodiment of heroism."

From the Loring home, they walked to the Jacksons, and on the way Mr. Loring again warned Miss Martineau of the danger which might be ahead, but as they approached the house they found only a dozen boys gathered. As soon as they had entered the house, the front door was bolted, and Mr. Jackson, Mr. Loring, and Mr. May remained in the front hall on guard after pointing out a way of escape at the rear of the house.

The Boston Female Antislavery Society more than filled the two drawing rooms, and Miss Martineau listened with interest as they carried on their meeting with reading from the Bible, a prayer, and the singing of a well-known antislavery hymn, written by Elizabeth Chandler. After the secretary had read her report, a note from Mr. Loring was handed to Harriet Martineau, asking if she would say a few words.

"The moment of reading this note," Miss Martineau recalled, "was one of the most painful of my life. I felt that could never be happy again if I refused what was asked o me; but, to comply was probably to shut against me every door in the United States, but those of the abolitionists. . . George Thompson was then on the sea, having narrowl escaped with his life; and the fury against 'foreign incendiaries' ran high."[19]

As she hesitated, Mrs. Loring whispered to her that sh should speak only if she felt it right to do so. Her answe was to rise with dignity and to say, "I have been requeste by a friend present to say something, if only a word, to express my sympathy in the objects of this meeting. I ha supposed that my presence here would be understood a showing my sympathy . . . . I will say what I have said throug the whole South, in every family where I have been, that I consider slavery as inconsistent with the law of God, and as incompatible with the course of His Providence. I should certainly say no less at the North than at the South, concerning this utter abomination – and now I declare that in your *principles*, I fully agree."

There was a murmur of satisfaction through the room, for it meant a great deal to hear a word of approval from a woman of such prominence as Harriet Martineau.

While, without doubt, her short speech was the climax of the meeting, there were other encouraging features, such as a letter from Lydia Maria Child telling of her contacts with the Philadelphia Society, through which help was being given to runaway slaves and free Negroes. She closed her letter with these challenging words, "Some will tell you that women have nothing to do with this question! . . . When Bonaparte told a French lady that he did not like to hear a woman talk politics, she replied, 'Sir, in a country where women are beheaded, it is very natural they should like to know the reason.' And where women are brutalized, scourged, and sold, shall we not inquire the reason? My sisters, you have not only the right, but it is your solemn duty; and may God bless you, according to the firmness with which you perform that duty."[20]

As Harriet Martineau anticipated, she paid dearly for her association with Boston abolitionists, reporting in her *Autobiography*, "For a considerable time, my intercourse was confined to the abolitionists and their friends, and my own former friends . . . but before the end of my stay, it seemed to be discovered that I was not the monster that had been described."[21]

Sharply criticized by the *Boston Daily Advertiser* for her abolitionist sympathies, she found an advocate in a highly respected Boston merchant, Mr. Minot, who sent a letter of protest to the *Advertiser,* calling attention to the fact that American travelers in England were allowed to express their opinions freely, and he hoped that Boston would not refuse a similar courtesy to a distinguished lady . . . to whom a debt of gratitude was owing for her writings.

Having heard all kinds of abuse of William Lloyd Garrison, Harriet Martineau felt it only fair to judge him for herself, and this she was able to do when Garrison and Samuel J. May called on her. "His aspect," she recorded in her *Retrospect of Western Travel,* "put to flight in an instant what prejudices his slanderers had raised in me. I was wholly taken by surprise. It was a countenance wholly glowing with health, and wholly expressive of purity, animation, and gentleness. . . . Garrison has a good deal of a Quaker air; and his speech is deliberate like a Quaker's, but gentle as a woman's."[22] When he thanked her for wishing to meet anyone with "so odious" a reputation, she replied that as she had become nearly as odious, it was fitting that they should meet. "Every conversation I had with him," she added, "confirmed my opinion that sagacity is the most striking attribute of his conversation. It has none of the severity, the harshness of his writing." She made it clear, however, that she did not like "the tone of his printed censures," that she could not use such language "toward any class of offenders, nor . . . sympathize in its use by others." Yet she was convinced that he was above passion and unrighteous anger and regarded his task as the "exposure of fallacy" and the "denunciation of hypocrisy." Asked later to describe Garrison, she replied that he was "the most bewitching person" she had met in the United States.

Garrison recorded his impressions of Harriet Martineau later in a letter to his wife, "She is plain and frank in her manners, and not less so in her conversation. I can assure you that we abolitionists need not fear that she will ever print anything, either in this country or in England, inimical to us, or in favor of the colonization society." Then he added, "She is now abiding under the roof of Dr. Channing and no doubt will do him much good."[23]

CHAPTER IV

"A Parcel of Silly Women"

The hospitable Chapman home on West Street had become a friendly meeting place for abolitionists. Here Garrison, Samuel J. May, the Lorings, and the Follens gathered for informal antislavery discussions, and occasionally Lydia Maria Child joined them. Both she and her husband were continuing their work for the cause. He was investigating the production of beet sugar to be used as a substitute for cane sugar raised by slave labor, and she had followed the publication of her *Appeal in Behalf of That Class of Americans Called Africans,* with an antislavery annual, *Oasis,* and two pamphlets, *Antislavery Catechism,* and *The Evils and the Cure of Slavery,* in which she quoted well-known Southerners on the subject and showed the satisfactory results of emancipation in the West Indies.

This group had for some time been disappointed in what they regarded as William Ellery Channing's lukewarm attitude toward slavery. The Chapmans were members of his congregation, drawn to him by his liberal theology, his deeply religious nature, and intellect. Mrs. Chapman did her best to bring Channing and Garrison together, feeling sure that if Channing knew Garrison and understood him as she did, he would appreciate him, but so far she had been unable even to arrange a meeting. Channing still recoiled from Garrison's harsh language, while Garrison was impatient with Channing's indecisiveness. When finally Garrison expressed a wish to hear Dr. Channing speak, she persuaded him to go to church with her one Sunday, and they sat in Stephen Higginson's pew, which she had permission to occupy. Garrison praised Dr. Channing's sermon, but had no opportunity to talk with him. So great was the feeling against Garrison that Mrs. Chapman the next day received a notice from Mr. Higginson that he could no longer allow her seats in his pew.

Then in November, 1835, Channing published his *Thoughts on Slavery*. Definitely a step in the right direction, it nevertheless provoked much discussion pro and con among abolitionists. Some, delighted to have a man of Dr. Channing's reputation speak out against slavery, even in a limited way, praised and distributed his book. In it, he made it very clear that although he regarded slavery as evil, he was not in sympathy with militant abolition nor immediate emancipation, that while he subscribed to the *Liberator*, he heartily disapproved of Garrison's harsh language. He also stated that while he honored abolitionists "for their strength of principle, their sympathy for their fellow creatures, and their active goodness,"[1] he was convinced that they did a great deal of harm by arousing bitter passions and fierce fanaticism. His great fear was that the efforts of militant abolitionists would lead to war — to civil war — which he regarded as a greater evil than slavery. In his opinion the removal of slavery should be left in the hands of the slaveholder.

The Chapmans and Garrison both sharply criticized Dr. Channing's *Thoughts on Slavery*, accusing him of using their arguments against the sin of slavery and then neutralizing them by repudiating their crusade. "He asks us," said Garrison, "to give up our watchword 'Immediate Emancipation,' to disband our societies, and to keep our publications from slaveholders."[2] Feeling that Channing's book misrepresented and retarded the cause, Garrison listed in the *Liberator* twenty-four reasons why abolitionists should not be deceived by it, criticizing Dr. Channing's unrealistic, inconsistent attitude toward slavery. Ellis Gray Loring, on the other hand, called the book "nineteen-twentieths sound in principle." John Quincy Adams, however, felt as strongly as Garrison and, commenting in his diary on its "Jesuitical complexion,"[3] said, "He treats the subject so smoothly that some Southern slaveholders have quoted it with approbation, as favoring their side of the question."[4]

Lydia Maria Child looked upon Dr. Channing's *Thoughts on Slavery* as the direct result of her *Appeal in Favor of That Class of Americans Called Africans.* This had so aroused Dr. Channing that he had come to see her repeatedly to discuss the subject, saying it made him feel he could no longer keep silent on slavery. Now, in an open letter to him published in the *Liberator,* she praised the militant abolitionists, whom Channing depreciated. "Had it not been for the honest enthusiasm of Wm. L. Garrison," she wrote, "I should never have felt, thought, or written on the subject. How far this is the case with Dr. Channing, no mortal, not even himself, can tell."[5]

So the debate continued, but Mrs. Chapman had much else to occupy her time and thought.

* * *

Mrs. Chapman and her sisters had introduced antislavery fairs to raise money for the cause, and the second annual fair was held late in December, 1835, at the home of her father-in-law, Henry Chapman. The women had pledged $1,000 and they raised it. These fairs became popular annual events and were widely patronized.

Mrs. Chapman and her colleagues in the Boston Female

Antislavery Society also circulated petitions urging the abolition of slavery in the District of Columbia. In fact, so many petitions were presented through the efforts of abolitionists that Southerners in the House of Representatives passed a Gag Rule, which was persistently fought by John Quincy Adams as endangering the sacred right of petition, guaranteed by the Constitution. In spite of the Gag Rule, Boston women continued to send petitions with many signatures to John Quincy Adams. One petition, drafted by Mrs. Chapman, read, "We respectfully announce our intention to present the same petition yearly before your honorable body that it may at least be a memorial of us, that in the holy cause of Human Freedom, 'We have done what we could.' "

With these petitions, sent out to women in Massachusetts for signatures, went a special appeal, written by Mrs. Chapman: "As *wives* and mothers, as sisters and daughters, we are deeply responsible for the influence we have on the human race. . . . Let us know no rest till we have done our utmost to convince the mind, and obtain the testimony, of every woman, in every town, in every county of our Commonwealth, against the horrible slave traffic, which makes the District of Columbia a disgrace . . . and exhibits, in the centre of a Christian country, an unrebuked wickedness, for which no other spot on earth affords a parallel."[6]

The Boston newspapers at once attacked and ridiculed this appeal, the *Commercial Gazette* declaring that the main object of the Boston Female Antislavery Society seemed to be " 'to lead captive silly women,' who would be more usefully and profitably employed at home . . . than stirring up discord and dissension, preaching on a subject about which they know no more than the man in the moon."

The Essex, Massachusetts *Register,* however, published

the appeal, giving it wider circulation, and earning the sharp rebuke of the *Commercial Gazette* for publishing the "absurdities and falsehoods" of "a parcel of silly women."[7]

The Gag Rule against antislavery petitions was only one of the indications of the South's increasing belligerence toward the activities of abolitionists. In his message to Congress, late in 1835, President Jackson had misrepresented the activities of abolitionists, had implied approval of mob violence against them, and had proposed closing the mails to their publications. As a result, Southern governors and legislatures bombarded those of the North with resolutions demanding action against abolitionists, whom they accused of inciting slaves to revolt. Falling in with their suggestions, Governor Everett, of Massachusetts, made this statement, "Whatever by direct and necessary operation is calculated to excite insurrection among the slaves may be prosecuted as a misdemeanor at common law."[8] Vigilance committees to prevent antislavery meetings were formed in some New England towns, and in Cincinnati a mob destroyed the office of James G. Birney's antislavery paper, *The Philanthropist.* Churches, following the lead of those in the South, spoke out with few exceptions against antislavery activities and closed their doors to antislavery meetings. Nevertheless the numbers of abolitionists increased and new societies were formed.

In March, 1836, the Massachusetts Antislavery Society asked for a hearing before the committee of the legislature to which Southern demands against abolitionists had been referred. Mrs. Chapman and her group of antislavery women, as well as Harriet Martineau, attended the hearing and listened with pride to the statements of Ellis Gray Loring, Samuel J. May, William Lloyd Garrison, and Dr. Follen, whose forthright remarks caused Chairman Lunt to adjourn the hearing. At the request of the abolitionists, a second hearing was granted. This, too, was adjourned in an uproar of conflicting opinions. However, the report of the committee did not recommend any legislative action against abolitionist activities, although it called abolitionists "disunionists, agitators, visionaries . . . enemies of peace and the Constitution."[9]

Mrs. Chapman was delighted to find both Dr. Channing and Harriet Martineau at this meeting and made use of this opportunity to introduce them, remarking, as they shook hands, "Righteousness and peace have kissed each other."[10]

Antislavery meetings and conventions continued in Boston, but did not arouse mob violence as in 1835. In May, 1836, the New England Antislavery Society held a convention in the Salem Street Church, attracting women as well as men from all parts of New England, and making many converts. One of the women attending was Elizabeth Buffum Chace from Providence, who was a guest of the Chapmans. Mrs. Chace described Mrs. Chapman as "young and very beautiful," and added, "They were living on West Street in great simplicity of style, being devoted heart, soul, and purse to the Antislavery cause. . . . She had three little children, and, though so young, they seemed imbued with the antislavery spirit. . . . Her little boy was sitting on the floor, tearing a newspaper to pieces, and she said to him, 'Oh Henry, you must not tear that paper.' He exclaimed, 'Why, it isn't the *Liberator,* mother.' "[11] Mrs. Chace also reported that Mrs. Chapman had confessed to her that since the antislavery riot she was afraid to walk on Washington Street alone because she was often insulted by clerks coming out of shops and she also admitted that she and her husband no longer had any social standing in Boston because of their antislavery activity.

* * *

Free Negroes in trouble and fugitive slaves also claimed the attention of Mrs. Chapman and the Boston Female Antislavery Society. In July, 1836, some Negroes unloading a brig at one of the wharves noticed two Negro women frantically signaling them from a porthole. Unable to go aboard, but suspicious that two free Negroes were to be taken back into slavery, they got in touch with their antislavery friends, who obtained a writ of habeas corpus by means of which the women were transferred to the Leverett Street jail, pending trial. There, members of the Boston Female Antislavery Society visited them. "Knowing so many painful facts respecting the seizure of free persons of color as slaves," Mrs. Chapman reported, "we felt great sympathy with these women, and determined to give them, at the trial, whatever comfort our presence might afford. . . ."[12] Five members of the Society were in the courtroom when the trial commenced. It was claimed that the two women were the property of John B. Morris, of Baltimore, and must be returned to him. Samuel Sewall, acting as counsel for the women, argued that the Bill of Rights was the basis of the practice of law in Massachusetts, and that, under the Bill of Rights, all are born free and have the right of engaging counsel and defending their liberties. Thereupon the audience, mostly Negroes, responded with applause. Judge Shaw, delivering his decision, declared that the question in the case was simply this, "Has the captain of the brig, *Chickasaw,* a right to convert his vessel into a prison?" When he announced that the prisoners were to be discharged, all in the courtroom rose. For a moment it looked as if the Southern agent would seize the prisoners, but suddenly there was a shout, Go! Go!, and the Negroes in the courtroom surrounded the women and took them away.

Later, Mrs. Chapman and her colleagues talked with these women and learned that the Southern agent on the brig, posing as a Methodist minister, had talked with them, asked to see their free papers, and destroyed them.

When asked by Mrs. Chapman why they had come North, one of them replied, "I thought I should not be in danger of falling into slavery again, if I could but get into the free states. I did not expect to meet such troubles the moment I got here: — nor to meet such friends to care for me either."

Then Mrs. Chapman asked her how the slaves thought freedom would come to them.

"They are waiting," she replied, "to see God do it for them, in some wonderful manner as he did for the Israelites. . . . We pray to him and have faith in him only: for the whole world seems to have forgotten us."

Talking with these women, Mrs. Chapman was impressed by their moral sense and piety. When she showed them some of the antislavery publications, they seemed surprised at the correctness of the description of the condition of the slaves. "Only," added one of them, "it is impossible to put such dreadful sufferings properly into print."

The part which members of the Boston Female Antislavery Society played in this affair was sharply criticized by the Boston *Centinel and Gazette:* "We learn that, in the Courtroom, the disgusting spectacle was exhibited of white abolitionists, accompanied by females, white and black, giving aid and countenance to violence on the part of the Negroes. . . . Among the principal actors in this attempt to disturb the peace, were a parcel of silly women, whose fondness for notoriety has repeatedly led them into scenes of commotion and riots. They deserve straight petticoats, as do their husbands, fathers, and guardians, who allow them to excite commotion in the city."

The *Courier, Transcript, Post,* and *Atlas* also expressed their disapproval of the women in exaggerated language, so much so that Mrs. Chapman, in reporting the story of those days in *Right and Wrong in Boston,* declared that this record would be useful in showing the character of the opposition, "useful as proofs of the existence of a spirit, in the pro-slavery party at the North in 1836, which, after abolition shall have taken place, will be strenuously denied: so incredible will it seem."

Another legal undertaking by the Boston Female Anti-slavery Society was the famous Med case, which developed when it came to the attention of the Society that a family in Boston, recently from the South, had a slave child with them and intended to return soon to the South with the child. Realizing that here was an opportunity to free the child, while she was in a free State and under the protection of the Massachusetts' Bill of Rights, the Society felt itself duty-bound to take this case to court and asked Ellis Gray Loring and Samuel Sewall to act as their counsel. Mrs. Chapman's mother-in-law, Mary Gray Chapman, contributed the necessary funds. Again, the members of the Boston Female Anti-slavery Society filled the courtroom and, to their great satisfaction, won the case and saw the child freed. The press condemned these women for leaving "the holiness of the fire-side," called them fanatics, and accused them of cruelty for separating the child from her mistress and from her slave mother in the South. To this they replied that since the slave-owner claimed the child was his and not the mother's, he was liable at any time to separate them by selling the child. This court action, on the other hand, not only freed the child, but proved to all colored persons in Massachusetts that they were free under its jurisdiction and could not be claimed by their former masters in the South.

Ellis Gray Loring regarded the decision in this case as "not exceeded in interest or real moment by any decision made within the last half-century." That this decision had come about through the efforts of "a female agency" he thought worthy of notice, and added, "It ought to be a strong argument with the females of our land to unite in societies, gathering as they may from union, a moral strength adequate to such important results. I have never doubted that the Female Antislavery Societies were a very valuable addition of power to us, — but it is a very pleasant assurance to see, year after year, tangible proof of it."[13]

The history of the Boston Female Antislavery Society, recorded by Maria Weston Chapman, was published in 1836 by Isaac Knapp of the *Liberator* press, under the title, *Right and Wrong in Boston.* This record was continued yearly through 1839, after which the Boston Female Antislavery Society merged with the Massachusetts Antislavery Society — for by that time many of the men were ready to welcome women as members. Mrs. Chapman gave as her reasons for preserving the record of the Society, "to promulgate Truth," and to remind those active in the cause of details they might easily forget in the onrush of events. She also felt that much that had happened would not be credited in the future, so impossible would it then seem. To Mrs. Chapman and her colleagues the cause had deep religious import and they carried on their work with evangelical zeal, "believing slavery to be in direct violation of the laws of God."[14]

Mrs. Chapman also published in 1836, *Songs of the Free,* a collection of antislavery hymns and poems, among them a few poems of her own. Believing that poetry and music had through the ages brought comfort, consolation, and strength to those working for the good of the race, she hoped that *Songs of the Free* would likewise meet the need of those "laboring for the freedom of the American slave."

* * *

There was romance as well as writing and discussion in the Chapman home at this time. Ann Terry Greene, who had lived with her uncle and aunt since the death of her parents, was now twenty-three years old, pretty and vivacious, a good conversationalist, a great favorite socially, and wealthy as well. She had become as ardent an abolitionist as her guardians, was a member of the Boston Female Antislavery Society, and had faced the mob in 1835. Late that year she traveled by stage to Greenfield with her cousin, Mary Grew, and Mary's fiancé, James Alford, who had persuaded his friend, Wendell Phillips, to accompany them as her escort. James Alford had described Ann Greene to Wendell Phillips in most flattering terms, warning him, however, that she was a devoted abolitionist. This Wendell Phillips soon found out for himself, but concluded that her beauty and charm had been underestimated. They were a handsome pair. Ann with her long brown hair, blue eyes, and good color, and Wendell, a veritable Apollo, tall and handsome, with ruddy complexion and reddish-blond hair.

The son of one of Boston's first families and a Harvard graduate, Wendell Phillips was at that time practicing law. He had watched with dismay and disapproval the mob on Washington Street breaking up the meeting of the Boston Female Antislavery Society.

This he and Ann Greene discussed, and as they talked, he took note of her intelligence and hearty laugh. He had read Mrs. Child's *Appeal* and had been greatly impressed by it. He was leaning toward abolition, and now Ann Greene heightened his interest. During the next few months, he was a frequent caller at the Chapman home and here he met William Lloyd Garrison for the first time, commenting later that this was a turning point in his life. At the time however, Ann Greene was his all-absorbing interest.

In addition to his law practice, he was filling lecture engagements, and in January, 1836, when he lectured in New Bedford, where Deborah Weston was teaching, he stayed at her boarding house. "Wendell, I like," she wrote her sister. "There seems to be a great deal of straightforwardness and simplicity about him. Intercourse with abolitionists I think will do him good. His lecture . . . was considered very fine, slightly whiggy and rather conservative. . . . He did better than I expected. . . . I think Ann Terry has done very well."[15]

During the summer, Ann became ill and often was too ill to see Wendell. Hearing in the fall that she was in a critical condition, he went straight to Mr. Chapman and insisted on seeing her. According to Mrs. Chapman "He went upstairs, saw her alone 20 minutes and came down a fiancé. Ever since this time he has been with her two hours each day and she is getting much better."[16] To a friend, Ann confessed later, "When I first met Wendell, I used to think, 'it can never come to pass, such a being as he is could never think of me.' I looked upon it as something as strange as a fairy tale."[17]

As the weeks went by, he became more and more of an abolitionist. He attended the convention of the Massachusetts Antislavery Society, held in the loft of a stable because all halls in Boston were closed to abolitionists, and he made his first antislavery speech in Lynn. Soon Maria Weston Chapman was able to tell her friends that he had subscribed to the *Liberator*.

As it became known in Boston that Wendell Phillips had abolitionist sympathies, his law practice was adversely affected, many of his former friends spurned him, and some of his family thought him insane. He had without doubt ruined his political, professional, and social future, but the cause both of the slave and freedom of speech had so gripped him that there was no thought of turning back.

Ann Terry Greene and Wendell Phillips were married in October, 1837, with only the Chapman and Phillips families present. According to Anne Weston, Ann Greene "in embroidered muslin with pink scarf and belt" was radiant and the picture of health. That Wendell's mother was unhappy over his marriage to an abolitionist, in spite of her wealth and social standing, was indicated by Anne Weston's comment, "The old lady Phillips . . . behaved like a perfect dragon."[18]

* * *

Less than two months later, the nation was stirred by the mob murder in Alton, Illinois, of Elijah Lovejoy. In the words of John Quincy Adams, it gave "a shock as of any earthquake, throughout this continent." Lovejoy, a young Presbyterian minister from Maine and a graduate of Princeton Theological Seminary, had started a religious paper, the *Observer,* in St. Louis. Seeing slavery at first hand, he began to write on the subject, advocating gradual abolition and colonization. Then, seeing a slave, accused of a crime, burned alive by a mob, he spoke out in his paper against the outrage. As a result, his office was destroyed and his press thrown into the Mississippi. Moving to Alton, Illinois, to continue his crusade for freedom of the press, he at once met opposition. Three of his presses were destroyed, and he was murdered defending the fourth.

When the news reached Boston, a group of leading citizens, headed by Dr. Channing, asked for the use of Faneuil Hall to hold a protest meeting, not as abolitionists, but as advocates of free speech and freedom of the press. Permission to use the hall for this purpose was refused, on the grounds that such a meeting would result in confusion and injure the city's reputation. So strong, however, were the protests by prominent Bostonians that permission to use Faneuil Hall was finally granted, and at ten o'clock on the morning of December 8, five thousand gathered there, among them not only defenders of free speech and abolitionists, but also those eager to rouse the mob spirit.

"It was a noble sight, that hall on that day," recorded Harriet Martineau. "The morning sunlight never streamed in over such a throng. . . . I went (for the Woman Question) with fifteen others. The indignation at us was great. People said it gave the meeting the air of an abolition gathering to have women there; it hung out false colors. Shame! when it was a free discussion meeting and nothing more, that women should have given color to the idea that it was for abolition purposes. Good is it not that sixteen women can give character to a meeting of 2,500 men."[19]

Wendell Phillips was there with Ann and Mrs. Chapman. Nothing could have kept him away. He was prepared to make a speech, for he had been increasingly troubled by indications that freedom of speech and the press were being threatened and that people were being mobbed and lynched for speaking their minds on slavery. This, in his opinion, was undermining the principles on which the nation had been founded.

He listened attentively as the chairman, Jonathan Phillips, opened the meeting, as Dr. Channing spoke briefly, and as resolutions drafted by Dr. Channing were offered, condemning "the fearful progress of lawless force in the country." Before the resolutions could be put to a vote, the Attorney General of Massachusetts, James Austin, began a rabble-rousing harangue, comparing the Alton mob with the Boston Tea Party of 1776. He accused Lovejoy of exciting the passions of men, of unwise, rash, and unchristian conduct which led directly to his murder. He warned that the people of Massachusetts would follow the example of the Alton mob, should "their lives be threatened by these abolitionist conspirators." Lovejoy, he added, "was a fool working with those conspirators and died a fool's death."[20]

Roaring applause, interrupted by hoots of derision, followed, giving every indication that the resolutions would be voted down. This so roused Wendell Phillips that he started toward the platform. Ann, seizing his arm, asked what he intended to do, and he replied hurriedly, "I am going to speak if I can make myself heard." Pushing his way through the crowd, he reached the platform. As he stood there calmly, youthful and handsome, the noisy audience became quiet, curious as to what would happen next. Addressing the chairman, he began, "We have met for the free discussion of these resolutions and the events which gave rise to them."[21] Then he expressed his surprise at the sentiments of the last speaker and the applause they received. "A comparison has been drawn," he continued, "between the events of the Revolution and the tragedy at Alton. . . . The mob at Alton were met to wrest from a citizen his just rights — met to resist the laws. We have been told that our fathers did the same, and the glorious mantle of Revolutionary precedent has been thrown over the mobs of our days. . . ." Pointing to the portraits on the walls of Faneuil Hall, he continued, in scornful, icy tones, "When I heard the gentleman lay down principles which place the murderers of Alton side by side with Otis and Hancock, with Quincy and Adams, I thought those pictured lips would have broken into voice to rebuke the recreant American, the slanderer of the dead. . . . For the sentiments he has uttered, on soil consecrated by the prayers of Puritans and the blood of patriots, the earth should have yawned and swallowed him up."

At this, the uproar was so great he could not be heard, but finally he was able to continue under heckling, as he appealed to the patriotism of the audience, reminding them of the ideals and principles of the founders of the Republic. Lovejoy, he declared, died because he dared put his convictions into print – that was all – and no American could criticize him for that. His great achievement was to show Americans the value of the freedom of the press.

This turned the tide. The resolutions, which had seemed doomed to defeat after Austin's speech, were now passed, and as the vast audience left the hall they talked more about Phillips than Lovejoy. For many, as well as for Ann and Mrs. Chapman, it was a thrilling experience. It established Wendell Phillips' reputation as an orator, and he was in continuous demand. It placed him in the public mind on the side of the abolitionists. That evening, Mrs. Chapman, realizing his importance to the cause, persuaded him to cast his lot wholeheartedly with the abolitionists.

The Lovejoy meeting brought another young Bostonian from one of the first families into the abolition fold – Edmund Quincy, the son of Josiah Quincy, then President of Harvard. He had been sympathetic to abolition, but had been troubled by Garrison's strong language denouncing slaveholders. The Lovejoy tragedy led him to speak and write for abolition and to become an active colleague of the Chapmans and the Weston sisters, whose loyalty to Garrison never wavered.

After the Lovejoy meeting, Mrs. Chapman sent her comments to the English Quaker abolitionist, Elizabeth Pease, who had expressed such interest in the cause in America. Lovejoy, she wrote her, had been killed in a free state for the crime of being an abolitionist. "You can hardly realize the feelings of the abolitionists," she added. "We feel there is no law for us." She described the meeting at Faneuil Hall as very nearly a mob and yet with free discussion carrying through. "We went home," she continued, "with a feeling of security for life and property for the present. But I fear when I see the strength of slavery here and how the institutions of the South are interwoven with our free ones, not openly indeed, but like the roots of giant trees, beneath the soil, — I fear that abolition will be resisted by the South to her own destruction, and by the North till the last possible day of Grace. May God strengthen us to endure."[22]

To another friend in Scotland, she wrote at this time, referring to the murder of Lovejoy, "Dreadful tidings from the West! . . . I feel deep regret that the principles of non-resistance were not adopted by our friend. . . . I sometimes fear that this is but the prelude to a wholesale slaughter of abolitionists."[23]

In Lynn, Massachusetts, a young Quaker, Abby Kelley, a teacher in the Friends' School, was so deeply stirred by the Lovejoy murder that she increased her activities as secretary of the Lynn Female Antislavery Society to such an extent that Maria Weston Chapman wrote her praising "the Lynn spirit."[24]

Born in Pelham, Massachusetts, January 15, 1811, of Quaker-Irish parents, Abby, when a young child, moved to Worcester with her family and then to a farm near the city. She attended the public school in Worcester, but completed her education at the Friends' School in Providence. She taught school in Worcester, in Millbury, and, for five years in Lynn. Here she heard Garrison speak on colonization as no remedy for slavery. Later, Arnold Buffum, the first agent of the New England Antislavery Society, moved her deeply by his speech in Lynn. "From this time on," she tells us, "I did whatever I could to carry forward the work, circulating petitions to State Legislatures and Congress, distributing our publications, soliciting subscriptions to our journals and raising funds . . . explaining our principles and measures, by private conversation, in season and out of season, taking more and more of my time left from school duties."[25]

She heard George Thompson lecture in 1835, and when a hostile mob interrupted him, throwing stones through the windows and forcing open the doors, she was in the group of antislavery women who surrounded him to shield him and hurried him to a nearby house, where he was hidden until it was safe for him to leave. This was her introduction to mob violence, which was to become a common occurrence to her in the years that followed.

Writing to her family in 1837, mentioning the Lovejoy murder, her interest in abolition, peace, and temperance, she added, "It's a great joy to see the world grow better in anything. Indeed I think endeavors to improve mankind is the only object worth living for."[26] Searching for a life work, dedicated to improving mankind, she found it in the antislavery movement.

CHAPTER V

Voices from the South

While all this was happening in New England, Sarah and Angelina Grimké were growing up in Charleston, South Carolina, where slavery was accepted as a matter of course. They, however, even as children, looked upon slavery as evil and often wept over its cruelty and tragedy.

Sarah, the sixth of fourteen children was born in Charleston, November 26, 1792. Her father, John Grimké, of German Huguenot descent, was a wealthy slave-owner, a brilliant, independent man, a judge of the supreme court of the state. Impressed by Sarah's superior mind, he paid special attention to her, guiding her and discussing serious subjects with her. He became the hero and friend of her youth, as did her brother Thomas, six years her senior, with whom she studied Latin and Greek, subjects then considered unsuitable for girls. Eager for wider knowledge, she begged to study law, but instead was obliged to busy herself with social activities. Her mother, who was of strictly orthodox English background was so hard-pressed by the management of the household and its many slaves that she had little time to show affection or understanding toward her children. Often impatient with the slaves, she had them severely punished, and this made a vivid impression on Sarah, who wept and prayed over each whipping. Sarah herself treated the slave children as her equals and often at night in her bedroom, with the keyhole covered so no one could see, taught them to read, although this was in defiance of state law.

At sixteen, instead of being able to study the subjects she longed to master, she was, as she expressed it, "initiated into the circles of dissipation and folly."[1] Far from satisfied with a life of extravagance, vanity, and frivolity, she turned to religion for comfort, and not finding it in the Episcopal Church, which she attended with her mother, reached out for help to the local Presbyterian minister. This was the beginning of her almost continuous soul-searching. About this time, her father, who was seriously ill, went to Philadelphia for consultation and treatment. Because she had nursed him so devotedly at home, he took her with him, and she found comfortable lodgings for them with a Quaker family. He did not recover, and when she returned home after his death, weighed down by her grief, she struggled again to find comfort in religion, turning first to the Methodists and then to the Quakers. The sin of slavery weighed heavily on her conscience. Unhappy at home, where she was ridiculed for her seriousness, her long face, and her drab clothing, she decided to return to Philadelphia, where she was invited to make her home with a Quaker family. However, she returned frequently to Charleston and to her beloved younger sister, Angelina,[2] who had become a gay, fashionable, intelligent, self-reliant young girl. Angelina, too, had sought peace and satisfaction in religion, for she found a life of frivolity empty. The punishment of slaves troubled her more at this time than the institution of slavery itself, which she still believed was sanctioned by the Bible. As a child, she was so distressed after witnessing severe whippings, that she stole away after dark to the slave cabins to soothe the burning welts with oil.

In 1828, she visited Sarah in Philadelphia, where she too came under the influence of the Quakers. Occasionally she returned to Charleston, each time finding slavery more intolerable and confiding to her diary that it was a heavy burden on her heart. When in Charleston, she longed for the north as for the promised land, because it was a land of freedom. Eager to become more familiar with the religious thought of the Quakers, she read Woolman's works. She also read the antislavery pamphlets which Sarah sent her, and these brought her in touch with the antislavery movement in the North. Gradually she made the decision to leave Charleston for Philadelphia, and, in the fall of 1829, left, never to return. At that time, she had no thought of affiliating with the antislavery movement. Her object was to get away from slavery and to be able to express herself freely on the subject. In Philadelphia, she lived with Sarah in the home of Catherine Morris, a devout Quaker, and found that Sarah was still agonizing over her sins, such as her fear of speaking in Meeting. Angelina also became a member of the Society of Friends, although not completely in sympathy with all its practices, such as the ungrammatical use of "thee" and "thou" which she never followed, nor the Quaker dress which she wore but felt to be an empty gesture. Yet, in spite of her independence, which troubled her more orthodox sister, she began to prepare for the ministry, for she discovered that she could speak with ease and effectiveness in Meeting. She took part in Quaker activities, visiting prisons and hospitals, but this did not satisfy her yearning for useful work to which she could give her whole self. The attitude of Orthodox Quakers toward slavery was disappointing to her. Although Quakers had been among the first to recognize the evil of slavery and had freed their own slaves, they were cautious about advocating a solution to the problem. In general, they favored gradual emancipation and colonization, and were warned to avoid all contention. Ministers like Lucretia Mott, who mentioned abolition, caused great uneasiness. All this troubled the forthright Angelina, whose keen mind was searching for the great work to which she felt she was called. For a short time she taught an "infant" school, and began corresponding with Catherine Beecher in Hartford in regard to further preparation as a teacher. She was now 27 years old, a tall, slender, attractive young woman with blue eyes and chestnut ringlets.

In the summer of 1832, she went to Hartford where she talked with Catherine and Harriet Beecher, attended some of Catherine Beecher's classes, and was assured that a six-months course would prepare her for teaching. Planning to study with Catherine Beecher, she returned to Philadelphia to encounter stiff opposition among the Friends, who warned her against coming under other than Quaker influence. Reluctantly she gave up her plans, but she had had a glimpse of the outside world which gave her food for thought. Much was happening in that world. In 1833, slaves in the British West Indies were emancipated, and later that same year the American Antislavery Society was organized in Philadelphia. Then the students at Lane Seminary, in Ohio, debated slavery, colonization, and emancipation with such fervor and effectiveness that further debate on this controversial subject was banned by the Trustees, with the approval of the Seminary's president, Dr. Lyman Beecher. This led to the withdrawal of some able students, among them Theodore D. Weld and Henry B. Stanton, who soon began lecturing for the American Antislavery Society with evangelical zeal. As Angelina thought over these happenings, she wrote her brother, Thomas, asking for his opinions on colonization and on the antislavery movement. Thomas Grimké, an able lawyer, had served in the South Carolina Legislature and was known for his liberal progressive views. He did not approve of slavery, and regarded colonization as only an aid, not a solution, but he realized that antislavery agitation would eventually shake the very foundations of the country. He planned to make a thorough study of the whole subject and come to definite conclusions. This, however, was cut short by his untimely death in 1834. For Angelina and Sarah, it was as if the light had gone out. They now must work out their own salvation.

* * *

They made a point of getting acquainted with the few colored members of the Friends' Society and became especially fond of Sarah Douglass. These Negro Friends were assigned to separate seats in the Meeting House, in a corner and under the stairs. At first, neither Angelina nor Sarah found this objectionable, but within a few years denounced it. The more independent Angelina took a great interest in the antislavery movement in the North, keeping in touch with it through the *Liberator*. She heard George Thompson speak and was greatly impressed. In May, 1835, she wrote in her diary that for a long time she had regarded the subject of abolition as utterly hopeless, but had changed her mind since examining antislavery principles. "I have found them," she added, "so full of the power of truth, that I am confident not many years will roll by before the horrible traffic in human beings will be destroyed. . . . My earnest prayers have been poured out that the Lord would be pleased to permit me to be instrumental of good to these degraded, oppressed, and suffering fellow-creatures. Truly, I often feel ready to go to prison or death in this cause of justice, mercy, and love. . . ." She kept asking herself, "What can I do?"[2]

When she read of the animosity toward George Thompson in Boston, she impulsively dashed off a letter from the heart to Garrison, expressing her sympathy in this "alarming crisis" and adding that she had viewed the violence of the past weeks with deep concern, fearing it would drive abolitionists into confusion. His *Appeal to the People of Boston* had reassured her. "I thanked God," she continued, "and took courage, earnestly desiring that thousands may adopt thy language and be prepared to meet the Martyr's doom. . . . If persecution is the means which God has ordained for the accomplishment of this great end, *Emancipation:* then . . . let it come, for it is my deep, deliberate conviction that this is a cause worth dying for. I say so, from what I have seen, heard, and known, in a land of slavery. . . ."[3]

Such a letter from a Southerner, a member of the prominent Grimké family, was unexpected feature material for the *Liberator,* and Garrison immediately published it, commenting upon it editorially with enthusiasm. It was of such interest to abolitionists that it was widely distributed as a broadside. Her letter caused a stir among Philadelphia Friends, most of whom heartily disapproved, among them Sister Sarah, who was grieved by Angelina's bold step away from orthodoxy. The publication of her letter was a surprise to Angelina and troubled her when she found it roused Sarah's disapproval, but she stood by her principles.

She continued to read everything she could find on the subject of abolition and took several practical steps, trying unsuccessfully to buy some of her brother's slaves from his widow in order to free them. She ceased using the products of slave labor, urging other abolitionists to do the same, and she offered $100 toward setting up a free cotton factory. When she was convinced that the principles of the abolitionists were "entirely pacific" and not aimed at inciting slave insurrections, she joined the Philadelphia Female Antislavery Society.

In the spring of 1836, both she and Sarah went to a Yearly Friends' Meeting in Providence, Rhode Island, and in that more liberal atmosphere found great encouragement and comfort. At a Friends Meeting which they attended in Newport, Angelina's views on slavery made such an impression that she was asked to remain to become an antislavery missionary in the Society of Friends, but she was led to return to Shrewsbury, New Jersey, for the summer, to the home of her friend, Mrs. Parker, with whom she discussed slavery day after day. More and more she realized the important role women could play in the antislavery movement. She had read Mrs. Chapman's *Right and Wrong in Boston* and was impressed by the religious zeal and courage of the antislavery women and by the numbers of Female Antislavery Societies that had been organized. She longed to have her Southern sisters read *Right and Wrong in Boston* so that they would understand that the women of the North had undertaken their work from a sense of religious duty and would carry it through until it was accomplished. She recalled how one lone woman in England, Elizabeth Heyrick, had expressed her ideas on immediate emancipation in a pamphlet which had led Wilberforce "to plead the cause of the oppressed African" and devote himself to freeing the slaves in the West Indian colonies. She remembered the support this cause had received from the Ladies' Antislavery Societies in England and Scotland. As she though this over, she saw clearly that Southern women must be awakened to their duty.

"God has shown me what I can do," she announced one morning to Mrs. Parker. "I can write an appeal to Southern women, one which . . . will touch their hearts and lead them to use their influence with their husbands and brothers. I will speak to them in such tones that they *must* hear me, and through me, the voice of justice and humanity."[4]

She began at once to write, but was interrupted by a request from the secretary of the American Antislavery Society,

Elizur Wright, that she come to New York to talk to women in their sewing circles about slavery. The doors were now opening, but, timid and inexperienced, she shrank from the challenge. She prayed over it and consulted with Sarah, who offered no advice, but left her free to follow whatever course she felt to be right. Much relieved that there was no opposition from Sarah, she wrote Elizur Wright that she was considering his suggestion, but must first finish her *Appeal to the Christian Women of the South,* which, she thought, would make a pamphlet of about twelve pages, and which she hoped the American Antislavery Society would publish. She sent it off to Elizur Wright, as she had sent her letter to Garrison, "with fervent prayers that the Lord would do just as He pleased with it," and she added, "I believe He directed and helped me write it."[5]

Elizur Wright was enthusiastic about the *Appeal,* as were all the members of the executive committee of the American Antislavery Society. They published it in 1836 and it was widely distributed and acclaimed. Later it was reprinted in England with a foreword by George Thompson. That a Southern woman from a prominent family should speak out frankly and boldly on the subject of slavery was highly important and her *Appeal* made many converts. Elizur Wright called it "a patch of blue sky breaking through the storm-cloud of public indignation which had gathered so black over the handful of antislavery workers."[6]

Orthodox Friends in Philadelphia, however, denounced Angelina because of it, even intimating she might be disowned. One bright spot was Sarah's attitude. She showed no signs of disapproval and soon left Philadelphia to join Angelina in Shrewsbury.

Many copies of Angelina's *Appeal to the Christian Women of the South* were received in South Carolina by mail and were publicly burned by postmasters, and she became an outlaw in her native state, warned that should she try to return, she would be arrested and imprisoned.

She had written her *Appeal to the Christian Women of the South* as one of them. "I am going to tell you some unwelcome truths," she began, "but . . . I do not believe the time has yet come when Christian women will not endure sound doctrines even on the subject of slavery, if it is spoken to them in tenderness and love. . . ." She then reminded them of the doctrine of their forefathers, expressed in the Declaration of Independence, that "all men are created equal" and that they have "certain inalienable rights," and she prophesied that very soon it would be "acknowledged by all the virtuous and candid that, in principle, it is sinful to hold a human being in bondage," whether he be born in Carolina or in Africa.

Because it was so generally believed in the South that the Bible sanctioned slavery, she attempted to disprove this for them, as she had disproved it for herself. The hereditary, perpetual, uncompensated, compulsory slavery of the South, she pointed out, was utterly unlike the servitude among the Hebrews, as recorded in the Bible, and she made definite comparisons of the two systems. "We have seen," she continued, "that the code of laws framed by Moses was designed to *protect them as men and women,* to secure to them their *rights as human beings,* to guard them from oppression and defend them from violence of every kind."

On the other hand, she maintained, the Southern slave system, robbed the slave of his rights as a man, reducing him to a chattel and upholding his master in the exercise of the most unnatural and unwarrantable power over him. The result was to deny that Negroes are human beings. She cited the restrictions on manumission, the breaking up of families, the laws keeping them from education, and the oppression of free Negroes. She bluntly declared that there was little difference in guilt between the despised slave dealer and the so-called Christian who kept him in business by buying his slaves or by selling slaves to him.

Then she explained to them the true motives of the abolitionists, so often misrepresented and denounced in the South as "insurrectionary and mischievous, fanatical and dangerous." She herself, she said "had taken the precaution, before joining an antislavery society, of becoming acquainted with some of the leading abolitionists, of reading their publications, and attending their meetings." This fully convinced her that their principles were entirely pacific, and their efforts only moral. "Since that time," she continued, "I have regularly taken the *Liberator* and read many Anti-Slavery pamphlets, and papers and books, and I can assure you I never have seen a single insurrectionary paragraph, and never read any account of cruelty which I could not believe. . . . I lived too long in the midst of slavery, not to know what slavery is. . . . I am not at all afraid to assert that Anti-Slavery publications have not overdrawn the monstrous features of slavery at all, and many a Southerner knows this as well as I do."

Next she indicted the North, declaring that Northern statesmen were no more innocent of the crime of slavery than Pilate was of the murder of Jesus. "Northern merchants and manufacturers," she continued, "are making their fortunes out of slavery. . . . How can these men bear testimony against slavery without condemning themselves?" Amalgamation, as the result of emancipation, she regarded as the great fear of the North, arousing Northerners against emancipation without expatriation. For this reason, she added, many Northerners opposed abolitionists.

"You may ask," she continued, "why I appeal to women.

. . . I know that you do not make the laws, but I also know that you are the wives and mothers, the sisters and daughters of those who do; and if you really suppose you can do nothing to overthrow slavery you are greatly mistaken. You can do much in every way . . . you can read on this subject . . . you can pray over this subject . . . you can speak on this subject . . . you can act on this subject." She urged them to discontinue cruelty to slaves, such as corporal punishment and inadequate clothing and food. She suggested that they free their slaves, or, should their slaves wish to remain with them, they should be paid wages. She reminded them of the courage of women in past ages in the cause of freedom, justice, and righteousness, and called upon them to create a correct public opinion in the South. "It is manifest to every reflecting mind," she added, "that slavery must be abolished and that this can be accomplished either by moral power or physical force." The choice, she warned them was theirs. "Slavery always has and always will produce insurrections, wherever it exists," she told them, "because it is a violation of the natural order of things, and no human power can much longer perpetuate it."

She then asked, "Can you not, my friends, understand the signs of the times: do you not see the sword of retributive justice hanging over the South, or are you still slumbering at your posts? . . . If there were but one Esther at the South, she might save her country from ruin."

* * *

The *Appeal* now written and cast upon the waters of public opinion, Angelina looked forward to going to New England to work with the Friends there, and wrote to a Quaker manufacturer of Uxbridge, Massachusetts, asking whether she could be of use in persuading the Friends to give up the manufacture and use of the products of slave labor. He made it clear that it would be futile to work among Friends in New England and suggested that she devote her time to writing for the American Antislavery Society.

This door closed to her, she gave serious thought to Elizur Wright's suggestion that she come to New York to speak to the women and discussed this with Sarah, who, not yet fully in sympathy with the antislavery movement, gave all the reasons why she opposed her going to New York. However, Angelina persisted, feeling that she had a call from God to undertake this work. Sarah, as she talked with her, was so impressed by her dedication, that she yielded, saying, "Where thou goest, I will go. What thou doest, I will, to my utmost aid thee in doing."[7]

In the fall of 1836, they both went to New York, and at the Antislavery Office were told what their work would be — to organize a National Female Antislavery Society, to travel about talking to groups of women, and to distribute tracts. They insisted on paying all their own expenses in this work, but accepted gladly the hospitality of Dr. and Mrs. Cox, devoted abolitionists. The men they met at the Antislavery Office made a most favorable impression on them, so superior were they in education, experience, and liberality to the Philadelphia Quakers and Charleston slaveholders. Here they met Arthur and Lewis Tappan, Theodore Weld, Henry B. Stanton, and the Southerner, James G. Birney. A whole new world opened to them when they attended the antislavery agents convention at which about thirty antislavery agents were present. These talented, zealous young men, many of them Lane Seminary students, headed by Theodore D. Weld, were preparing to spread the gospel of abolition throughout the country. Thinking in biblical language, as was their habit, they saw themselves as the "seventy" sent out by Jesus with the challenge, "The harvest is truly great, but the laborers are few." The convention held three sessions a day for two weeks, all of which Angelina and Sarah attended, listening eagerly to the discussions. They were the first women to be included among the Seventy. It was at this convention that Angelina heard her future husband, Theodore D. Weld, speak for the first time, on "What is Slavery?" and wrote to a friend, "I never heard so grand and beautiful an exposition of the nobility of man in my life."[8] Introduced to him after the meeting by Garrison and called by him "my dear sister," she felt as if he were truly a brother in the holy cause. Sarah, as well, was inspired by the convention and by the dedication of those taking part. After hearing Theodore Weld's "Bible Argument," Sarah began to write *An Epistle to the Clergy of the Southern States,* which was published in December, 1836, as a pamphlet refuting the claim that the Bible sanctioned slavery, calling upon the Church to awake to the sin of slavery, and pointing out the success of immediate emancipation in the British West Indies.

* * *

Now looked upon as among the Seventy, Angelina and Sarah were invited to speak, whenever and wherever they thought it proper, on their own experiences with slavery. They began their work as agents in New York, speaking to small groups of women in their homes, but so great was the desire to hear them that a large meeting place was necessary and a Baptist minister, the Rev. Mr. Dunbar, offered the lecture room of his church. For women to speak in a lecture room, even to women, was so unheard of that some abolitionists protested, among them the liberal, Gerrit Smith, who feared it would be looked upon as a Fanny Wright affair. The Friends also protested and Angelina and Sarah were urged to give up the meeting, even though notices had been sent out. Then Theodore Weld came to the rescue, sympathizing with and encouraging them. Angelina confessed that she felt utterly unfit and unprepared for public speaking, but Weld assured her the Lord would put the words in her mouth. "His visit was really a strength to us," she reported, "and I felt no more fear. We went to the meeting at three o'clock, and found about three hundred women there. It was opened with prayer by Henry Ludlow; we were warmly welcomed by brother Dunbar."[9] After this the two clergymen left the room so that the impropriety of women speaking before a mixed audience would be avoided. Then Angelina spoke for about forty minutes, "entirely unembarrassed," as she expressed it. Sarah followed, and both answered questions. So successful was the meeting that plans for another were made immediately. This was probably the first gathering of women, other than Quakers, in a public hall in the United States to be addressed by women.

Every week until spring, Angelina and Sarah spoke to groups of women in New York, and as these groups grew larger the Reverend Mr. Ludlow offered his church to them. "Our meetings in New York," Sarah wrote a friend at this time, "have been better attended than we expected, but it is a hard place to labor in; ten thousand cords of interest, are linked with the Southern slaveholder. Still there are some warm-hearted abolitionists there and I believe the fire of Emancipation will increase. . . ."[10]

It did increase. Now and then an interested man slipped into the church to listen to the two women, but usually was asked to leave. When one refused to leave, Angelina was not disturbed, and commented, "I did not find his presence embarrassing at all, and went on just as though he had not been there."[11]

Neither Angelina nor Sarah were experienced speakers, but Theodore Weld, who was an exceptional orator, continued to give them helpful suggestions. Angelina was an apt pupil and soon held her audiences spellbound. Sarah, however, never spoke loud enough to be heard easily, nor learned how to make her talks interesting. She was completely happy in the work, nonetheless, and wrote a friend at this time, "I would not give up my abolition feelings for anything. They are entwined with my Christianity. They have given a new spring to my existence."[12]

After the New York meetings, they spoke in New Jersey, and Gerrit Smith, who by this time was completely converted to meetings of women addressed by women, accompanied them up the Hudson River so that they might speak in Hudson and Poughkeepsie. Then they returned to New York for a much needed rest before helping prepare for the Anti-slavery Convention of American Women to be held there in May, 1837.

CHAPTER VI

The First Antislavery Convention of American Women

The interest aroused by Angelina and Sarah Grimké in the abolition movement further proved the value of women in this work and inspired female antislavery societies to increase their activities. This led Maria Chapman, of the Boston Female Antislavery Society, to propose to the Philadelphia Society that a convention of antislavery women be called. Although expressing willingness to cooperate, the Philadelphia Society stated plainly that many of its members preferred "proper recognition of female members in the American Society to a separate organization of women."[1]

About the same time, Lewis Tappan wrote the Boston Society suggesting that women hold an antislavery convention in New York. "This coincidence of opinion, respecting women's duties," was very encouraging to Mrs. Chapman and her colleagues, and plans were soon underway for the first Antislavery Convention of American Women.

The Grimké sisters, at the helm in New York, corresponded with Boston women about the convention, Sarah writing to Anne Weston in April, 1837, "All who reflect on the subject . . . must feel that our meeting together as a national convention is a step of great importance. The eyes of many will be fixed upon us, watching for halting, and it is exceedingly desired that all the strength we have should be consecrated at that time. We hope to have the company of some of our colored sisters from your city." Philadelphia, she added, would send colored delegates, believing that association would break down prejudices. "The modest worth and unassuming yet dignified deportment of many of our colored friends," she continued, "could make the whites blush."[2]

About one hundred women from ten states met in New York for three days, May 9–12, 1837, during which they freely and thoroughly discussed the ways and means of abolishing slavery and encouraged the timid to bolder action. Philadelphia was well represented by Lucretia Mott, Mary Grew, Sarah Pugh, and a Negro, Sarah Douglass. Even from as far West as Ohio, a few women made the long journey to New York. Boston sent Maria Weston Chapman, Anne Weston, Mary S. Parker, Henrietta Sargent, and Lydia Maria Child, who felt it her duty to be there even though she had little interest in conventions. The active Lynn Female Antislavery Society contributed one of the most effective speakers of the convention, Abby Kelley.

Lucretia Mott asked the delegates to consider whether they could continue to use the products of slave labor without becoming "a partaker in other men's sins." She herself had renounced the products of slave labor. The convention took no action on the issue. A special plea was made that all prejudice against color be renounced and that colored women be invited to join Female Antislavery Societies and be treated as equals. The delegates were urged to visit the schools and churches of free Negroes and, in their own churches, to sit in the pews assigned to Negroes, instead of sitting with the white aristocracy. "The abandonment of prejudice is required of us as a proof of our sincerity and consistency," declared Mary S. Parker of Boston, who had been elected president of the convention. The attitude of Northern churches was discussed — the apathy of some, the unchristian opposition of others to antislavery efforts — and delegates were asked to appeal to their churches to declare slavery a sin, to wipe out prejudice against color, and to cease assigning separate seats to Negroes. Their most important work, they decided, was to get signatures for petitions to Congress, asking for the abolition of slavery in both the District of Columbia and the Territory of Florida and for the abolition of interstate slave trade. Attention was called to the Gag Rule, passed by the House of Representatives in 1836, which provided that all abolition petitions be laid on the table. To bring about the repeal of this unAmerican limitation of the right of petition, the convention called upon women to send their Congressmen an overwhelming number of petitions. Those who feared that petitions signed by women would receive no attention were reassured when they were told of the response of parliament to petitions of British women; and they were encouraged by the remark of a Southern Congressman, who confessed that he dreaded the influence of women on this subject more than any other influence.

The convention adopted a resolution which stated definitely that it is "the province of woman" and her "duty . . . to plead the cause of the oppressed and to do all that she can by her voice, and her pen, and her purse, and the influence of her example, to overthrow the horrible influence of American slavery."[3]

Emphasizing the importance of the participation of women in the antislavery movement, Angelina Grimké made a special appeal to the women of the North, which was afterward published as a pamphlet by the convention under the title *Appeal to the Women of the Nominally Free States.* She made it clear that the women of the North were deeply involved in slavery by their prejudice against color, by their use of slave products, and by their support of the colonization movement. She urged them to become better informed on the subject, to read and circulate antislavery papers and leaflets, to realize how Negro women suffered under slavery. She reminded them that slavery corrupted the morals of the North as well as the South and was completely out of character in a Christian nation. "No intelligent woman," she declared, "ought to be ignorant of this great subject – no Christian woman can escape the obligation now resting upon her, to examine it for herself. . . . The denial of our duty to act in this cause is a denial of our right to act; and if we have no right to act, then may we well be termed 'the white slaves of the North,' for like our brethren in bonds, we must seal our lips in silence and despair."

She refuted the argument that because the abolition of slavery is a political subject women should have nothing to do with it. "Every citizen," she continued, "should feel an interest in the political concerns of the country, because the honor, happiness, and well-being of every class are bound up in its politics, government, and laws. Are we aliens because we are women? Are we bereft of citizenship because we are the mothers, wives and daughters of a mighty people? Have women no country – no interest staked in public weal . . . no partnership in a nation's guilt and shame?"

With this challenge she brought the question of women's rights definitely into the antislavery movement. She saw that the struggle for the Negro's rights and women's rights were inseparable as part of the larger struggle for human rights – equal rights for all human beings. The majority of women attending the convention were completely in sympathy with these views.

When it was suggested that a national organization of women be formed, this was voted down in favor of an annual convention which it was thought would accomplish the same objectives without the cumbersome machinery of a society, and Philadelphia was chosen for the next convention, to be held in May, 1838.

Reports of this first convention of women were read eagerly by Harriet Martineau, who was following closely the activities of the American antislavery women. "It will stand," she wrote, "as a great event in history." The press, however, felt differently, ridiculing and misrepresenting the women, and the clergy at once began denouncing their antislavery activities as contrary to the Bible.

* * *

Meeting and talking with the Grimké sisters had been even more rewarding for most of the women than the convention itself. Invitations for them to speak poured in from the West as well as from New England. The Boston group immediately made arrangements with them to come to New England, sending out a letter to Female Antislavery Societies highly recommending them. In this letter, signed by Mrs. Chapman, the importance of women's participation in the antislavery movement was emphasized. She said of the Grimkés: "One thing . . . which marks them as eminently qualified for the promulgation of antislavery principles" is "the elevated and Christian point of view from which they behold the condition of woman; her duties and her consequent rights. It is of paramount importance that both men and women should understand their true positions and mighty responsibilities to this and to coming generations."[4]

The Grimkés spent a social evening at the Chapmans, after which Angelina reported to a friend, "I had a long talk with the brethren on the rights of women, and found a very general sentiment prevailing that it is time our fetters were broken. L. M. Child and Maria Chapman strongly supported this view; indeed, very many seem to think a new order of things is very desirable in this respect. . . . I feel that it is not only the cause of the slave that we plead, but the cause of woman as a moral, responsible being."

So many women came to hear the Grimkés in Boston that parlors and drawing rooms were inadequate for their meetings. From Boston they moved on to nearby towns, speaking in the town hall in Dorchester and to over a thousand in the large Methodist Church in Lynn. Gradually other churches were opened to them. Men slipped into the meetings, ostensibly to find out how dangerous they were, among them the Congregational clergyman, Amos Phelps. He was enthralled when he heard them speak in Lynn, but such pressure was brought against him by the orthodox clergy that he tried to influence the Grimkés to lecture to women only. Even the liberal, Samuel J. May, was doubtful about their addressing mixed audiences, but he "looked the facts fully in the face," and reasoned that "here had come two well-informed persons of exalted character from the midst of slavedom to testify to the correctness of our allegations against slavery, and to tell more of its horrors than we knew. And shall they not be heard because they are women?" His answer was to invite them to visit his home in Scituate and to speak in his church. After Angelina had spoken from his pulpit to a large audience for two hours, all doubts left him, and, on his recommendation, she spoke to six hundred in the Methodist Church in Scituate and then in the Baptist Church in Hanover. "If there was a person there who went away unaffected," was his comment, "he would not have been moved though an angel instead of Angelina had spoken to him . . ."[5]

"The experience of that week," he added, "dispelled my Pauline prejudice. I needed no other warrant for the course the Misses Grimké were pursuing than the evidence they gave of their power to speak so as to instruct and deeply impress those who listened to them. I could not believe that God gave them such talents . . . to be buried in a napkin."

They spoke to fifteen hundred in Lowell, to one thousand in Methuen, and so on. "Remarkably large audience . . ." Angelina wrote Henry Wright from Methuen, "Many men seemed to come out of curiosity and from time to time walked out. . . . Also mischievous boys gave a serenade outside. . . . I went on as though nothing was disturbing me."[6] In Andover, a great many students came to hear her. "I felt," she wrote, "as if I were speaking before an array of learning and talent and prejudice, but after a while forgot the fear of man." The continuous travel and speaking were wearing, and Sarah was obliged to rest for a time, but Angelina persisted, determined to fight the "battles of women and the slave through to the end," and it was a comfort to find the friends of the cause everywhere like brothers and sisters.

* * *

New England women often walked from two to eight miles to hear the Grimké sisters. The fact that they had lived in the midst of slavery and could tell about it first-hand was their greatest drawing card. Occasionally they spoke in churches, arousing such interest in abolition that the clergy became alarmed and began closing their churches to them. Orthodox churches generally were proslavery in their thinking, maintaining that the Bible sanctioned slavery and that antislavery lecturers stirred up strife. Yet, in spite of this, a few courageous clergymen allied themselves with the antislavery movement. However, as the Grimkés continued to speak, the clergy's concern increased, for this, in their opinion, defied Paul's admonition, "Let your women keep silence in the churches; for it is not permitted unto them to speak."

They were disturbed as well by Garrison's criticism of the Church in the *Liberator*. Although Garrison was deeply religious and often quoted the Bible, he had no patience with what he considered the Church's unchristian position on slavery. The popular Lyman Beecher's moderate abolition, his leaning toward colonization, and his opposition to immediate emancipation seemed to Garrison inconsistent with Christianity and he repeatedly reprimanded Beecher in the *Liberator* and spoke out plainly and harshly against what seemed to him the hypocrisy of the Church. Nor did his unorthodox, freely expressed views regarding the observance of the Sabbath help matters. More and more he was rated a heretic by the Church. Some of the clergy who had been independent enough to become abolitionists pleaded with him to be less outspoken, for there were definite signs of a division in antislavery ranks on religious grounds.

Now Catherine Beecher, following in the moderate abolition footsteps of her father, expressed her disapproval of Angelina Grimké's antislavery activities in her *Essay on Slavery and Abolitionism with Reference to the Duty of American Females,* published in Philadelphia, in 1837. She had read Angelina's *Appeal to the Christian Women of the South* and she heartily disapproved of her lecturing in the North. Because Angelina had come to her some years before for advice about teaching, she now felt it her duty, as a more experienced woman, to guide her and show her why women should not organize abolition societies.

Catherine Beecher told Angelina Grimké plainly that her estimate of the attitude of Northern women toward slavery was incorrect, that they did look upon it as unchristian, but believed in gradual, not immediate emancipation. She felt that it was wrong for Northern women to preach against the sins of the South unless they went South with their message of reform and reasoned directly with the people. She disapproved of abolition societies because they aroused angry passions and unchristian sentiments, but she did respect the abolitionists' strong sense of religious duty and their stand for free discussion. The methods of William Lloyd Garrison, however, she deplored, and she urged abolitionists to adopt more of the spirit of the great British abolitionist, Wilberforce.

She criticized the attitude of abolitionists toward the "benevolent" Colonization Society and toward Negroes, to whom they sent the *Liberator,* which taught them to feel injured and abused. She disapproved of the attempt to found a college for Negroes in Connecticut near Yale University and of the manner in which Prudence Crandall established her school for colored females in a town such as Canterbury. She questioned the wisdom of James G. Birney when he established his antislavery paper, the *Philanthropist,* in Cincinnati, where there was bound to be violence. All this forced her to the conclusion that abolitionists did encourage violence and compared unfavorably with the wise and talented British abolitionist statesmen "who had the intellect, knowledge, discretion, and wisdom demanded for so great an enterprise." In other words, she approved of abolition as handled by the British, but heartily disapproved of militant American abolitionists.

Then she poured forth a tirade against the participation of women in the antislavery movement, pointing out "the place woman is appointed to fill by the dispensations of heaven." Under the divine order, she explained, man was appointed the superior sex, woman the subordinate, and women should conform. Even so, this did not mean that woman's influence was to be less important, but that her mode of gaining influence and exercising power should be altogether different and peculiar. "Woman is to win everything by peace and love," she continued, "by making herself so much respected, esteemed, and loved, that to yield to her opinions and gratify her wishes, will be a free-will offering of the heart."

Women's participation in the antislavery movement, she pointed out, took them out of their appropriate sphere, making them partisans in a conflict, exposing them to the violence of mobs, to sneers and ridicule in public places, and leading them "into the arena of political collision as combatants, not as mediators." Petitions to Congress, circulated by Female Antislavery Societies, she regarded as "entirely without the sphere of female duty." In her opinion, petitioning was the task of men. Women's part in the antislavery movement, she concluded, should be only as mediators and peacemakers.

"Catherine's arguments are the most insidious things I ever read," declared Angelina Grimké impatiently in a letter to a friend. "I know not how to find language strong enough to express my indignation at the view she takes of woman's character and duty."[7] She answered Catherine Beecher promptly in a letter in the *Liberator,* June 23, 1837. Other *Letters to Catherine E. Beecher* followed and were published as a small book in 1838, restating briefly and forcefully her arguments against slavery, and taking a positive stand for woman's rights. "The great fundamental principle of Abolitionists," said Angelina, "is that man cannot rightfully hold his fellowman as property. . . . We hold that the North is guilty of the crime of slaveholding – We assert that it is a *national* sin. . . . We hold that slaveholding laws violate the fundamental principles of the Constitution of the United States."

Pleading for immediate emancipation, she continued, "I have seen too much of slavery to be a gradualist. . . ."

Theodore Weld

Emancipation, she explained, means to pay the laborer his hire, to deny him no longer the right of marriage and the right to his own children, to deny him education no longer, nor to forbid his reading the Bible. It means to put the slave under equitable laws.

Explaining why she and other abolitionists began their work in the North, she said, "Proslavery men of the North are to the system of slavery just what temperate drinkers were to the vice of intemperance. Temperance workers did not begin their labors among drunkards, but among temperate drinkers." Just so, she continued, "Antislavery reformers did not begin their labors among slaveholders, but among those who are making fortunes out of the unrequited toil of the slave. . . . As soon as we reform the recreant sons and daughters of the North, as soon as we rectify public opinion at the North, then I, for one, will promise to go down into the midst of slaveholders themselves to promulgate our doctrines in the land of the slave."

"What man or woman of common sense," she asked, "now doubts the intellectual capacity of the colored people? Who does not know that, with all our efforts as a nation to crush and annihilate the minds of this portion of our race, we have never yet been able to do it."

Then she commented on Catherine Beecher's moralizing on woman's sphere. "My doctrine," she declared, "is that whatever it is morally right for a man to do, it is morally right for a woman to do. . . . I recognize no rights but human rights — I know nothing of men's rights and women's rights; for in Christ Jesus, there is neither male nor female." Prophecying that the signs of the times clearly indicated a vast and rapid change in public sentiment regarding the role of women, she added, "Sure I am that she is not to be, as she has been, *'a mere second-hand agent'* in the regeneration of a fallen world, but the acknowledged equal and co-worker with man in this glorious work. . . . Then it will be seen that nothing which concerns the well-being of mankind is either beyond her sphere, or above her comprehension. Then it will be seen 'that America will be distinguished above all other nations for well-educated women, and for the influence they will exert on the general interests of society.' . . . That thou and all my countrywomen may better understand the true dignity of woman is the sincere desire of Thy friend, A. E. Grimké."

This was strong woman's rights doctrine and it was being expressed as well by Sarah Grimké in a series of *Letters on the Province of Women* in the *New England Spectator,* which were later published as a book, addressed to Mary S. Parker, President of the Boston Female Antislavery Society, who had urged her to write them.

Theodore Weld, who had been corresponding frequently with the Grimké sisters, and who had been strongly attracted to Angelina since he first met her in New York, now commented on her reply to Catherine Beecher. He felt a protective interest in her which he tried to explain to himself as brotherly. She thought of him as the best of friends, but love, as well as friendship, was fast developing between them in spite of their efforts to resist it. "Your letters to Catherine Beecher," he wrote her, "I like greatly and yet I wish they were better." Then he made suggestions regarding the choice of words, adding, "You see I am at my old tricks of fault finding with you. Be patient."[8] In the same letter he expressed strong approval of her public speaking, "God give thee a mouth and give wisdom to prophecy like the daughters of Philip, like Huldah and Deborah. If the men wish to come, it is downright slaveholding to keep them out."

Thanking him for his comments and wishing he had been

at hand to correct the *Letters* before they were sent out, she told him about some of her speaking engagements and confessed to a feeling of incompetence before speaking. "I often feel in our meetings," she wrote him, "as if I was 'as a lamb led to the slaughter,' sometimes so sick before I rise that it seems impossible for me to speak ten minutes; but the Lord is at my right hand . . . and he sustains me and fills my mouth. At times when I feel so miserable and little and incompetent, I remember what thou told me about thy feelings before speaking and am really strengthened. . . ."[9]

She appealed to him not to justify their public speaking on the ground that this was Quaker peculiarity. "We want thee to sustain us," she said, "on the high ground of moral right. . . . We do not stand on Quaker ground, but on Bible ground and moral right. What we claim for ourselves we claim for every woman whom God has called and qualified with gifts and graces. Can't thou stand just here side by side with us?"[10]

While she wrote this, the opposition of the Church was fast building up. "It is really amusing," commented Sarah, "to see how the clergy are arrayed against two women who are telling the story of the slave's wrongs. . . . They think to frighten us from the field of duty, but they do not move us."[11]

CHAPTER VII

The Pastoral Letter

In the eyes of the clergy, the situation had become so serious that in June, 1837, the General Association of Congregational Ministers met in North Brookfield, Massachusetts, to take action. Convinced that the authority of pastors was being undermined as outsiders brought the discussion of abolition into the churches, they made this pronouncement: "Your minister is ordained by God to be your teacher, and is commanded to feed that flock over which the Holy Ghost hath made him overseer. If there are certain topics upon which he does not preach . . . it is a violation of sacred and important rights to encourage a stranger to present them." Even more concerned were they over the dangers threatening the female character. "The appropriate duties and influence of woman is in her dependence," they declared. "But when she assumes the place and tone of a man as a public reformer . . . we put ourselves in self-defense against her, she yields the power which God has given her for protection and her character becomes unnatural."[1]

They decried the mistaken conduct of those who encouraged women to bear an "ostentatious" part in reform or who "countenance any of that sex who so far forget themselves as to itinerate in the character of public lecturers and teachers." They mentioned no names, but there was little doubt that they were referring to the Grimké sisters. Particularly offensive to them was Angelina Grimké's reference in her lectures to the immoral relationship which so often existed between slave owners and young female slaves, and they commented, "We especially deplore the intimate acquaintance and promiscuous conversation of females with regard to things 'which ought not to be named.' "

They drew up a Pastoral Letter to be read in the churches, issuing it in July. Young Lucy Stone, then teaching in North Brookfield, sat with her cousin in the gallery of the Congregational Church when the Pastoral Letter was read. She blazed with indignation at every aggravating sentence, vowing that if she ever had anything to say in public, she would say it all the more because of the Pastoral Letter. Her sympathy with abolition had been strengthened by the few copies of the *Liberator* she had read and her interest in woman's rights was fast building up.

The Pastoral Letter was followed by several Clerical Appeals, the first of which, *The Appeal of Clerical Abolitionists on Antislavery Measures,* was signed by five ministers who, although they were abolitionists, could not condone Garrison's criticism of the clergy in the *Liberator*. The second Clerical Appeal, issued by the faculty of Andover Theological Seminary, condemned "public lectures of females" as "departure from propriety." These pronouncements of the Church, while they influenced some, were in large measure rendered ineffective by the progressive thinking of the day.

John Greenleaf Whittier made his protest in a poem of fourteen verses, "The Pastoral Letter":

So this is all – the utmost reach
Of priestly power the mind to fetter!
When laymen think – when women preach –
A war of words – a "Pastoral Letter!"
Now shame upon ye, parish Popes![2] . . .

Maria Weston Chapman, not only recorded in *Right and Vrong in Boston,* 1837, the story of the Pastoral Letter but he too turned to verse to ridicule the clergymen who opposed he participation of women in the antislavery movement. Her poem, "The Times That Try Men's Souls," rollicked hrough ten verses in this vein:

> Confusion has seized us, and all things go wrong
> The women have leaped from their spheres
> And instead of fixed stars, shoot as comets along,
> And are setting the world by the ears! . . .
> They've taken a notion to speak for themselves,
> And are wielding the tongue and the pen . . .[3]

Mrs. Chapman, as well, called upon women to take their tand on this issue. "It is not necessary for us, at this late day," he said, "to declare our theory with regard to the sphere of voman. It is sufficiently evident in our practice. We entreat ll women . . . to examine this subject attentively, for we ee that women, generally, cannot become other than aboli-ionists in the abstract, till their sentiments respecting the ights and consequent duties of women are the growth of heir own minds." Scripture, she maintained, had been misin-erpreted for women, and as a result women "have been fet-ered in body and in mind by commentators and translators, nd by partial reasoners, but by revelation never . . . What is he sphere and duty of woman, it rests with each one for her-elf to determine. . . ."[4]

In protesting against the Pastoral Letter, Samuel J. May pointed out to the clergy that they had overlooked the fact hat women were the bravest as well as the most devoted of esus' disciples. The *Liberator* expressed its disapproval by eprinting the Pastoral Letter in the "Refuge of Oppression" ection, with appropriate comments by Oliver Johnson and Garrison.

The Grimké sisters, against whom the Pastoral Letter was directed, were troubled by it only because it brought controversy over women into the antislavery movement. It strengthened their conviction that they must take a firm stand for women's rights. "I cannot help feeling some regret that this should have come up before the Antislavery question was settled, so fearful am I that it may injure the cause," Angelina wrote Theodore Weld, "and then again I think, it must have been the Lord's time and so therefore the best time."[5]

Sarah, who was taking a firm stand for woman's rights in her *Letters on the Equality of the Sexes,* published in the *New England Spectator,* devoted ample space to repudiating the Pastoral Letter. "An extraordinary document," she called it, and added, "When the minds of men and women become emancipated from the thralldom of superstition and 'traditions of men,' the sentiments contained in the Pastoral Letter will be referred to with as much astonishment as the opinions of Cotton Mather and other distinguished men of his day, on the subject of witchcraft." Protesting against the false translation and perverted interpretation of New Testament passages, quoted so glibly by clergymen as authority for defining the sphere and duties of women, she declared, "Man and woman were created equal; they are both moral and accountable beings, and what is right for man to do is right for woman." Not only did she thoroughly repudiate the Pastoral Letter in her *Letters on the Condition of Women and the Equality of the Sexes,* but she dealt with other topics relating to women, such as the status of women in the United States, Asia, and Africa, the intellect of woman, her heroism, her legal disabilities, the ministry of women, and so on. In fact, it was the first book published in the United States which thoughtfully and courageously appraised women, their rights, and their place in society. Lydia Maria Child had published, a few years before, a *History on the Condition of Women*, but she had made it clear that this was not "an essay on woman's rights, or a philosophical investigation of what is or ought to be the relation of the sexes." In contrast, Sarah Grimké gave her readers strong women's rights doctrine, and Lucretia Mott, eagerly reading it, rated it[6] as a work on the woman question second only to Mary Wollstonecraft's *Vindication of the Rights of Women*.

* * *

In spite of the Pastoral Letter, the Grimkés continued to lecture in New England during the summer and fall to good audiences, but churches were quite generally closed to them. In Pepperell, they spoke in a barn, "crowded almost to suffocation." The clergyman who opened the meeting with prayer left immediately, remarking afterward that he would as soon rob a hen-roost as hear a woman speak in public. The Reverend Mr. Lincoln Gardiner, however, asked Angelina to occupy his pulpit. The result was gratifying, and he commented, "Never before or since have I seen an audience so held and so much moved by any public speaker, man or woman, and never before or since have I seen a Christian pulpit so well filled, nor in the pews seen such absorbed hearers."[7]

Angelina was thirty-two years old at this time, handsome and graceful, as described by a fellow abolitionist, Oliver Johnson. "In her simple Quaker garb," he added, "her intelligent face lighted up with animation, . . . [she] presented a most lovely picture of womanhood. She was entirely self-possessed . . . and a mistress of her facts . . . without a suggestion of masculine assurance."[8]

Sarah, on the other hand, made no such favorable impression, in spite of her keen mind. She was then forty-four, somber, repressed, angular, and physically unattractive. She did not speak with ease or hold her audiences. Often in poor health, she lectured less and less. Angelina bore the brunt of their strenuous life, as they held five or six meetings a week, driving over rough roads, rain or shine, in wagons or in the stagecoach, speaking for two hours, and then driving back to their lodgings.

They both lectured in Amesbury, where they were guests in Whittier's home. "We met the mother, aunt and sister of brother Whittier," commented Angelina. "They received us at their little cottage with sincere pleasure. . . . He was absent, serving the good cause in New York."[9] Whittier met them shortly after, and later recalled, "How well I remember, dear Angelina when she first came to New England, the brave beautiful young woman! How we all admired and loved her." During their first lecture in Amesbury, two young men, who had just returned from the South, challenged them to debate on the subject, "Are the slave laws of the United States contrary to God's laws?" They accepted the challenge, and at a second meeting, which packed the hall, the young men argued that slavery was justified by the Bible and that the condition of slaves was no worse than that of Northern mill workers. The sisters readily refuted their claims, but this public debate with men aroused much criticism, so much so that when Henry B. Stanton, greatly impressed by Angelina's ability, suggested that they arrange a meeting at which they would both speak, she felt it best to refuse. "We have given great offense," she wrote a friend, "on account of our womanhood, which seems to be as objectionable as our abolitionism. The whole land seems aroused to discussion on the province of women, and I am glad of it. We are willing to bear the brunt of the storm, if we can only be the means of making a breach in public opinion, which lies right in the way of women's true dignity, honor and usefulness."

The abolitionists for the most part upheld them, and Mrs. Chapman, Garrison, and Henry C. Wright spurred them on. Henry C. Wright helped them plan their lecture engagements and reported their meetings in the *Liberator* in his column "The Labor of the Misses Grimké." Sometimes, to their dismay, he even published Sarah's letters to him. Theodore Weld was troubled because Wright made nonresistance, clericalism, woman's rights, and other reforms too appealing to the sisters. In fact, Angelina even went so far as to suggest to Wright, "What wouldst thou think of the *Liberator* abandoning abolition as a primary object and becoming the vehicle of all these grand principles? I trust brother G will be divinely directed." There were many crosscurrents. They talked over the possibility of a paper advocating woman's rights with Mrs. Chapman, Mrs. Child, and others, but concluded that "as long as we are not shut out from the men's papers we will use them. We do not want to separate the sexes any more into different organizations if it can be avoided. When they refuse to publish for us, as I expect they will, we may then find it best to have a medium of communication with the public for ourselves."[10] Appreciating Mrs. Chapman's strong stand for woman's rights, Angelina hoped she would soon begin to lecture, for she did not want the spark kindled on the woman question to die out.

Under strong pressure from fellow clergymen, Amos Phelps again suggested that the Grimkés advertise their meetings for women only. Angelina opposed this suggestion, saying they ought not retreat, as that would make it harder at some future day.

Invitations continued to come to them to speak in all parts of Massachusetts, so many in fact that they could not accept them all. Sometimes crowds were so great that a second hall or church was provided and Angelina would speak in one and Sarah in the other. One evening when Sarah was too ill to accompany Angelina, Abby Kelley came to her rescue and drove her to her meeting on a dark rainy night. On the way they met crowds of men bound for the meeting. "It seemed as if I could not realize they were going to hear me," Angelina wrote a friend. "This was the first large meeting I ever attended without my dear sister, and I wonder I did not feel desolate, for I knew not a creature there. Nevertheless, the Lord strengthened me, and I spoke with ease for an hour and a quarter."[11]

The strain of the many meetings and the continuous travel so exhausted Angelina that by November a rest was imperative and she and Sarah were grateful for the hospitality of Samuel and Eliza Philbrick for a few months of comfort and complete rest on "a delightful farm" in Brookline, as Sarah described it. The Philbricks were Quakers, Samuel being a retired Boston merchant.

Hearing of Angelina's exhaustion and illness, Theodore Weld was troubled and wrote at once for news of her. He urged Angelina and Sarah to spend the winter in the warmer climate of Philadelphia, begging Angelina not to speak at any more meetings until she had completely recovered.

Sarah replied at once assuring him that Angelina's illness was not serious and that she was steadily improving. Living in Philadelphia, she explained, would be out of the question, as their interest in abolition had deprived them of their home there. She told him of their comfortable quarters at the Philbricks, "To us, it appears like the home provided for us by our heavenly father. We have a comfortable chamber warmed by a furnace, and have nothing to take us out unless the weather is suitable . . . It is a comfort indeed that we can look back upon the labors of the past summer with feelings of unmingled satisfaction. . . . Now, although we do not contemplate public speaking this winter, we do not wish or expect to be idle. . . . Thou sayst thou can cut out work enough to employ a dozen; what wilt thou allot to us?"[12] Angelina added a few lines to reassure him.

Theodore, eager to keep them busy on straight abolition, set them to work revising Angelina's *Appeal to the Women of the Nominally Free States,* suggesting it could be cut one-third or even one-half and be more forceful. A republication of the *Appeal,* he felt, was greatly needed, and would be widely read because written by a Southerner.

Their correspondence continued, full of solicitude for each other's welfare, Theodore showing concern for the sisters' health, and they for his and for his overwork and loneliness in New York. Angelina wrote him, "How is it my brother that H. B. Stanton tells us thou are now working far harder than is good for thee? I feared it by thy own account of thyself. . . . We wished thou hadst a comfortable home to go to after thy labors. . . ."[13] Their most serious disagreement was on the subject of mixing woman's rights and abolition.

Although Theodore was completely in sympathy with woman's rights per se, he felt strongly that woman's rights and abolition should be kept separate. His good friend, John Greenleaf Whittier, felt as he did, and in August, 1837, had written the sisters, asking why they had become controversial writers on the subject of woman's rights. "Does it not look, dear Sisters," he continued, "like abandoning in some degree the cause of the poor and miserable slaves . . . ? I would not for the world interfere with you in matters of conscientious duty, but I wish you would weigh candidly the whole subject, and see if it does not seem an abandonment of your first love." He then reminded them that their lectures t crowded and "promiscuous" audiences were "practical an powerful assertions of the right and duty of woman to labo side by side with her brother for the welfare and redemptio of the world."[14]

His assumption that there was no need at this time t discuss woman's rights, troubled Angelina and Sarah ver much, as did Theodore's letter which followed the next day Theodore made it clear that basically he advocated woman' rights, but felt it should not be injected into antislavery di cussions. Pointing out to them that as Southerners and forme slaveholders they had a special mission as abolitionists an therefore could do "ten times as much as Mrs. Child or Mr Chapman in convincing the North," he urged them to leav the lesser work to others. He ended on this note, "Let us firs wake up the nation to lift millions of slaves of both sexe from the dust . . . then . . . it will be an easy matter t take millions of females from their knees and set them o their feet."

Later he wrote, "What is done for the slave and huma rights in this country must be done now, now, now. Delay madness, ruin, whereas woman's rights are not a life an death business, now or ever. Why can't you have eyes t see this?"[15]

Angelina could not see this at all. In fact she was so angr that she dared not reply at once, but soon, in a joint lette to Weld and Whittier, she pointed out that the Pastora Letter, and not they, had been responsible for bringing u the subjects of woman's rights and duties. "What did yo do?" she asked them, "when you were told a few years ag that you had no right to discuss the subject of slavery. Di you take no notice of this assertion? Why no! With one hea and one voice you said we will settle this right before we g one step further. . . . We must establish this right, for if we do not, it will be impossible for us to go on with the work of Emancipation."[16]

The same was true in the case of women, she maintained. "If we are to do any good in the Antislavery cause, our right to labor in it must be firmly established, not on the ground of Quakerism, but on the only firm basis of human rights, the Bible . . . We cannot push Abolition forward with all our might until we take up the stumbling block out of the road. . . . Now we entreat you to weigh candidly the *whole subject,* and then we are sure you will see, this is no more an abandonment of our first love than the effort made by Antislavery men to establish the *right* of free discussion."

Woman's rights was in the air, so much so that in December, 1837, there was a public discussion of the subject at the Boston Lyceum before an audience of 1,500. Angelina and Sarah had not been asked to take part in the discussion, but were in the audience with Samuel Philbrick. Afterwards Angelina commented, "A very noble view throughout. The discussion has raised my view of the woman question. It was conducted with respect, delicacy, and dignity, and many minds were roused to reflection. . . ." The question was put to a vote and, as Angelina reported, "was decided against us by acclamation, our enemies being our judges. It was like a meeting of slave-holders deciding that slaves are happier in their present condition than they would be freed."[17]

* * *

Angelina and Theodore, in their frequent letters, continued their arguments on woman's rights. They could not agree, but, so strong was the respect and affection between them and so strong their genuine desire to be divinely guided, that no rift in their friendship developed.

Occasionally, Theodore was very harsh in his criticism o Angelina. One letter in particular rankled and hurt her, a she thought it indicated he did not care for her as she wa beginning to care for him and more than ever realized tha her love for him must be held in check. Philosophizing ove his criticism, she wrote him, "How often I have thanked Goc for such a friend as you have proved to me, one who will tel me my faults. I solemnly believe there is, there can be, nc true friendship without it. . . . If we ever meet and car talk those things over, I think it will do my heart good. . . There will be no use writing about it — *We Can Not Under stand Each Other*. . . ."[18]

Theodore's reply, marked Private, was a complete sur prise. After telling her how much her last letter had movec him and how much it distressed him that she felt further dis cussion of disputed points would be futile, he added impetu ously, "I know it will surprise you and even amaze you Angelina, when I say, as I now do, that for a long time, yo have had my whole heart. . . . Your letter to Wm. Lloyc Garrison formed an era in my feelings and a crisis in m history that drew my spirit toward yours by irrepressibl affinities. I read it over and over and over. . . . Though had never seen you, my heart turned toward you with a unwavering steadfastness. . . . I strove long against it. . . From the time that I met you in New York to this momen . . . this same state of mind has continued unvarying, excep that it has gathered strength with every day. . . . I have *n expectation* and almost *no hope* that my feelings are in an way *reciprocated by you*. . . . When I found the strength o my affection for you, I strove against it till weary with con flict and convicted of sin. . . . It has often occurred to m that God may have ordered it in his providence as a crownin trial to test my love to Him. . . . If (and I have hardly hope that it is otherwise) your heart, Angelina, does not reciprocate my love, I charge you before a risen Lord not to shrink for a moment through fear of giving me pain from declaring to me the *whole truth.*"[19]

Angelina, expecting to find his reply pointing out to her some sin or some fault, was astonished to find a declaration of love. Yet, as she confessed to him, his love was not a complete surprise because in the depths of her own heart there was a response which she thought and hoped might be produced by his feelings toward her. It was her love for him, she explained, which made his criticism of her cut so deeply.

Then she admitted that two years before a letter of his in the *Liberator* had drawn her spirit to his. "I felt," she wrote, "there was a kindred mind, a congenial soul and I longed to hold communion with you. . . . You talk too of 'the long conflict' you have had with yourself on account of your affection for me. I confess I have had the same on account of mine for you." Then she told him how frightened she had been in New York when she found her happiness was bound up in him. "Do you believe," she asked him, "that our Father ever begets such pure and holy feelings in one heart without touching the other? I feel dear Theodore that we are the two halves to one whole . . . and that the Lord has given us to each other."[20]

After receiving Angelina's letter, Theodore was so overcome by emotion that he could not reply for four days. Then he wrote, "Angelina, instead of writing you, I should at once have gone to see you . . . but I cannot see you. I dare not see you yet." So intense was their love for each other that they often feared they were idolaters. While they wrestled with this problem of idolatry, the antislavery movement moved forward.

CHAPTER VIII

Angelina Grimké Overrides the Woman Question

Angelina and Sarah Grimké were among the several hundre
women who attended the "great Texas meeting" in Bostoı
early in January, 1838, in Faneuil Hall, called by the Mass
chusetts Antislavery Society to protest the annexation c
Texas. Since the Republic of Texas had declared its ind
pendence from Mexico in 1836, there had been continuoı
agitation for its annexation to the United States, both on th
part of its own citizens and the South. Abolitionists oppose
annexation, realizing how much it would strengthen th
power of the slave states in Congress.

So impressive were the Texas meeting and further meetin
of the Massachusetts Antislavery Society that the Massach
setts Legislature appointed a committee to consider petitior
before it relating to the abolition of slavery. As thousanc
of women had signed these petitions, Henry B. Stantoı
lining up the speakers, asked Angelina Grimké if she woul
not like to speak before the committee. Not expecting her t
accept, he was surprised, and troubled as well, when she r
plied that if the friends of the cause thought well of it, sh
would speak. Some of the abolitionists hesitated. "Even th
stout-hearted tremble when the woman question is to b
acted out in full," was Angelina's comment. "Jackson, Fulle
Phelps, and Quincy were consulted," she added. "The first i
sound to the core, and went right up to the State House t

ıquire of the committee whether I could be heard. Wonder-ıl to tell, the Chairman, James C. Alford, said yes without ıe least hesitation, and actually helped to remove the scruples f some of the timid-hearted abolitionists. . . . I feel this is ıe most important step I have ever been called upon to take: nportant to women, to the slave, to my country, and to the orld."[1]

On February 21, 1838, the halls of the Massachusetts Leg-lature were opened for the first time to a woman. "My heart ever quailed before," Angelina confessed in a letter to Theo-ore, "but it almost died within me at that tremendous hour . . but our Lord and Master gave me his arm to lean upon ıd in great weakness, my limbs trembling, I stood up and oke nearly two hours. . . . So far as intellect and power f language was concerned, I did not excel – it was not one of ıy happiest efforts; but my heart broke over the wrongs of ıe slave . . . and many were melted to tears. It was just ıch a meeting as I had tried to pray for. Many of our dear bolitionist friends did indeed travail in spirit for me, wres-ing in earnest prayer and M. Chapman's 'God strengthen ou my Sister' just before I rose was a strength to my faint-ıg spirit."[2]

A large crowd had assembled for the hearing and many ere turned away. Angelina Grimké's strong, melodious voice ached every part of the hall. Here was "pathos and power ogether," reported Maria Weston Chapman for the *Lib-rator,* "with a play of countenance whose strength and obility of expression I never saw equalled."[3]

"I stand before you," Angelina Grimké began, "as a citi-n, on behalf of 20,000 women of Massachusetts whose ames are enrolled on petitions which have been submitted the Legislature. . . . These petitions relate to the great ıd solemn subject of American slavery. . . . Because it is a political subject, it has often been tauntingly said that women have nothing to do with it . . . I hold, Mr. Chairman, that American women have to do with this subject, not only because it is moral and religious, but because it is political, inasmuch as we are citizens of this republic, and as such our honor, happiness, and well being are bound up in its politics, government, and laws.

"I stand before you as a Southerner, exiled from the land of my birth by the sound of the lash and the piteous cry of the slave. I stand before you as a repentant slaveholder. . . ."

The audience was visibly moved. "A sudden glow came to men's faces," reported Mrs. Chapman, "the flush of mingled shame and enthusiasm; the eyes of gray-haired men filled with tears."

According to Wendell Phillips, who was in the audience, "It gave Miss Grimké the opportunity to speak to the best culture and character of Massachusetts; and the profound impression then made on a class not often found at our meetings was never wholly lost. It was not only the testimony of one most competent to speak, but it was the profound religious experience of one who had broken out of the charmed circle, and whose intense earnestness melted all opposition. The converts she made needed no after-training."

Feeling she had still more to tell, Angelina asked for and was granted another hearing. Again people were turned away from an overcrowded hall. She felt calm and confident at this second hearing, as she stood before the Speaker's desk and looked into the faces of the audience. At first there was hissing from the doorways, but the audience in the hall was quiet and expectant. She was asked to stand in the Speaker's place, so that she could be seen as well as heard, and she spoke for two hours, without the slightest interruption, on the dangers of slavery, the safety of emancipation, and the character of the free people of color and the cruel treatment they received because of prejudice. Still needing more time, she asked for a third hearing, which was granted.

"What the effect of these meetings is to be, I know not," she wrote her Negro friend, Sarah Douglass. "This I know that the Chairman was in tears almost the whole time I was speaking. . . . No doubt great numbers who have attended them come out of mere curiosity; some to make fun of . . . a Woman's addressing a Committee of the Legislature; they came despising me and my cause. . . . We Abolition Women are turning the world upside down. . . . It has been an inexpressible comfort and strength to me to find how deeply the Abolitionists have sympathized with me and how they have been bound in exercise and prayer with me. I did not expect it to the extent to which it has been manifested. I feel that when I am speaking I am surrounded by a bodyguard of hearts faithful and true and by an atmosphere of prayer."[4]

* * *

Soon after the hearings, Theodore came to Boston to spend a few days with Angelina. Meanwhile, they had been agonizing in their letters over their faults, their unworthiness, and their fears of disappointing each other. All this was dispelled by their happy days together and the plans for their marriage in Philadelphia in May. Sister Sarah's approval filled their cup of joy to the brim. When Theodore returned to his work in New York, Angelina prepared for a series of lectures to be delivered in Boston, at the Odeon, the old Boston Theater which had been converted into a music hall. These lectures were arranged for her, because it was generally agreed that her speaking had done more than anything else to advance the cause of abolition in Massachusetts.

Unfortunately, Sarah delivered the first lecture before an

audience that packed the Odeon to overflowing. Expecting to hear Angelina, they were bitterly disappointed and showed it. The abolitionists in Boston hesitated to speak to Sarah about this, not wishing to hurt her, but Theodore came to the rescue, thus saving the rest of the meetings. As kindly as possible he explained the situation to Sarah by letter, adding, "The lack of interest in your lectures was not at all for lack of interesting matter, but for lack of an interesting and happy manner of speaking . . . Your manner is monotonous and heavy, and instead of increasing the power of the truth uttered, it weakens it. . . . I know you will take this from me just as I give it in abounding love. . . . I am persuaded you will agree with me the only . . . question to be thought of for a moment . . . is which of you shall produce the best effect."[5]

Sarah, valuing Theodore's friendship and judgment, replied, "Our adored A. shall deliver the other lectures at the Odeon."[6] Almost immediately afterward, Sarah gave up lecturing. It had always been hard for her, and she began to realize that writing was her field.

Angelina delivered the remaining five lectures at the Odeon, and according to Wendell Phillips, "Angelina . . . possessed a rare gift of eloquence, a calm power of persuasion, a magnetic influence over those that listened to her, which carried conviction to hearts that nothing before had reached . . ."[7]

Reporting to Theodore on the last meeting at the Odeon, Angelina wrote, "I felt I had an audience who had come to hear, not out of idle curiosity, but the want of information. It was a far more quiet meeting . . . not the least attempt at disturbance within. I spoke about one and a half hours. The Lord helped me. . . . Dearest it was a great strength to me last night to feel and know that you were praying for me.

Your prayer, I believe, was answered, tho' I don't think my lecture was one of my best efforts. Somehow I think my *best* efforts are over." Then she added, "I tho't yesterday, perhaps our marriage was to be my dismission from *public* service. O! how I should rejoice at it, if the Master should say, 'It is enough.' "[8]

Mrs. Chapman had suspected that Theodore's and Angelina's interest in each other was leading to marriage and so told Angelina, but spoke of it only to a few friends and her sister, Anne Weston, who immediately exclaimed that Theodore had risen fifty percent in her estimation. Anne was sure the match was made in heaven. "Altho' a great many will go to hear you, and may admire you . . ." she told Angelina, "yet I have believed you had thrown yourself entirely beyond the ordinary lot of women, and no man would wish to have such a wife." In Anne Weston's opinion, Angelina's engagement to Theodore was "a complete triumph over the pastoral brethren who threaten such women with the entire withdrawal of man's protection."[9]

Angelina's public speaking and advocacy of woman's rights had put many men on the defensive, so that Theodore reported that nine-tenths of his New York abolitionist friends regarded her as "utterly spoiled for domestic life."[10] He told her of a man who had great respect for her principles and character, but could not believe it possible for a woman of her "sentiments and practice as to the sphere of woman to be anything but 'an obtrusive clamorer' in the domestic circle, 'repelled and repelling,' " and felt it impossible for a man of high and pure feeling to marry her.

Later, when Theodore wrote her that even Lewis Tappan thought he was showing great moral courage in marrying her, she replied, "Why, didst thou not know that no other man would marry me—no, not even a good abolitionist? . . . I agree with Lewis Tappan perfectly. But thou art blind to the *danger* of marrying a woman who feels and acts out the principle of *equal* rights."[11]

Then she added, "Beloved, I believe thou wilt find me *most* happy in our little cottage and in the kitchen of that cottage when duty calls me there . . . May the Lord Jesus help me for thy sake and for *woman's* sake to prove that well regulated minds can with equal ease occupy high and low stations and find *true happiness* in both."

* * *

The last week in April, 1838, Angelina and Sarah left the Philbricks' comfortable home in Brookline for Philadelphia, to prepare for the wedding. Sarah was welcomed into the home of Angelina's dear friend, Jane Smith, while Angelina stayed with her sister, Anna Frost, in whose home her wedding was to take place. She had written her sister just what kind of a wedding she and Theodore felt it their duty to have, adding that if she were willing to have such a wedding under her roof, they would be happy to be married there. They chose May 14 as the date of the wedding, as many of their friends would be in Philadelphia at that time for the opening of Pennsylvania Hall and the second Antislavery Convention of American Women.

In the meantime, while Theodore was delayed in New York by an antislavery convention, he and Angelina corresponded about their future home and its furnishings. Theodore had found a house at Fort Lee, New Jersey, on the Hudson River, not far from New York. A small boat provided transportation to and from the city, and, when he could, Theodore went up to supervise the repairs and painting, and planted a garden. He now wrote Angelina that many of his friends who had come to the convention rejoiced over their approaching marriage, all but Henry C. Wright, who "looks as tho' his heart was broke when he speaks of it."[12] Angelina, on the other hand, reported, "I am told that my abolition friends here are almost *offended* that I should do such a thing as to get married. Some say *we* were both public property and had no right to enter into such an engagement. Others, that I will now be good for nothing henceforth and forever to the cause. . . ."

Sarah, too, in spite of her fondness for Theodore, was finding it difficult to face the marriage, even though she felt it ordained of God. So long had her life been bound up with Angelina's that any change in their relationship was difficult. Angelina understood, writing Theodore, "She has had a hard struggle for many weeks. May the Lord help her and me too. I know I do not feel right about the trial she feels in anticipation of our union."

As the wedding day approached, Theodore was concerned about his wedding suit, confessing he was an ignoramus about such matters. "Just tell me your preferences about my dress on that occasion," he wrote Angelina. She suggested a brown coat, white cravat (which Sister Anna would tie for him as they presumed he had never done this), white waistcoat, white or light-colored pantaloons, and white stockings – quite an order for a man who all his life had been indifferent to how he looked, but he complied.

Angelina and Theodore sent their friends a handwritten invitation to their wedding, reading in part, "Wilt thou grant us thy presence and sympathy and prayer on that solemn occasion."[13] This was signed by both and written on paper headed by a picture of a slave, a woman, with her hands manacled. As Angelina could not conscientiously consent to be married by a clergyman, Theodore, a member of the Presbyterian Church, yielded to her views, asking only that both a colored and a white Presbyterian clergyman offer prayers. Since, under Pennsylvania law, a marriage was legal if witnessed and attested by twelve persons, they gathered their friends about them and, as Sarah wrote to a friend in England, had the marriage solemnized "as a religious act in a religious and social meeting."

Because neither Theodore nor Angelina wished to repeat a set form of words, they carried through the ceremony as the Spirit moved them. Theodore addressed Angelina in a solemn tender manner, alluding to the unrighteous power vested in a husband by the laws of the United States over the person and property of his wife and renouncing all such authority. Angelina declared she would honor him, prefer him above herself, and love him with a pure heart fervently. Then all knelt while both Theodore and Angelina offered prayers, as did a colored and a white Presbyterian minister. Then William Lloyd Garrison read with dignity the marriage certificate which all of the witnesses signed.[14]

"A more interesting service, it never was my fortune to witness," wrote Mrs. Chapman to an English friend. "It was a mingling of what was most interesting in the marriage-rites of the Friends and other sects . . . with much that was individual. . . . It was in short an abolition wedding."[15]

Outstanding abolitionists attended, among them the Lewis Tappans, the Birneys, Henry B. Stanton, Maria Weston Chapman, Abby Kelley, several Negro friends, and Whittier, who stepped outside during the ceremony to avoid being disowned by the Quakers. Angelina was disowned for marrying a Presbyterian and Sarah for attending the wedding. "We feel no regret," Sarah confided to a friend, "believing that the discipline which cuts us off from membership for an act so strictly in conformity with the will of God and so sanctioned by his word . . . must be anti-Christian, and I am thankful for an opportunity to testify against it."[16]

"The evening," Sarah added, "was spent in pleasant social intercourse. Several colored persons were present, among them two liberated slaves, who formerly belonged to our father, had come by inheritance to sister Anna, and had been freed by her. They were invited guests, and thus we had an opportunity to bear our testimony against the horrible prejudice which prevails against colored persons. . . ."

* * *

They continued to bear testimony the next day, at the Second Antislavery Convention of American Women. This convention was held in Philadelphia at Pennsylvania Hall, one of the finest buildings in the city, recently erected and financed by abolitionists and friends of free speech, who had found the halls, lecture rooms, and churches of Philadelphia closed to them. From five hundred to six hundred women had gathered for the convention from all parts of the country, three times as many as had assembled for the convention in New York, in 1837. Mary S. Parker of Boston was elected President, and a program was mapped out.

While there was much proslavery sentiment in Philadelphia, no disturbance developed until the evening meeting of May 16, which was open to the public. The announcement of the speakers, William Lloyd Garrison, Angelina Grimké Weld, and Maria Weston Chapman, at once aroused antagonism, and placards were posted about the city urging interference with the meeting. Although this was regarded as the work of only a few malcontents, the police were alerted. As an audience of three thousand filled the hall, a noisy crowd gathered outside, growing more belligerent as they saw Negroes enter and sit next to whites. When Garrison opened the meeting with a short speech, the mob spirit broke loose and stones and bricks were hurled through the windows. Mrs. Chapman rose to speak in the midst of shouts and the breaking of windows. It was her first speech before an audience of men and women. She stood there with the bearing of a queen, a red shawl about her shoulders, pleading for a hearing for herself and others. Her red shawl was a badge of courage to an audience ready to panic, and as one delegate remarked, "I kept my eye on that shawl. . . . I made up my mind that until that shawl disappeared, every man must stick by his guns."[17]

Angelina Grimké Weld came forward next, calm and unmindful of the uproar, speaking with earnestness and eloquence. The mob howled and hissed, hurled bricks, and tried to force the doors. "What is a mob?" she asked. "What would the breaking of every window be? Any evidence that we are wrong, or that slavery is a good wholesome institution? What if the mob should now burst in upon us, break up our meeting and commit violence upon our persons – would this be anything compared with what the slaves endure? No, No, . . ."[18] She continued for nearly an hour, ignoring the noise except to raise her voice so that she could be heard. Rebecca Moore, a Quaker, followed her; then the intrepid, calm Lucretia Mott, and young Abby Kelley of Lynn, who explained that she had never before addressed "a promiscuous audience," but was now called by a still, small voice within, bidding her open her mouth for the dumb and "to plead the cause of God's perishing poor."[19] So eloquently and earnestly did she speak then and later during the convention, that Theodore Weld urged her to give up teaching and become an antislavery lecturer. "Abby," he said, laying his hand on her shoulder, "if you don't, God will smite you!"[20]

While she was speaking, the disturbance became so violent that the meeting was adjourned until the next morning, and as the audience filed out it confronted a dense noisy mob; but there was no violence until later when colored men in the streets were attacked.

The mob was on hand the next morning when the women assembled for another session of their convention. Lucretia Mott spoke of their "being a little disturbed last evening by the tumultuous sea of human passions around us,"[21] and reminded the delegates of the courage and perseverance of Jesus' disciples as they preached the Gospel. She called upon them to do likewise. Angelina Grimké Weld expressed her grief at the color prejudice she found in the free states and offered a resolution expressing sympathy for their colored friends in the city.

In the afternoon, as the disturbance by the mob increased, the president of the Pennsylvania Hall Association sent a message warning that the "colored sisters" for their safety should not attend the evening meeting. Lucretia Mott, although presenting this message, said that in her opinion colored women should not stay away and she expressed the hope that no one would be alarmed by the appearance of danger. She herself, she said, would attend the meeting, and Abby Kelley added that the New England delegation would be there. A colored woman then declared it would be selfish and cowardly for her people to stay away in the hour of danger. Angelina Weld suggested that as they left the hall, each one walk arm in arm with a colored friend. This they did, pressing through a dense crowd, and all reached their destinations unharmed.

So ominous were the demonstrations of the mob that the Mayor forbade an evening meeting in Pennsylvania Hall, taking the keys and asking the mob to disperse. A few of the women, holding a business meeting elsewhere that evening, suddenly heard a shout, "Fire!" Soon they discovered Pennsylvania Hall was in flames. After the Mayor had left the Hall, the mob had forced the doors and rushed in, destroying whatever was in their path and then, with a flaming torch, set the building on fire. The fire departments on the scene made no effort to save the hall, and so the "Temple of Freedom" was destroyed, as the mob marched through the streets singing a song of triumph.

By this time the women had reached the Mott home, where a number of abolitionists had taken refuge. In addition to Lucretia Mott, there were Mrs. Chapman, her sister, Anne Weston, and Sarah Pugh. As the rioters swarmed through nearby streets, it seemed as if an attack on the Mott house were imminent, but a friend of the Motts joined the mob, and crying, "On to the Motts'," led them in the wrong direction.

Describing this night of terror to an English friend, Mrs. Chapman wrote, "Hundreds of Southerners were seen spurring on a ferocious mob to raze the houses of abolitionists. Fortunately the sacrifices of the Friends of old were yet a power to stay the hand of devastation. The mob respected the dwellings of Quakers to which the body of abolitionists . . . of Philadelphia belong and nothing was destroyed but the beautiful spacious hall which had just been built."[22]

The next morning, the convention delegates, sad but undismayed, tried to meet in Temperance Hall, but found it closed to them. Then they walked some distance to the schoolroom of one of the delegates, Sarah Pugh, where they held their last meeting, which was opened with the reading of pertinent lines from II Corinthians: "We are troubled on every side, yet not distressed; we are perplexed, but not in despair; persecuted but not forsaken; cast down, but not destroyed." As these words rang out, the women were encouraged and strengthened, and rededicated themselves to the cause. After a prayer by Julia Tappan, Lucretia Mott spoke of the riot and how she felt when she heard that the mob was heading for her home, "I had often thought how I would sustain myself if called to pass such an ordeal. . . . I believe I was strengthened by God. I felt at the moment that I was willing to suffer whatever the cause required. . . . But the mob was not suffered to molest us, and I feel thankful that we slept a few hours in tranquility and peace."[23]

Once again, women had bravely faced a mob for the cause, and, as in Boston in 1835, the mob was not made up of the so-called lower classes and rabble, but of the "respectable," merchants and bankers who profited from trade with the South and of Southern medical students. As Harriet Martineau observed in her *Retrospect of Western Travel,* "Each State appears to have to pass through riot to rectitude on this mighty question."

The Convention of Antislavery Women adopted many resolutions, reaffirming that it was woman's duty to take an active part in the antislavery movement, that slavery was contrary to Christianity, that churches should exclude slaveholders from pulpits and communion tables, that it was women's duty to withdraw from churches that did not comply, that the North was deeply implicated in the slave system. They resolved that prejudice against color is the very spirit of slavery and that it was the duty of abolitionists to identify themselves with colored Americans, sitting with them in places of worship, appearing with them in the streets, on steamboats and stages, and visiting them in their homes. They rejoiced over the success of emancipation in the West Indies and resolved to continue their petitions for the abolition of slavery in the District of Columbia.

Some of the resolutions aroused doubts in the minds of a few abolitionists, as James and Lucretia Mott reported later in a joint letter to Mrs. Chapman, after the convention. "A few of our timid friends," they wrote, "have become greatly alarmed at the resolution passed by the woman's convention respecting the duty of abolitionists associating with and countenancing colored Americans and have endeavored to persuade the publishing committee to omit the resolution." This, however, could not be accomplished. "The prejudice against color that I have always felt lurking within me," James Mott confessed, "has, I believe, been entirely destroyed by the light of Pennsylvania Hall."[24]

To this Lucretia Mott added, "None of our thorough Antislavery friends are turning back and discouraging the colored people from co-operating with our movement. It is only our half-way Abolitionists and those who have never joined our societies who are quaking with fear."

At the convention, there was discussion of future gatherings of antislavery women. Some felt that separate conventions of women were no longer necessary, as from now on they would be included in men's conventions. The majority, however, voted to hold a Women's Convention in Philadelphia in 1839. As one delegate expressed it, "It is worth everything to Abolitionists, who have such a mighty work to accomplish, to be all acquainted with each other, and to be encouraged by each other's zeal, and strengthened by each other's strength."[25]

When the 1839 Antislavery Convention of American Women prepared to meet in Philadelphia, the Mayor approached Lucretia Mott to find out whether colored women would attend and suggested that to avoid disturbance there be no "unnecessary walking with colored people" through streets. To this Mrs. Mott replied that as she was in the habit of walking with colored people as the occasion demanded, she would continue to do so, and added that as she expected to have colored house guests during the convention, she probably would walk to the convention with them. In spite of this, the meetings, held in the hall of the Pennsylvania Riding School, were undisturbed. There were no evening meetings, as there was no way of lighting the hall. The convention adjourned, expecting to meet in Boston in 1840, but this was never convened, for by that time women as well as men were acceptable as delegates at antislavery conventions.

Of this Lydia Maria Child heartily approved. She had not attended either the 1838 or 1839 conventions, for as she explained to Lucretia Mott, "I never have entered very earnestly into the plan of female conventions and societies. They always seemed to me like a pair of scissors. This feeling led me to throw cold water on the project of the Boston Female Antislavery Society. You will remind me of the great good done by that society. I admit it most cordially. I am thankful that there were those who could work heartily in that way . . . I attended the first convention because I was urged by friends and feared I might fail in my duty if I obstinately refused. But I then thought the large sum necessarily expended in getting the delegates together might be otherwise expended with far more profit to the Antislavery cause. This opinion has been confirmed by the two conventions already held. For the freedom of women, they have probably done something; but in every other point of view, I think their influence has been very slight."[26]

Like Lydia Maria Child, but for different reasons, the Grimké sisters did not attend the 1839 convention, although especially invited and urged to take part. Angelina, after her strenuous years of lecturing, felt the need of a period of quiet, out of the public eye, and Sarah, who always shrank from public speaking, now devoted herself to writing.

Nor was Abby Kelley at the convention. She had felt it her duty to be with her mother in Millbury, Massachusetts, for a time. She had given up teaching at the Friends' School in Lynn, and was trying to decide whether or not to follow Theodore Weld's advice that she become an antislavery lecturer. Her family opposed it and put obstacles in her way, thinking she was under a delusion.

She wrote Theodore Weld that she would probably leave home in the spring if her mother's health continued to improve, but added, "Whether I shall go, I know not, and if the Lord be with me, I know I ought not to care even though I should not have 'where to lay my head'. . . . I have prayed earnestly that this cup might pass from me, not feeling I could drink it, How can I? I have nothing to start upon, nothing to commend me to the notice or favor of any, no name, no reputation, no scrip, neither money in my purse. The prospect is full of trials. But what is greatest is the feeling of my own inability for the work. I have not the gift. How can I make bricks without straw? I have waited thus long, hoping that I should be excused. No excuse comes. I *must* go . . . I often think that had I the qualifications of Sarah and Angelina, I could not wait another day, when the cry from the South is grating so harshly on our ears."[27]

CHAPTER IX

The Doors Open for Women

/hile Abby Kelley was pondering her future course, the oman question and theology were playing havoc in the anti- avery movement. William Lloyd Garrison's criticism in the *iberator* of the Pastoral Letter, the Clerical Appeal, and of ıe clergymen involved, increased in intensity, and, as a re- ılt, a definite rift developed in the Massachusetts Antislavery ociety, which soon spread to the American Antislavery So- ety, the national organization with headquarters in New ork. Garrison was denounced as an infidel, a Sabbath breaker, Fanny Wright man, advocating dangerous doctrines. In Iassachusetts, abolitionist clergymen proposed that a second ıtislavery society be formed which would devote itself exclu- vely to the abolition of slavery and would not involve the sue with woman's rights, nonresistance, and the many ex- aneous reforms advocated by the *Liberator*. In fact, the *iberator* was no longer acceptable to them and they made it lain that they would no longer support it. Garrison, accus- med to carrying on alone, was more than ever determined keep the paper in the hands of laymen and out of the ınds of the clergy. As before, in critical moments, his loyal, ealthy friends, Francis Jackson, Edmund Quincy, and Wil- am Bassett, came to the rescue with funds, and Oliver ɔhnson with editorial assistance. The *Liberator* was therefore ɔle to continue publication, even announcing two new de- ırtments — on nonresistance, the other on equal rights.

The latter had plenty of news to report after the New England Antislavery Convention which met in Boston at Marlboro Chapel, May 31, 1838. Marlboro Chapel, like Pennsylvania Hall, had been erected by abolitionists and dedicated to free speech, because public halls in Boston were closed to them. The dedication of Marlboro Chapel aroused the antagonism of proslavery groups, who distributed placards urging action against abolitionists, although this time police protection proved to be adequate. The only disturbance was in the convention itself, after Garrison suggested that women be invited to take part, and Oliver Johnson offered a resolution that "All persons present, or who may be present at subsequent meetings, whether men or women, who agree with us in sentiment on the subject of slavery, be invited to become members, and participate in the proceedings of the Convention."[1] When this was adopted without a single negative vote, eight orthodox clergymen withdrew from the convention, while others remained to protest against the introduction of the woman question, which they regarded as foreign to the platform. Even Whittier, reporting the convention for his *Pennsylvania Freeman,* wrote that the question of admitting women had nothing to do with "the professed object of the Convention."

The next disturbing action was the election of Abby Kelley to serve on a committee which would memorialize New England ecclesiastical bodies to bear testimony against slavery. Although there was opposition to the committee's draft of the Memorial because it was proposed by "an unscripturally woman-ruled Convention,"[2] it was nevertheless accepted.

Hearing that women had been made voting members at the New England Antislavery Society and that Abby Kelley had been appointed to serve on an important committee

Angelina Grimké Weld expressed her satisfaction in a letter
o Anne Weston, "I believe this can no more be driven back
rom the field of investigation than the doctrine of Human
Rights of which it is a part. And New England will be the
battleground, for she is most certainly the moral lighthouse
of our Nation." Then, referring to Abby Kelley's appointment, she added, "We have heard that she spoke so frequently in the Convention as really to injure the cause . . .
hat she really made herself and it ridiculous. Now I don't
believe this, but I would like to hear how often she spoke to
Resolutions . . . and what effect was produced on the mind
of those with whom thou hast conversed. . . . I cannot help
hoping she will yet come out as a lecturer in the cause of the
poor slave. Such a practical advocacy of the rights of woman
are worth everything to every reform . . ."[3]

Nonresistance was the next extraneous reform advocated
by the *Liberator*. A great interest in the subject of peace had
been aroused by a series of lectures by Unitarian clergymen,
including William Henry Channing, and this led Garrison
o call a Peace Convention in Boston in September, 1838.
Both Abby Kelley and Mrs. Chapman took an active part in
he convention, much to the dismay of a few clergymen who
were confident this was contrary to the will of God. The New
England Non-Resistance Society was organized with men and
women as members. Its Declaration of Sentiments, published
in the *Liberator,* announced, "We cannot acknowledge allegiance to any human government. . . . We recognize but
one King and Lawgiver, one judge and ruler of mankind."[4]
t spoke out against war and self-defense, against holding
office in human government, and repudiated politics. These
statements were too radical even for some of Garrison's de-
oted followers, and Mrs. Chapman and her sister, Anne
Weston, realizing that the *Liberator* needed to be protected

from publishing too much on the subject of nonresistance, urged a separate journal. As a result, the *Non-Resistant* was established, beginning publication in 1839, with William Lloyd Garrison, Maria Weston Chapman, and Edmund Quincy as editors.

Nonresistance, the woman question, no-human government, and the growing antagonism between clergy and Garrison led to differences among abolitionists which greatly disturbed Mrs. Chapman. When she saw how the heretofore dependable Elizur Wright was being deceived by what she regarded as the "theological demon," she pleaded with him to stand by Garrison, writing him, "Garrison is *the cause* at this critical juncture."[5]

Distressed over James G. Birney's insistence on political action and what seemed to be his influence over Henry B. Stanton, she wrote to Sarah Grimké, urging her to use her personal influence with Stanton not "to join these fellows."[6]

When Angelina Grimké Weld wrote her, "The *Liberator* is an injury to the cause; dost thou not think so?" she was aghast. She replied at once, and to show Angelina how her views had changed, she enclosed a letter Angelina had written in 1836. To Abby Kelley, she commented, "I have had the basest letter from Angelina Grimké that you can conceive of. I shall cut her off from my communion shortly unless she repents. She has run almost to the bottom of the mill."[7] The Grimkés' retirement to their farm home in Belleville, New Jersey, was a great disappointment to many abolitionists, especially to the women. It was hard to understand how they could remain silent in this crisis in the antislavery movement, which was blamed by many on the woman question. In fact, Henry C. Wright, who had worked closely with the Grimkés when they began speaking in New England, now wrote Abby Kelley, "I long to see more women in the field pleading the

ause of Abolition and Non-Resistance. . . . I have no ex-
ectation that Sarah or Angelina will ever go forth again.
They have retired and are under an influence that has bound
nd fettered their souls."[8] He, like Garrison, had feared that
Theodore Weld's sectarianism would hamper the develop-
nent of the Grimké sisters. Now Angelina's criticism of the
iberator reflected Weld's impatience with Garrison's attacks
gainst the clergy and the Church.

* * *

The differences among abolitionists in Massachusetts came
o a head at the Convention of the Massachusetts Antislavery
ociety in Boston, early in 1839. First, a resolution was intro-
luced proposing a weekly official organ other than the *Lib-
rator.* This was voted down, but a short time later the
lissidents established a new paper, *The Massachusetts Aboli-
ionist,* with Elizur Wright as editor, and a new society as
vell, the Massachusetts Abolition Society. Neither were long-
ived, but a nucleus for an anti-Garrison group had been
ormed.

The refusal of some abolitionists to vote was also brought
ip at this meeting. Followers of Garrison regarded the anti-
lavery movement as primarily moral in character and non-
olitical. Their duty, as they saw it, was to stir the consciences
f the nation against slavery, and the nonresistants among
hem regarded voting as the acknowledgment of a govern-
nent that sanctioned slavery. In other words, political action
or them was out of bounds.

Now Henry B. Stanton, more and more an advocate of
olitical action, accused Garrison of lowering the standard of
bolition and being recreant to the cause and bluntly asked
im, "Mr. Garrison, do you or do you not, believe it a sin
o go to the polls?"[9]

Promptly Garrison replied, "A sin for me." Then turnin
to the audience, he asked with indignation, "Am I recrean
to the cause?"

"No! No!" they shouted.

Again Stanton questioned him, and Mrs. Chapman re
ported that the indignation of the astonished audience "ros
to an almost uncontrollable pitch; yet they did restrain it
for the winnowing time had not come and they must tak
careful note of men's conduct now that they might know
whom to trust hereafter." They asked themselves "Was th
true and original test of membership not an acknowledg
ment of the justice and necessity of immediate emancipation
Or was it a belief in the religious duty of voting at the polls?
These questions were not answered by this convention. In
stead, a compromise resolution on going to the polls wa
adopted.

Still another controversial subject was introduced – th
right of women to vote on matters before the convention, bu
the President, Francis Jackson, true to his convictions, an
unmoved by clerical pressure, announced, "The Chair rule
that it is in order for women to vote."

"Not a voice was raised in appeal" reported Mrs. Chap
man. "The Massachusetts Society dared not, for the slave'
sake – it would not for its own, exile any of its member
from its councils."

The Massachusetts Antislavery Society survived this storm
convention. Yet, as Mrs. Chapman expressed it, it was "lik
a ship struggling with a heavy sea."[10] The next big wave cam
in the disagreement over the method of collecting pledge
due the American Antislavery Society. The Massachusetts So
ciety had pledged $10,000, was still in arrears, yet hopefu
of redeeming its promise. The American Society untactfull
sent its agents into Massachusetts to collect. This was a grea

shock to Mrs. Chapman and to some of the members of the Boston Female Antislavery Society, who raised most of the funds through their antislavery fairs. Next came the resignation of the Rev. Amos A. Phelps from the board of managers of the Massachusetts Antislavery Society, on the grounds that the Society no longer devoted itself to the antislavery cause but espoused as well extraneous reforms such as women's rights and nonresistance. Phelps' action was hard to account for, as he had been one of the few clergymen who promptly condemned the Clerical Appeal. His defection at this time produced serious repercussions in the Boston Female Antislavery Society, of which his wife had been an organizer and active member.

Feeling it would be helpful to iron out the differences that had developed in the Boston Female Antislavery Society since Phelps' resignation, Mrs. Chapman asked for a special meeting, which the officers refused to call on the grounds that it would be unconstitutional. Heading the opposition was Mary S. Parker, hitherto so active in the good work of the Society and the Antislavery Conventions of American Women. Now completely under the influence of the clerical, anti-Garrison faction, she instinctively opposed requests of Mrs. Chapman and her group, whom she now looked upon as heretical Unitarians. At the regular annual meeting of the Society, the matter of raising $1,000 as usual for the Massachusetts Antislavery Society was considered, as was supporting the *Liberator* with subscriptions. Both propositions were voted down. As the minority group, including Mrs. Chapman and her sisters, could not be a party to such a decision, they met afterward separately and resolved to raise money for the Massachusetts Antislavery Society and the *Liberator* as in the past, by means of an antislavery fair. These fairs had become an annual project of the Boston Female Antislavery

Society, directed most successfully by Mrs. Chapman and her sisters. The division among members of the Boston Female Antislavery Society regarding policy continued to widen, reflecting the differences which were developing in the American Antislavery Society. Finally, when a definite rift came in the American Society, in 1840, the Boston Female Antislavery Society dissolved. It was at once reorganized by Mrs. Chapman, Mrs. Child, and Thankful Southwick, who could not let it lapse at a time when Henry Clay in the Senate was calling upon his "fair country women to desist from antislavery efforts."[11] Later, Mary S. Parker and her followers formed the Massachusetts Female Emancipation Society.

* * *

Continuing pressure against Garrison, his policies, and his influence threatened the future of the American Antislavery Society as it prepared to hold its Sixth Annual Convention in New York, in May, 1839. Lewis Tappan accused "the Massachusetts madman"[12] of ruining the Society. Birney, Stanton, and others kept up their pressure for political action on slavery. Financial matters as well were in a serious state, as debts piled up and agents went unpaid. The panic of 1837 had taken its toll among previously generous contributors such as the Tappan brothers and Gerrit Smith. Unable to finance its paper, *The Emancipator,* the executive committee of the American Society turned it over to the New York City Society. Local groups, as they became self-sufficient, decreased their contributions to the national organization. All in all, the zeal for reform, inspired by the religious revivals of the early 1830's, had lessened, and it became obvious that complete rededication to the antislavery cause or a change in methods was necessary. Then John Quincy Adams, who had willingly and persistently presented antislavery petitions to Congress, surprised abolitionists by offering a constitutional amendment for the gradual abolition of slavery. In an explanatory letter in the *National Intelligencer*, May 27, 1839, he attacked the doctrine of immediate emancipation as impractical, and recommended compensation to slaveholders. In addition, he conferred with William Ellery Channing about forming a new organization with gradual emancipation as its purpose. Such an organization never materialized, but to Garrison and his colleagues, dedicated as they were to immediate, unconditional emancipation, this seemed like outright betrayal.

Garrison was not blind to the signs of the times as he prepared for the annual convention of the American Antislavery Society in New York, in May, 1839. He had no intention of witnessing the dissolution of the national organization which he had helped to found, nor of allowing the goal of immediate emancipation to be weakened. Nor did he intend to see political action on slavery become the purpose of the national organization. Practical politician that he was, he lined up his supporters. He could count on the majority of members of the Massachusetts Antislavery Society, on many of the local societies in New England, and on the women. With him were his stalwart allies from Boston, Wendell Phillips, Ellis Gray Loring, and Francis Jackson, as well as Quakers from Pennsylvania and Rhode Island, and delegates from upstate New York.

Again, women delegates at the convention were a bone of contention, and a day and a half was spent discussing whether they should sit and act with the Society. Gerrit Smith, friendly to the women, presided. The chief opposition came from the clergy. In the final vote, 180 to 140, the women won, but the Reverend Amos A. Phelps continued his opposition by offering a resolution which would interpret the vote as not intending to permit women to speak or serve on committees.

This resolution was defeated, and commenting on the decision, Gerrit Smith declared, "If some prefer to send up here as delegates your Chapmans, your Kelleys, and your Barneys, have we the right to object? If a woman can do my work best, I wish to be at liberty to select a woman."[13]

Almost immediately, Elizabeth Barney, a Quaker from Nantucket, and Abby Kelley made use of this opportunity by addressing their fellow delegates, Abby Kelley following the advice of Lucretia Mott who had written her a few weeks before, "I should be very glad if women generally and men too, could so lose sight of distinctions of sex as to act in public meetings on the enlightened and true ground of Christian equality. . . . There is perhaps no better or speedier mode of preparing them for this equality than for those women whose 'eyes are blessed that they see' . . . to avail themselves of every opportunity offered them to mingle in the discussions. . . ."[14]

Reporting women's victory at the New York convention, the *Liberator* declared, "We hail it with unmingled satisfaction as an era in the history of human rights."

The matter of political action, however, was not settled so satisfactorily for the Garrison faction, but they left New York resolved to fight again another day.

Political action was carried further during the summer of 1839, when a group of abolitionists called a convention in Albany with the hope of forming a third political party. Although only a small number gathered, mostly from western New York, it was a first step toward nominating candidates for President. Alert to all these developments, Mrs. Chapman wrote to her English friend, Elizabeth Pease, "We are in a hot conflict with the political demon." She explained that a third party movement and nominations of antislavery candidates for President had been suggested and urged by the Democratic party to weaken the Whigs. "Some of the abolitionists," she added, "were deceived and instead of maintaining a position from whence they could influence the politicians, suffered the politicians to make use of them."[15] She was more fully convinced than ever of the wisdom of Garrison's policy of no political action, which she knew would again be opposed at the next antislavery convention.

* * *

Mrs. Chapman, however, was unable to join the faithful who gathered in New York, in May, 1840, for the annual convention of the American Antislavery Society, determined to wrest control from the political-action group and the clergy and to keep it true to its main purpose, immediate emancipation of the slaves. Instead, Mrs. Chapman was in Haiti with her husband, who was recuperating there from a serious illness. Her thoughts, however, were often on the issues she knew were being debated. Edmund Quincy kept her informed, urging her to write regularly for the *Liberator*.

Garrison, she knew, had taken no chances, and was prepared for the contest. He had called out his supporters with editorials and pamphlets explaining the crisis in antislavery ranks, and had arranged with railroads and steamship companies for extra trains and boats to take his supporters to New York. They did not disappoint him. More than a thousand delegates assembled at the Fourth Free Church in New York. Unwilling to preside at this meeting, Arthur Tappan turned the chair over to Francis Jackson, who then appointed a business committee of ten men and one woman, Abby Kelley. At once there were protests and a vote was called for, which upheld her appointment. This resulted in the resignation of three of the men appointed to serve with her, Lewis Tappan, Amos Phelps, and Charles Dennison, who stated,

"To put a woman on the committee with men is contrary to the Constitution of the Society . . . is throwing a firebrand into the antislavery ranks . . . is contrary to the usages of civilized society."[16] Then they left the hall, asking all who voted against Abby Kelley to withdraw to form a new society. Arthur Tappan joined them, as did the entire executive committee with the exception of the Quaker, James Gibbons.

Undaunted, the convention continued, approving the appointment of Lucretia Mott, Lydia Maria Child, and Maria Weston Chapman to take the places of the three men who had resigned from the executive committee. Then a resolution was adopted condemning political action, and another, stating that the election of neither Martin Van Buren nor William Henry Harrison could be countenanced by conscientious abolitionists, and still another, condemning churches for "giving undisguised sanction and support to slavery."[17] The Garrison faction had won complete control.

* * *

The men who walked out of the convention, protesting the appointment of Abby Kelley, immediately formed a new organization, which they called the American and Foreign Antislavery Society. Mrs. Chapman always slurringly referred to *it* as "New Organization" and regarded its members as traitors. Lucretia Mott wrote her that she would not "conceal from anyone her disapprobation of the proceedings from the beginning,"[18] but added that, like Mrs. Child, she wished that the local dissension and divisions had not been repeated so in detail in the *Liberator*. To Oliver Johnson, Mrs. Mott made it clear that she had no patience with those who called the *Liberator* an "Infidel Publication," and added that were she a poet, she would extoll the *Liberator* and Garrison in flowery language. She congratulated both for having triumphed over the conspiracy and stated that while she did not agree with all of Garrison's doctrines, including nonresistance, her opinion had "not changed in reference to the utility, the ability, and fidelity of his labor in the antislavery cause – nor in reference to the superiority of the *Liberator* over all other papers on the subject of abolition." Her letter was signed "Yours for the old organization."[19]

Lydia Maria Child, reflecting on the causes that led to the secession from the American Antislavery Society, wrote in a letter to the *Liberator* that she thought it odd that she and other women had been charged with a wish to use antislavery as a tool to advance what were called "woman's rights." "It needed," she added, "but a common portion of foresightedness to foresee that a struggle for the advancement of the principle of freedom would inevitably tend to advance all free principles, for they are connected like a spiral line, which if the top be put in motion revolves even to the lowest point."[20]

Whittier, once close to Garrison and a champion of women at the time of the Pastoral Letter, now stood aloof. In poor health, he had resigned as editor of the *Pennsylvania Freeman*. "I am glad I did not go to New York" he wrote his sister, "for I am sick of all this folly. . . . Our friend Abby it seems . . . was the bomb-shell that exploded the society. . . . Abby is a good girl after all – a little too enthusiastic – but honest and conscientious."[21] To Samuel J. May, he wrote, "My strong faith in my early fellow-laborers remains. . . . But I cannot see eye to eye with Garrison and Mrs. Chapman. They do injustice, as I think, to those who dissent from them. There is a dictatorial censorious intolerant spirit about them which I cannot fellowship."[22]

Theodore Weld also stayed away from the 1840 Convention, as did Angelina, who wrote Gerrit Smith, "We are hid here from the strife of tongues, and hear with . . . indiffer-

ence that our Antislavery light has gone out in total darkness."[23] Recoiling from the bitter controversy and unable to
work with Garrison or the new organization, they refused to
become involved. Invited by Lewis Tappan to speak at the
anniversary of the New-Organization, Weld refused, because
he protested "against the grounds upon which the society
at its organization was based, the denial of the rights of
women."[24] He saw it as such in spite of Lewis Tappan's efforts
to convince him that the split in antislavery ranks was not
solely on account of the woman question.

Regardless of the pros and cons, the woman question remained a live issue to be settled on the basis of human rights.

CHAPTER X

The World's Antislavery Convention

The woman question was raised again when delegates to the World's Antislavery Convention were being chosen. The call to the convention, to be held in London, June 12, 1840, had been issued in October, 1839, inviting all friends of the slave "of every nation and clime." The American Antislavery Society appointed Lucretia Mott as a delegate, as well as William Lloyd Garrison; Charles Remond, a free Negro who had proved to be an intelligent, able lecturer; and Nathaniel P. Rogers, editor of the *Herald of Freedom,* an antislavery paper published in New Hampshire. The Massachusetts Society chose a number of women to represent them – Mrs. Child, Mrs. Chapman, Abby Kelley, Ann Phillips, Emily Winslow, and Harriet Martineau, and, in addition, Wendell Phillips, George Bradburn, William Adams, and Isaac Winslow. The Childs, the Chapmans, and Abby Kelley were unable to accept. More women were appointed delegates by the Pennsylvania Antislavery Society and the Philadelphia Female Antislavery Society – Lucretia Mott, Mary Grew, Sarah Pugh, Abby Kimber, and Elizabeth Neall, all Quakers but Mary Grew.

When word reached London that women were coming as delegates, a second call to the convention was issued, specifying that societies send the names of the gentlemen who were to represent them and, in a letter published in both the *Emancipator* and *Liberator,* Joseph Sturge, the founder of the

British and Foreign Antislavery Society, made it plain that he hoped the sending of female delegates would be discouraged, as it would provoke adverse feeling in England. After reading his letter, Sarah Grimké wrote her English friend, Elizabeth Pease, that she greatly regretted the sending of women, as she feared it would stir up controversy on the woman question and divert attention from the primary purpose, the abolition of Negro slavery.[1]

Observations such as this and the absence of the Grimké sisters from the New York Convention led their old friend, Henry C. Wright, to send a public call to them in the *Liberator,* "Where are those women, Sarah M. Grimké and Angelina G. Weld, who, for a brief space, so powerfully advocated the cause of human rights with tongue and pen? . . . Is their light gone out in total darkness? Have they passed into oblivion? Oh that God would move them to speak once more in this crisis."[2]

The sisters had certainly retired from the world, and were enjoying their quiet life at Fort Lee and their efforts at housekeeping and cooking. "I cannot tell thee how I love this private life," Angelina wrote Elizabeth Pease, "how I have thanked my heavenly father for this respite from public labor or how earnestly I have prayed that whilst I am thus dwelling at ease I may not forget the captives of my land, or be unwilling to go forth again. . . ."[3] Then she assured her that, in spite of some rumors to the contrary, Theodore put no obstacles in her path. "My dear Theodore," she continued, "entertains the noblest views of the rights and responsibilities of woman, and will never lay a straw in the way of my lecturing."

The birth of Angelina's baby, Charles Stuart, in December, 1839, had necessitated a change of pace, but the sisters' light had not gone out, as Henry C. Wright had feared. Both had been helping Theodore compile first a pamphlet and then a book, *Slavery As It Is,* an accurate, vivid, and startling picture of the cruelty of the slave system. Theodore, obliged to give up lecturing because of the condition of his throat, had been editing *Antislavery Almanacs* and revising his *Bible Against Slavery* and *Slavery As It Is.* This kept the three of them busy, Sarah and Angelina spending six months, averaging six hours a day, examining Southern newspapers which Theodore brought home from the New York Commercial Reading Room. From them, they cut news items relating to slavery, speeches in Congress and state legislatures, trials and court decisions, and advertisements for runaway slaves. In addition, Sarah and Angelina related instances of cruelty they themselves had observed. The result was an impressive picture of overworked, undernourished, "inadequately sheltered slaves, neglected in sickness and old age, and often brutally punished." *Slavery As It Is: Testimony of a Thousand Witnesses* was much in demand in England as well as in this country. Close to a hundred thousand copies were sold before the end of 1839. Sarah had also been working on her *Letters on the Equality of the Sexes,* which she published in book form in 1839.

Early in 1840, the Welds moved from Fort Lee on the Hudson to a fifty-acre farm at Belleville, New Jersey, nine miles from New York, in the hope that farm work would improve Theodore's health and would be a means of support for the family. At this time, the American Antislavery Society did not have the funds to employ him regularly.

Among the first visitors at the Belleville farm were Henry B. Stanton and his bride of a few days, Elizabeth Cady, en route to the World's Convention in London. Henry B. Stanton's allegiance was to the new organization and political action. Even so he was sympathetic to the rights of women, and had encouraged Angelina's public speaking in New England.

His young wife was an enthusiastic, out-and-out advocate of the rights of women. Commenting on their visit, Angelina wrote Elizabeth Cady Stanton's cousins, Gerrit and Ann Smith, "We were very much pleased with Elizabeth Stanton, who spent several days with us, and I could not help wishing that Henry was better calculated to mould such a mind. . . . How we long to hear all that was done in the World's Convention and how our American friends worked or warred in it."[4]

* * *

The women who were chosen as delegates to the World's Antislavery convention prepared for their journey, undismayed by the warning that only gentlemen were expected. Lucretia Mott's only regret was that Maria Weston Chapman and Lydia Maria Child were unable to join them and she suggested that the Massachusetts Society add Mrs. Chapman's sisters, Caroline and Anne Weston, to their delegation. She and her Philadelphia colleagues appreciated Mrs. Chapman's keen mind and fearlessness, for in the words of Abby Kimber, "She does not spare to smite when the good of the cause is at stake, and the priesthood of all the sects fear her."[5]

Lucretia and James Mott sailed from New York, on the *Roscoe,* May 7, 1840, and with them were the delegates from Pennsylvania, Henry and Mary Grew, Sarah Pugh, Abby Kimber, and Elizabeth J. Neall; George Bradburn and Abby Southwick from Massachusetts; and Isaac Winslow and his daughter, Emily, from Portland, Maine. There were thirty-two cabin passengers and twenty-one in the steerage. Both Lucretia Mott and Mary Grew kept diaries. They told of the rough, stormy sea which they never tired of watching, of the good conversation, of singing in the evenings, of the generosity of Isaac Winslow who distributed oranges, lemons, and "other luxuries," of Elizabeth Neall, who was the life of the company.

After a voyage of twenty days, they landed in Liverpool and traveled by coach to London, stopping en route for sightseeing. In London, they found comfortable lodgings at Mark Moore's on Queen Street where they met other American abolitionists, among them J. G. Birney, H. B. Stanton, and "his nice Elizabeth." The next day Joseph Sturge breakfasted with them and urged the women not to ask to be seated as delegates. "We endeavored to show him,"[6] Lucretia Mott reported, "the inconsistency of excluding Women Delegates – but soon found he had prejudged and made up his mind to act with our New Organization; therefore all reasoning was lost upon him and our appeals made in vain." Their next caller was Elizabeth Pease, who had been corresponding with many American antislavery women and contributing articles to be sold at their fairs. "A fine noble looking girl," Lucretia Mott described her, later adding "I liked Elizabeth much."

The women were invited to meetings and tea at the Antislavery Rooms where they were greeted with friendliness. Here Lucretia Mott never failed to speak up for the women in her good-natured way, reminding Englishmen, for instance, that an Englishwoman, Elizabeth Heyrick, had been the first to advocate immediate emancipation. Here she also noted that Quakers were cold to her and realized that they must have been warned against her by the orthodox in America, for she and James were Hicksite, Unitarian Quakers and therefore were regarded as heretics. At the Antislavery Rooms, Mary Grew had the pleasure of meeting for the first time her new cousin, Wendell Phillips, who had married her cousin, Ann Greene. "I was quite delighted with him," she commented in her diary, "and every succeeding interview has increased my love and respect for his noble intellect and heart."[7] She was even more pleased with him as the convention progressed.

Representatives of the credentials committee called on the women at Mark Moore's repeatedly to plead with them not to present themselves at the convention as delegates. One of them, an American Baptist minister, the Rev. Nathaniel Colver, bluntly told them that women were constitutionally unfit for public or business meetings. To this Lucretia Mott replied that it was often said that "the colored man was constitutionally unfit to mingle with the white man."[8] At this Colver left the room in anger.

Lucretia Mott soon found she was being supported in her arguments with the clergy by another champion of women, Elizabeth Cady Stanton, who felt "no question was so important as the emancipation of women from the dogmas of the past, political, religious, and social."[9] It was hard for Mrs. Stanton to understand how "abolitionists who felt so keenly the wrongs of the slave could be so oblivious to the equal wrongs of their own mothers, wives, and sisters, when, according to common law, both classes occupied a similar legal status." On the voyage to England with her husband and J. G. Birney, Elizabeth Stanton had heard from Mr. Birney only the most uncomplimentary remarks about the women delegates from Pennsylvania and Boston. She found them charming, intelligent, and stimulating. The feeling was mutual, for Lucretia Mott wrote in her diary, "Elizabeth Stanton gaining daily in our affections."[10]

* * *

Delegates from many countries, including the women from America, gathered in Freemasons Hall, on June 12, 1840, for the World's Antislavery Convention. "We" [the women], reported Lucretia Mott, "were kindly admitted behind the bar, politely conducted to our seats and introduced to many."[11] As Elizabeth Cady Stanton described "behind the bar," it was space at the far end of the hall, screened off by a rail and a curtain, like a choir.[12] Here, in all modesty, women could listen and learn. While Elizabeth Cady Stanton sat there next to Lucretia Mott, Ann Phillips and her husband joined them. Meeting Mrs. Phillips for the first time, Mrs. Stanton was impressed by her earnestness and her beauty, and later described her, "She had a profusion of brown hair, large loving blue eyes and regular features. She was tall, graceful, and talked with great fluency and force. Her whole soul seemed to be in the pending issues."[13] As her husband left her, she laid her hand on his shoulder, reminding him, "No shillyshallying, Wendell. Be brave as a lion."[14] The women counted on him to plead their case at the convention.

While the veteran abolitionist, Thomas Clarkson, opened the convention, they watched and listened with interest. Then Wendell Phillips rose to speak. Tall, handsome, and commanding, he moved that a committee be appointed to prepare a correct list of the members of the convention, including all persons bearing credentials from any antislavery body. He urged the acceptance of the fully qualified women delegates. This opened a spirited discussion which lasted the rest of the day. Next to speak for the women was John Bowring, a distinguished Englishman, who reminded his fellow delegates that the sovereign rule of his country had been placed in the hands of a female who exercised her influence in opposing slavery, and added, "I look upon this delegation from America as one of the most interesting, the most encouraging, and the most delightful symptoms of the times. I cannot believe that we shall refuse to welcome gratefully the cooperation which is offered us." William Ashurst, another

Englishman, pointed out the inconsistency of calling a World's Convention to abolish slavery, and at its threshold depriving half the world of their liberty.[15]

By this time the clerical delegates were fully aroused and voiced their opposition with vigor. The Reverend J. Burnet, an Englishman, appealed to the American ladies to conform to English customs, adding, "It were better that this Convention be dissolved at this moment than that this motion be adopted."

To this, Mary Grew's father, the Reverend Henry Grew, gave his approval, declaring, "The reception of women as part of this Convention would, in the view of many, be not only a violation of the customs of England, but of the ordinance of Almighty God."

After listening to this and much more in the same vein, it was a relief to the women "behind the bar" to hear the strong voice of George Bradburn, of Massachusetts, speaking for them. "Women," he said, "have furnished most essential aid in accomplishing what has been done in the State of Massachusetts. If, in the Legislature of that State, I have been able to do anything in furtherance of that cause, it was mainly owing to the valuable assistance I derived from the women. And shall such women be denied seats in this Convention?" Then he told how these same women had helped George Thompson, when "gentlemen of property and standing" had attempted to drive him out of Boston, "putting his life in peril." George Thompson then entered his plea for the women, telling of Angelina Grimké's speech before the Massachusetts Legislature. "Let us," he said, "contrast our conduct with that of the Senators and Representatives of Massachusetts who did not disdain to hear her. It was inconsequence of her exertions . . . that that interest sprung up which has awakened such intense feeling throughout America." However, even he, in spite of his praise of women as capable hard-working abolitionists, suggested that Phillips withdraw his motion, and in this others joined him, but Wendell Phillips would not yield. "When we have submitted to brickbats and the tar tub and feathers in America," he replied, "rather than yield to the custom prevalent there of not admitting colored brethren to our friendship, shall we yield to parallel custom or prejudice against women in Old England? We cannot yield this question if we would; for it is a matter of conscience. . . ."

Then the clergy declared it was a matter of conscience with them as well and waxed eloquent as they pompously declared that the admission of women would be contrary to the word of God. Listening with growing indignation with the women "behind the bar," Elizabeth Cady Stanton now heard her husband's voice speak out for women, the only member of the New-Organization delegation to do so. However, one voice was missing among those that spoke for the women, that of William Lloyd Garrison, who was still on his way to the Convention, his ship delayed by severe storms.

When finally a vote on Wendell Phillips' motion was taken, it was defeated by an overwhelming majority and the women delegates were excluded. "It was really pitiful," reported Elizabeth Cady Stanton, "to hear the narrow-minded bigots, pretending to be teachers and leaders of men, so cruelly remanding their own mothers, with the rest of womankind, to absolute subjection to the ordinary masculine type of humanity. I always regretted that the women themselves had not taken part in the debate before the Convention was fully organized and the question of delegates settled."[16]

* * *

Women's American champion, William Lloyd Garrison, now arrived at the convention, five days late. He had left America in a hopeful mood, feeling that with a young woman on the throne of Great Britain, the convention could hardly presume to bar delegates because of their sex. Nor could he believe that any assembly would regard "that almost peerless woman, Lucretia Mott," unqualified to take part. In London, however, he came face to face with the stern realities. In protest, he refused to take any part in the convention, and with the companions of his sea voyage, Charles Remond, William Adams, and Nathaniel Rogers, sat in the gallery as an observer. At first Lucretia Mott argued against this, feeling his voice should be heard at the convention, but he would not yield, "We felt," he reasoned, "that in rejecting the credentials of those who were delegated with us, the London meeting did really dishonor our own. We felt that we had no more right there than was possessed by our rejected delegates, and we would not go in as a matter of favor."[18] For this he won the gratitude of the women who frequently went up to the gallery to sit with him. "Lady Byron," reported William Adams, "was among the first to venture up to our small gallery and informed us who the speakers were; for we were so far away that we could not hear."

Far from crushed by their defeat, the American women made the most of the opportunities offered, making many friends, among them Amelia Opie, Elizabeth Fry, Elizabeth Pease, Lady Byron, and the Duchess of Sutherland. "Our delegation," wrote Mary Grew in her diary, "is regarded as quite a phenomenon which everyone is anxious to see. We are almost every day introduced to numbers of persons who request this *privilege,* and who look upon us with countenances of mingled astonishment and respect. Publicly and privately, we are edified with laudatory allusions to the sacrifices we have made in leaving our homes, 'braving the dangers of the Atlantic' to come hither for the sake of the antislavery cause etc. . . . (little thought we of its dangers, when we had the happiness to be upon it)."[19]

They felt very much honored by the attention of Thomas Clarkson, who asked to call on them and who in a note to them acknowledged "the obligations which our sacred cause owes to the American Ladies, for having so warmly taken it up and protected it on their side of the water against the attacks of its adversaries and this in times of threatened persecution." The Irish orator and leader of the Catholic emancipation movement, Daniel O'Connell, also showed his interest and friendliness, when, in one of his speeches, he referred to the exclusion of the women delegates and expressed a hope that it would be reversed.

Wendell Phillips tried twice to introduce Garrison to the convention, but was put off in order that there be no further discussion of the woman question; yet the subject could not be put down. A protest against the exclusion of the women, drawn up by Professor Adams of Harvard, and signed by Wendell Phillips, James Mott, George Bradburn, and others, was presented to the convention by Wendell Phillips, but was laid on the table and refused a place in the printed proceedings.

Attempts by American women to hold a meeting with Englishwomen were discouraged, although they merely wanted to discuss what more they could do to help free the slaves. Orthodox Quakers, many of whom attended the Convention, feared the influence of Lucretia Mott, whom they regarded as a heretic. In fact, an English Quaker, William Howitt, maintained that the women delegates were excluded not because of their sex, but because most of them, not orthodox Quakers, were tainted with Hicksite doctrine.

In his opinion this so influenced the many Quakers at the convention that they could not tolerate the presence of the women. Both James and Lucretia Mott felt this to be the case.

This also influenced the painter, Benjamin Robert Haydon, who had been commissioned to paint a picture of the convention and who asked those who attended to sit for him. "Lucretia Mott, the leader of the delegate women from America sat," he wrote in his diary, "I found her out to have infidel notions, and resolved at once, narrow-minded or not, not to give her the prominent place I first intended. I will reserve that for a beautiful believer in the Divinity of Christ."[20]

Nevertheless, according to Garrison, Lucretia Mott was winning "golden opinions" in spite of "the ceaseless efforts of the Orthodox Quakers to obstruct her course."[21] Richard D. Webb, in an article in the Dublin *Weekly Record,* called her "the lioness of the Convention . . . one of the most remarkable women in the whole assembly. . . . She is a thin, petite, dark complexioned woman, about fifty years of age. She has striking, intelligent features and bright, vivacious eyes. This lady has the enviable celebrity of being one of the undaunted, consistent, able, and indefatigable friends of the slave."[22]

Harriet Martineau, who, when she was in America, had met Lucretia Mott, looked forward to renewing their acquaintance at the convention, but when the time came, she was too ill to attend and this was a great disappointment to her. "I cannot be satisfied,"[23] she wrote Lucretia Mott, "without sending you one line of love and sympathy. I think much of you amidst your present trials; and much have I thought of you and your cause since we parted." She urged Lucretia and James to call on her if possible before they left England

and this they were able to do. In spite of her illness, Harriet Martineau kept in touch, through friends, with what happened at the London convention, and wrote Maria Weston Chapman, "Garrison was quite right to sit in the gallery of the Convention. I conclude you think so. It has done much I am persuaded. You will live to see a great enlargement of our scope of usefulness . . . but it will be hard work to assert our liberty. I will, however, until I die – and so will you – and so make it easier for some few to follow." Then she assured her, "I feel in my soul the honor of the appointment of delegate. . . . I beg to assure my constituents that there is in me no lack of willingness to serve our cause in any capacity."[24]

Elizabeth Cady Stanton, who promised to send news of the convention to the Grimké sisters, wrote them, "We have been very kindly received here and treated with great attention. I have seen your dear friend Elizabeth Pease. . . . I have had much conversation with Lucretia Mott and I think her a peerless woman. . . . Lucretia Mott has just given me a long message for you, which condensed is that she thinks you both have been in a state of reticency long enough, and that it is not right for you to be still, longer; that you should either write for the public or speak out for *oppressed* woman. Sarah, in particular, she thinks should appear in public again as she has no duties to prevent her. She says a great struggle is at hand and that all the friends of freedom for woman must rally around the Garrison standard. . . . I am often asked if you have not changed your opinions on woman's rights and I have invariably taken the liberty to say no, though John Scoble has always contradicted me. Who is right?"[25]

After receiving this letter from Elizabeth Stanton and other letters about the convention, Sarah Grimké reversed somewhat her earlier opinion regarding the sending of women as delegates. "It seemed to be at first view," she wrote Elizabeth Pease, "that it was cause for regret that the woman question, as it is called, was introduced, as it has, I fear, carried with it some of those unchristian feelings which characterize the controversy in this country. . . . It may induce an examination of this subject which may be a blessing to the women of Britain. Certain it is that we are under bondage to man and that our rights and privileges as human beings are little understood and less appreciated by our own as well as the other sex. I apprehended injury to the cause of the slave, the cause which called the convention together, but it may be the means of extending the usefulness of women in that very cause. One thing is very clear, I think, viz. that the convention had no right to reject the female delegates . . . unless it could be proved they were not persons."[26]

Lucretia Mott wrote Maria Weston Chapman that she was convinced that the British public would not have been as outraged over the admission of women as delegates as members of the convention had been led to believe, for she herself had spoken in public in London several times, and in Birmingham her "appearance on the platform of a large meeting at the Town Hall was heartily cheered."[27] She also spoke at a Temperance meeting in Dublin where the cheers were long and loud. This, she thought, showed that the objections to the admission of women were all hollow, and she added, "A World Convention has yet to be held."

Abby Kelley, at home, hearing reports of the convention, was inclined to be critical of Lucretia Mott because she had not taken a stronger stand for women by personally presenting her credentials, and she wrote William Lloyd Garrison to ask whether Lucretia Mott had not "sacrificed Principle at the altar of peace."[28] Commenting on this in a letter to Mrs. Chapman, Lucretia Mott confessed, "I have sometimes shrunk from a defense of our rights when others have gone forward . . . and I am very willing to crown those with laurels I may not deserve. . . ." Even though she herself did not present her credentials to the convention, she rejoiced that Wendell Phillips and Ann "were not so easily put by, and that he came forth manfully to plead for the right." Then she continued, "I shall ever love Ann Phillips for her earnest to her husband to stand firm in the hour of trial, and him for so doing. Tell Abby Kelley if I am not much bold myself, I respect those most who are so."[29]

For this same reason, she loved and respected her new friend, Elizabeth Cady Stanton, with whom she had many stimulating discussions. When the convention adjourned, they left arm in arm, deep in conversation, resolving that as soon as they returned home they would hold a convention and form a society to advocate the rights of women. "The action of this convention," Elizabeth Cady Stanton later reported, "was the topic of discussion in public and private for a long time and stung many women into new thought and action, and gave rise to the movement for women's political equality both in England and the United States."[30]

CHAPTER XI

Women to the Rescue

While the women who attended the World's Antislavery Convention were traveling in England, Scotland, and Ireland, making warm friends among abolitionists, Maria Weston Chapman, Lydia Maria Child, and Abby Kelley picked up the pieces left after the split in the American Antislavery Society and began strengthening the movement, each in her own way. The Garrison faction had won control of the Society, keeping it a moral, evangelical movement rather than political, but it was practically without funds to carry on its work. The organ of the Society, *The Emancipator,* had previously been transferred to New-Organization supporters. Therefore it seemed imperative to establish a paper in New York to take its place, to serve as the organ of the American Antislavery Society, and to reach a wider field than the *Liberator*. In fact, the *Liberator* had not satisfied many New Yorkers.

To finance such a paper was a difficult problem which Mrs. Chapman and her husband attempted to solve. They could not, as in the past, count on the help of Francis Jackson and other wealthy, generous abolitionists who had preferred the *Liberator* above all other papers. The only solution was for Mr. Chapman to borrow the money and for Mrs. Chapman to repay it gradually by means of her antislavery fairs. This she did, raising substantial sums.

She next faced the critical financial situation of the Amercan Antislavery Society and persuaded the Boston Female Antislavery Society to turn over to the American Society the $500 raised by means of its last antislavery fair. In a sense she had become the general manager of the antislavery movement, carrying out Garrison's policies, helping edit the *Liberator* in his absence with the able assistance of Edmund Quincy, and keeping abolitionists busy and in line. As Edmund Quincy observed to Richard D. Webb, "Commands must be obeyed, and we that are tied . . . to Mrs. Chapman's apron strings, must do as she bids us."[1]

Turning her attention to the New York headquarters of the American Antislavery Society, she conferred with James C. Jackson, an antislavery lecturer from western New York, who then took over for the Society the old Antislavery Depository on Nassau Street for $500, supplied it with books and pamphlets, and engaged an elderly Quaker abolitionist, Isaac Hopper, as agent. In June, 1840, Jackson began the publication in New York of the *National Antislavery Standard*. The *Liberator* recommended it wholeheartedly to "the true and tried friends of the cause in every part of the country," and published a poem by Mrs. Chapman, "The Consecration of the *Standard*," in which she called upon friends of the slave to raise the "rescued banner, to meet the coming fight." That the American Society had been deprived of its popular organ, *The Emancipator*, by a last minute transfer to a New-Organization group continued to rankle, and like Wendell Phillips, many old-organization abolitionists regarded this transfer as an outrage.

Garrison's friend, Nathaniel P. Rogers, served as editor of the *Standard*, as soon as he returned from the World's Convention in London, but he made it plain that this would be only temporary, as he wished to return to New Hampshire and his *Herald of Freedom*. Isaac Hopper's son-in-law, James

S. Gibbons, was the *Standard*'s first printer, adding this to his regular employment as bank teller, and so devoted was he that, during a critical period, he mortgaged his furniture to buy paper and necessary supplies for the *Standard* to keep it in circulation. Because of his association with this antislavery paper, he and his family were read out of Friends Meeting.

* * *

Early in 1841, Rogers insisted on returning to New Hampshire, and a new editor had to be found. To Rogers and Garrison, David Lee Child, with his wife to assist him, seemed the best possible choice. Both were sincere, devoted abolitionists. Child had had editorial experience on the Whig paper, the *Massachusetts Journal,* and was a forceful writer, while his wife's literary reputation was established. In addition they understood, as few people did, the value of the American Antislavery Society — its weaknesses and its divisions. David Lee Child was far too busy with his beet-sugar experiments on his Northampton farm to serve as editor, but Mrs. Child was urged to undertake the task, at a salary of $1,000 a year. Although she had often longed for a more challenging field, she was reluctant to leave her home and her husband. The salary was an inducement, for they were deeply in debt. She left for New York with a feeling of great desolation, mitigated somewhat by the contract she signed en route with the Boston *Courier* for weekly letters from New York. The way was further smoothed for her when the American Antislavery Society arranged for her lodging and board with the Isaac Hopper family. Their friendliness and congeniality made the separation from her husband somewhat easier.

In the *Standard* of May 6, 1841, the outgoing editor, N. P. Rogers, congratulated his fellow abolitionists on securing the services of the distinguished, extraordinarily able Lydia Maria

Lydia Maria Child

Child, adding that he believed it to be woman's first assumption of the editorial chair in the great antislavery movement

Mrs. Child, in her first editorial, May 13, 1841, replied
"Such as I am, I am here — ready to work according to my
conscience and my ability; providing nothing but diligence
and fidelity; refusing the shadow of a fetter on my free expression of opinion, from any man, or body of men; and
equally careful to respect the freedom of others, whether as
individuals or societies." This was truly a declaration o
independence, to which she adhered.

She made it plain that the principles and object of the
Standard were identical with those of the American Anti
slavery Society, as expressed in its Constitution, adopted in
1833, and that she would conduct it "on the broad principle
of the universal fraternity of the human race, irrespective o
sect, party, sex, color, or country. She also spoke out agains
the New-Organization and the Massachusetts Abolition Society, whose formation she regarded as "inimical to the broad
and noble platform from which the Antislavery enterprise
first started."[2]

She then proceeded to make the *Standard* a well-edited
family paper with something for the young and the old, for
the politician, the moralist, the religious, the economist, the
literary, and the uneducated. It required continuous hard
work to plan each four-page edition, to write editorials and
whatever else was needed. She tried to give readers a cros
section of the world, with emphasis on the abolition of slav
ery. She had to be alert to all national and world news, and
keep watch of Congress. David helped with the news from
Washington and wrote editorials such as "The Florida War,"
"The Texas Question," and "The Tariff." She herself chose
to write about capital punishment, the treatment of the insane, and the new social communities, such as Brook Farm. In

an editorial, "The Society of Friends," she criticized the disowning by the Friends of James S. Gibbons and Isaac Hopper. In another, "Speaking in Church," she recalled the lectures of the Grimkés in New England, writing, "Evangelical sects have highly approved of female prayer meeting, and urged women to support missions and distribute tracts. They have turned the household utensil to a living, energetic being and they have no spell to turn it into a broom again."[3]

Regarding the "woman question," she wrote, "A budding conscience must struggle for human rights," but added that she herself preferred "quietly and unobtrusively to take her freedom without disputing about it."

She upheld the "Old Organization" and opposed a third political party. She said, however, "I am far from believing that all who are interested in this political movement are so from motives of personal ambition. . . . It is the misfortune of our country that nearly all its teachings tend to give undue importance to politics, so that men tend to trust in management rather than in principles and calculate contingencies instead of relying on truth." Then she added, "No reformer can make use of political machinery as a means to effect his ends without moral injury to himself and serious detriment to the cause he advocates."[4]

She reported the Welcome Home meeting in Boston, in July, 1841, for Wendell and Ann Phillips, who had remained in Europe two years because of Ann's health, and for the Chapmans, who had returned from their second visit in Haiti. She quoted Garrison's speech, in which he declared that slavery dreaded no spirit more than Maria Weston Chapman's, and that none could discover more quickly than Mrs. Chapman the signs of the enemy and none could more fearlessly combat them.

* * *

Notices of the *Standard* were gratifying. The *Liberator* had words of high praise for its editor. The Boston Female Antislavery Society, in its annual report, expressed satisfaction at the good it was accomplishing, beyond their most sanguine hopes. "Its circulation," the report stated, "already equals that of any other antislavery paper, while its excellence gives promise of a more extensive one than our former national organ, the *Emancipator*."[5]

Lucretia Mott praised the way Mrs. Child was "acquitting herself in the editorial chair" and "thereby advancing the cause of woman. It is one of the best things we have done to secure her services."[6]

"The ultra, the moderate," wrote Wendell Phillips, "the half-converted, the zealous, the indifferent, the active, all welcome the *Standard,* and it is fast changing them all into its own likeness of sound, liberal, generous, active, devoted men and women."[7]

When even the critical Mrs. Chapman praised Mrs. Child, she replied, "I rejoice that you approve of my editing, I thought I was too cautious to please you, but my caution plagues New-Organization more than anything."[8]

This praise was very sweet, and yet Mrs. Child felt hard-pressed and lonely, confessing to Deborah Weston, "My life here is monotonous and secluded in the extreme . . . The tedious paper brings the same duties every day . . . The task is a very irksome one to me."[9] Yet the work had its compensation when she saw what the *Standard* accomplished among lukewarm abolitionists in New York. She had found the movement there "pretty much defunct," and added "There is no Old Organization except the James S. Gibbons and Isaac Hopper's families. As for New-Organization, it scarcely seems to keep up the semblance of life. Yet, for all these discouraging appearances, I believe our antislavery work is being rapidly done in the community. I am inclined to think there is more real though less perceptible progress than ever."

Leaving New York for a short business trip to Northampton, in November, 1841, she found she was more attached to the *Standard* than she realized. "I find," she wrote, "that the paper itself has become to me as a favorite child from which I am not well content to be absent."[10]

The financial situation of the *Standard*, however, continually added to her worries. Starting out with a paper deeply in debt, she had followed her own way of doing business, choosing the safe ground. Her economical way was soon overruled by the appointment of a general agent to widen the paper's sphere of operation, but the debts piled up, and her own salary was always in arrears. For the first three months she was paid only twenty dollars. Troubled and hard-pressed by the continuous work, she wrote her good friend, Ellis Gray Loring, "I question the morality of letting one's soul thus be ground up for a cursed reform. It is a beggarly sort of business to work for benevolent societies."[11]

There was some relief and refreshment for her in her rambles about New York, with young John Hopper, looking for subjects for her *Letters from New York* for the Boston *Courier*. The *Letters* were also published in the *Standard* and aroused great interest. People were curious about this rapidly growing city, and eagerly read Lydia Maria Child's vivid descriptions of busy, crowded Broadway, the Bowery, the tenements, the prisons, the beggars, the street musicians, and the newsboys, as well as the celebrities, such as the Norwegian violinist, Ole Bull, to whose music she was devoted.

The overcrowded city, with its influx of immigrants and inadequate housing, was ripe for social reform, and Mrs. Child's *Letters*, throwing light on its deficiencies, encouraged interest in reform. New York newspapers reprinted some of her *Letters* and Horace Greeley, in his newly established *Tribune,* made use of them in furthering his own plans for the city's improvement.

Mrs. Child herself described the *Letters* as "an honest record of my own views and impressions on subjects which most interest me."[12] Reading them, James Russell Lowell observed, "A great heart is here that dares go into the prison, the slave hut, the alleys of sin, and to bring into each, or to find there, some line of the never completely out-trampled divine."[13] Margaret Fuller, commenting on the *Letters* in the *Dial,* rated them as "really a contribution to American literature."[14]

For some of the more militant Massachusetts abolitionists, among them Mrs. Chapman and Garrison, there was too much sweetness and light in the *Standard.* They wanted more controversial matters discussed, more agitation, more condemnation of backsliders. When there was talk, late in 1841, of merging the *Pennsylvania Freeman* with the *Standard,* Mrs. Child strongly opposed this, because the *Freeman* wanted three columns a week for subjects chosen by them and discussed as they saw fit. She intended to keep control of her paper. "The *Freeman,*" she wrote Mrs. Chapman, "is a betwixt and betweenity. It pats both organizations, and winks at the third party. If the *Standard* cannot be kept clear of this, I drop all interest in it forthwith."[15]

More differences developed after Garrison, at a large meeting in Faneuil Hall, in Boston, offered three incendiary resolutions, one prophecying the dissolution of the Union. This followed shortly after John Quincy Adams had presented to the House of Representatives a petition from citizens of Haverhill, Massachusetts, not abolitionists, asking that the Union be speedily dissolved. At once Southerners threatened Adams with a vote of censure, which was blocked, but dissolution of the Union was in the air, and newspapers made the most of it, spreading exaggerated reports and blaming abolitionists. The New York press accused the American Antislavery Society of calling for the dissolution of the Union. Feelings ran high in the city, so much so that Mrs. Child and James Gibbons, then chairman of the Executive Committee of the American Antislavery Society, feared riots and the destruction of the office of the *Standard*. Therefore they issued statements to the press and distributed a circular disassociating the *Standard* and the American Antislavery Society from the doctrine of dissolution of the Union, explaining that this was an object entirely foreign to the purpose of the Society — the abolition of slavery. This brought strong criticism from Mrs. Chapman and Garrison. In reply, Mrs. Child wrote to Mrs. Chapman, "I received your vehement letter of the 8th and smiled at the great fluster you were in, where it seemed there was not the slightest occasion. There is no separation whatever between us and the Massachusetts friends, and never has been. . . . You seem to consider that it was intended to rebuke Garrison, when its sole purpose was to correct a false impression in the minds of the citizens of New York. . . . I have no disposition 'to wash my hands of Garrison,' for the simple reason that I have the highest respect for his ability, the most perfect confidence in his integrity of purpose and a general unity with his principles. I am not willing to be mobbed for him, though I am for any *principles* that we hold in common."[16]

Differences of opinion over the circular persisted as the *Liberator* commented on it, expressing "unfeigned surprise, deep mortification, and extreme regret."[17] Mrs. Child, however, insisted that she still considered the circular "proper, justifiable, and absolutely necessary," and added, "Every day

that I live, I thank God more and more that he gives me th
power and will to be an individual."[18]

Letters on the subject continued, Mrs. Child writing, "A
agitator, I am not, and never will be. I find no fault wit
those who are, nay, acknowledge their great usefulness."
Then she warned that when the *Standard* became the orga
of agitation, it would have to find another editor. "For my
self," she added, "I would like to leave it tomorrow, an
accept the propositions of the booksellers here; but my at
tachment to antislavery principles would lead me to wish t
stand by it, so long as the Society were content to have it
good family antislavery newspaper, not intended to meet th
wants of ultra abolitionists, but to gain the ear of people a
large."[19]

This the *Standard* was accomplishing under her edito
ship. Its circulation had doubled that of the *Liberator*.

Garrison kept the subject of disunion alive in the *Liber
ator,* but it was discussed in the *Standard* very cautiousl
Mrs. Child objecting to the phrase, "Dissolution of th
Union," because it involved a threat. "I do not believe," sh
added, "that evil was ever overcome, or ever can be, by forc
or fear." In an editorial, "Prospects of the Antislavery Cause,
she wrote, "We love the old platform of the American Sc
ciety and we have stood by it through many shocks an
temptations, because it is so broad that all may stand upo
it with perfect unity of principle and purpose."[20]

Abolitionists, however, were showing less interest in th
old platform of the American Society than in political actio
While the *Standard* was converting more people to the anti
slavery cause, converts were joining the Liberty party and th
Whigs, as pressure for the annexation of Texas built up. A
the 1842 anniversary meeting of the American Antislaver
Society approached, Mrs. Child in the *Standard* urged mem

bers to take counsel and pray for wisdom. She wrote, "Our mission, as of old, is to purify a corrupted public sentiment and enlighten the misled opinions of the people; and never, never had we so much need of zeal and energy, well-tempered with a most loving discretion. . . . Come to the meeting."[21]

Garrison stayed away from the anniversary meeting, where disunion was nevertheless thoroughly discussed but not acted upon, although a majority, including Abby Kelley and Wendell Phillips, favored it. Discussion continued at the New England Antislavery Convention in Boston, and the *Liberator* began to carry this motto above its editorial column: "A repeal of the Union between Northern liberty and Southern slavery is essential to the abolition of the one and the preservation of the other."

* * *

Mrs. Child was feeling more and more out of tune with the militant abolitionists. Again she faced the *Standard*'s critical financial situation, which she felt was due primarily to the fact that so much money had been spent by the Massachusetts group to send out agents to get more subscribers. She wrote them, "Either the American Society is worth supporting, or it is not worth supporting. If not . . . you should have been more sparing of promises. I write in perfect freedom in this matter, because I have nothing at stake. Personally, it is of no consequence to me whether the *Standard* exists another week. . . . Whether things can be arranged as to still continue it as a useful instrumentality to the cause, it is for the Society to determine. But it is not fair for any Association to place a Committee in the situation in which we have been placed for the last year; and no person of principle, or the least pride of character, can consent to remain on it."[22]

When David came to New York reporting that his beet-sugar venture had gone into bankruptcy and he had been obliged to sell most of their belongings, she despaired. He went directly to Washington to size up the political situation for abolitionists and the *Standard*. The annexation of Texas[23] was being strongly urged by Southerners and was the policy of the Tyler administration.

While he was in Washington, Mrs. Chapman sent him more of their back salary and praised Maria's editorial on colonization, suggesting, however, that the New-Organization should be treated in the same way and indicating that he soon might be called upon to serve as editor.

Early in 1843, after the Massachusetts Antislavery Society had resolved that "the compact that exists between the North and the South is 'a covenant with death and an agreement with hell' . . . and should be immediately cancelled," and Garrison had been elected chairman of the executive committee of the American Society, Mrs. Child realized that there would be even more interference with her editorial policy and that she must resign. She published her *Farewell* editorial in the *Standard* of May 4, 1843. She had served as editor for two years. "I find much peace in reviewing what I have done," she wrote. "I have a peaceful consciousness of undeviating rectitude of intention. I have doubtless made mistakes, but none of them have originated in personal or partisan feeling." Then she listed the complaints against her: that she spoke of the Liberty party with courtesy, not accusing it of intrigue, duplicity, and meanness; that she did not attack New-Organization, the Church, or the clergy; that the large amount of literary material in the paper was to increase her personal popularity.

Again she emphasized the fact that the *Standard* was a paper for the people, not just for abolitionists, as were the

Liberator and the *Herald of Freedom;* that she had edited it so that many might be induced to subscribe; and that in the selection of material, her aim was "to elevate and enlarge the soul," and "to glorify humanity." She thanked those who urged her to remain as editor, but explained, "The freedom of my own spirit makes it absolutely necessary for me to retire. I am too distinctly and decidedly an individual to edit the organ of any Association, and so I bid you all an affectionate farewell."

She told her readers that she could not yet announce her successor, who would be chosen at the annual meeting of the American Society, but she begged abolitionists not to give up the *Standard* until it had been tried another year under new guidance. "There is a great amount of intellect, ability, and moral excellence in the antislavery cause," she added, "which could support the *Standard.*"

"The forcing of Mrs. Child from the editorship was the most fatal calamity that ever befell the antislavery cause," wrote James Gibbons to Abby Kelley. "I say this as the result of deliberate reflection, enlightened by observation and by a better knowledge of the circumstances. . . . Those who grow dissatisfied with Mrs. Child in one year, will grow discontented . . . in six months with any other Editor."[24]

David Lee Child was asked to succeed Maria, and he was listed as editor on August 3, 1843. Maria remained in New York, helping him in the selection of articles, especially when he was in Washington to report on the political situation, but she had nothing to do with editorial policy. In accepting the appointment, Child wrote the executive committee that on some occasions he would have admitted more controversial material than Maria had, but warned "I must be left in full freedom to speak as conscience dictates."[25] Expressing his opinion regarding political parties, he acknowledged both the Whigs and Democrats were bad, but added, "What either do to help the cause in States or Congress should be acknowledged and welcomed," and in his opinion the Whigs had made nearer approaches to abolitionist standards. This, and his letters from Washington, led Garrison to believe that Child was a Whig at heart. Mrs. Chapman also recognized that he was a Whig in principle, and called him her "favorite Whig." To Sydney Gay, she observed, "I like Mr. Child's paper very much."[26]

To other friends she wrote, "Disagreeing with Mr. Child as I do, I yet know him for as true a soul as breathes to his convictions of duty. I know many a 'come-outer' who is less true. I say it though I am a believer in the duty and the policy of sundering all connections with bodies whose course is mainly wrong. . . . Mr. Child has made it clear he would not vote for pro-slavery candidates. A further advance . . . out of the parties is in my view desirable, but I have no right to ask for more."[27]

Soon, however, she, as well as Garrison, became more and more critical of Child, especially when he stated in an editorial that he doubted he would ever "come out" of the political party he thought least objectionable. "If at any time," he added, "that party nominates an abolitionist, I will vote for him."[28] He also urged abolitionists to stick to the broad principles of their organization and not to require qualifications for fraternizing. Such tolerance disturbed Garrison, Mrs. Chapman, and Abby Kelley, the latter having become a strict "come-outer," leaving her church and political party because both condoned slavery. Child saw the handwriting on the wall and came to the conclusion that he would resign unless he received a vote of confidence from the American Antislavery Society at its annual convention in May, 1844. This convention decided the matter for all concerned with its endorsement of Garrison's resolution that "No Union with Slaveholders" be the watchword and battle cry of the organization and that no member should vote for or support a political party dedicated to the preservation of the Union. There was strong but futile opposition to this resolution by David Lee Child, Ellis Gray Loring, James S. Gibbons, and others. Child immediately resigned as editor of the *Standard* and was replaced by an editorial board of three, consisting of Sydney Howard Gay of Boston, a young ardent abolitionist, Edmund Quincy, and Maria Weston Chapman.

CHAPTER XII

Garrison's Lieutenant

Maria Weston Chapman was now not only one of the editors of the *National Antislavery Standard* which she had initiated and financed in June, 1840, but she was continuing to finance it by means of Antislavery Fairs and Bazaars. She had first introduced these fairs in 1834 to raise money for the cause and they had been carried on successfully through the years with the help of her sisters, Anne, Caroline, and Deborah Weston. The first fairs were held in Faneuil Hall. Decorated with evergreens and well-stocked with attractive Christmas gifts, Faneuil Hall was transformed into an attractive meeting place, and the bazaars became popular social events. Articles contributed by antislavery friends in Great Britain and France were greatly in demand. As many who came to buy or to meet their friends had little or no interest in the cause, it was important to reach them with antislavery propaganda. This was possible through evening meetings at which Wendell Phillips, Samuel J. May, Abby Kelley, and others spoke, and through the sale of *The Liberty Bell,* an attractive gift book with a golden bell on its cover. *The Liberty Bell,* edited by Mrs. Chapman, was in demand year after year, not only in Boston, but in other cities as well. It was a compilation of poems and articles by "Friends of Freedom," among whom were many well-known writers, such as Harriet Martineau, Elizabeth Barrett Browning, Fredrika Bremer, Henry Wadsworth Longfellow, Eliza Lee Follen, Theodore Parker, and James Russell Lowell. Whittier, known throughout the world as an antislavery poet, never contributed because he was repelled by Mrs. Chapman's intolerance of those who disagreed with her kind of abolition. She had called him "either a knave or a fool" for advocating political action, and the antagonism between them increased. Some years later he called her Garrison's "evil genius," acting "through him her evil plans."[1]

James Russell Lowell saw her in a very different light. In his poem, "Letter from Boston," describing Boston's Antislavery Bazaar of 1846, he wrote:

> The great attraction now of all
> Is the "Bazaar" at Faneuil Hall,
> Where swarm the antislavery folks. . . .
> There's Garrison, his features very
> Benign for an incendiary. . . .
> There was Maria Chapman too
> With her swift eyes of clear steel blue,
> The coiled-up mainspring of the Fair
> Originating everywhere
> The expansive force, without a sound,
> That whirls a hundred wheels around . . .
> A noble woman, brave and apt . . .
> Who might with those fair tresses shorn,
> The Maid of Orleans' casque have worn;
> Herself the Joan of our Arc,
> For every shaft a shining mark.[2]

He continued with a description of others, including Abby Kelley:

> A Judith there, turned Quakeress,
> Sits Abby in her modest dress
> Serving a table quietly,
> As if that mild and downcast eye

Flashed never with its scorn intense. . . .
No nobler gift of heart and brain,
No life more white from spot or stain,
Was e'er on Freedom's altar laid
Than hers – the simple Quaker Maid.

So successful were the fairs and bazaars in Boston that they encouraged antislavery groups in other cities and towns to undertake them. Boston's fair in 1840 raised $1,100, and in succeeding years the amounts greatly increased. At first, the Quakers questioned the moral influence of selling trinkets, but Lucretia Mott, realizing the need of raising money for the cause and observing the unselfish service of those working for the fairs, persuaded Quaker abolitionists in Philadelphia to hold fairs, but to call them sales.[3] Between 1840 and 1861, these sales in Philadelphia raised about $32,000, and at the same time aroused interest in abolition.

In this way, women played an important role in financing the antislavery movement.

* * *

While Mrs. Chapman was busy superintending antislavery bazaars, helping to edit the *Liberator,* editing *The Liberty Bell,* and watching over the *Standard,* her personal life was saddened by the illness of her husband. For a time, after their return from Haiti in 1841, he seemed to improve, then grew steadily worse, so that in 1842 she wrote her sister Deborah that she left him only to go to market, adding "I have only to endeavor not to despair."[4] They were then living at 39 Summer Street with their three children. Their marriage of twelve years had been a very happy one, free from financial worries and devoted to the antislavery cause. "He adored her," observed Edmund Quincy, "and she was the tenderest and most devoted of wives to him. Her devotion to him dur-

Maria W. Chapman

ing his last illness was truly beautiful." He died in October, 1842. The Boston newspapers gave high praise to Henry Grafton Chapman, extolling his character, his kindness, and his devotion to duty. *The National Antislavery Standard* reported that when he became an abolitionist he had given up his trade in cotton. The *Liberator* commented on the loss of a "faithful, early and widely known friend and benefactor."

With her characteristic courage and stoicism, Mrs. Chapman turned from grief to even more intensive antislavery work. She told Edmund Quincy that she had no feeling of separation, and he soon saw the household fall back "into its usual liveliness." To Richard D. Webb, Quaker abolitionist in Dublin, Quincy wrote, "I doubt whether you will easily find the equal of the family of 39 Summer Street, anywhere you may look for it. Mrs. Chapman and her sisters unite the highest education and the first of abilities with the purest philanthropy. They have warm hearts, clear heads, wit, human spirit, and . . . beauty. Mrs. Chapman, I consider as standing at the head of the human race, men or women. She is the most perfect creature morally, intellectually, physically that I ever knew."[6]

Mrs. Chapman was of great assistance to Quincy in editing the *Liberator* while Garrison was lecturing in western New York trying to build up the American Antislavery Society and *Liberator* subscriptions. In the summer of 1843, she reported in its columns the Bunker Hill celebration at which Daniel Webster was the principal speaker. Webster was highly praised by the Boston press, but Mrs. Chapman dissented, calling Webster's speech "an audacious exhibition of national hypocrisy, equalled by nothing in history . . . dissimulation, cant, bombast, and impudence."[7]

She also commented on the national scene in *Ten Years of Experience,* published as pamphlet and small book, late in 1842. This was a sequel to *Right and Wrong in Boston,* 1836 and 1839, which reported the activities of the Boston Female Antislavery Society. As many who would read *Ten Years of Experience* knew little of the beginnings of the antislavery activities of Boston women, she filled in the background for them, explaining that a few women, convinced that slavery was a sin against God and man, organized the Boston Female Antislavery Society in 1832 to combat this sin. They found the churches almost solidly against them, and, because of this opposition, many women held themselves aloof, preferring to remain neutral on the subject. In Mrs. Chapman's opinion, this showed an incredible ignorance of the practical requirements of the Christian religion, and she called upon women to awake, to become informed, to read Dr. Channing's pamphlet, *Emancipation,* and Mrs. Child's *Appeal,* and to talk about the subject in their homes and to their friends. She admitted that in so doing women would be criticized for straying beyond their sphere, but she asked, "Do I hear such language in a civilized age, and in a land of Christianity? What . . . is woman's work? It is to be a minister of Christian love. . . . It is to keep alive in society some feeling of human brotherhood."

Then she called attention to the fact that in national politics the tide seemed to be running higher against the antislavery cause than in the past, or Henry Clay would not have been nominated for the Presidency. She reminded them that Senator Clay had appealed to women of the North to keep silent on the subject of slavery and had himself said he never would listen to a proposition for emancipation. She herself had then written Clay a strong letter, which she repeated in full in *Ten Years of Experience,* and she urged women to be awake to Clay's influence in politics and to discuss this with their husbands and sons, so that they would not vote for proslavery candidates. "We are bound to this cause," she told them, "as to our religion. . . ."

The Latimer case next absorbed her attention. George Latimer, a mulatto, had escaped with his wife and child from Norfolk to Boston, where he lived for several years. Suddenly, he was arrested on the street without a warrant and jailed, on the order of his alleged owner in Virginia. This was the first case in Massachusetts under the Fugitive Slave Law since the U.S. Supreme Court decision in the Prigg case, which held that under the Constitution Congress had exclusive jurisdiction in the matter of fugitive slaves. Boston abolitionists at once turned to Samuel E. Sewall to defend Latimer. Judge Shaw, in view of the Prigg decision, denied Latimer a trial by jury and turned him over to a Federal Court. From then on, free Negroes in Boston lived in terror, fearing that they too might be seized and sent back into slavery.

Indignant abolitionists called a public meeting in Faneuil Hall to protest and rouse public opinion. They posted placards throughout the city and circulated handbills reading, "Bostonians! Friends of the rights of man! Descendants of the Pilgrim Fathers! Shall Boston, shall Massachusetts be made the hunting ground of Human Kidnappers, Shall our soil be polluted by the foot prints of Human Slavery?"[8]

Mrs. Chapman, involved in this agitation, reported it in the *Liberator,* and attended the Faneuil Hall meeting where a turbulent, unfriendly crowd tried to hiss down abolitionists, until once again Wendell Phillips came to the rescue. Mrs. Chapman heard him lash out against the Constitution for upholding slavery, and approved when he shouted, "Many of you, I doubt not, regret to have this man given up – but you cannot help it. There stands the bloody clause in the Constitution. . . . I say my curse be on the Constitution of these United States."[9]

Mrs. Chapman continued to agitate through the *Liberator* for the freedom of Latimer, who was saved when Henry Bowditch raised the money for his purchase. The Latimer case roused public opinion far beyond Massachusetts and in Massachusetts led to the adoption of a Personal Liberty Act in 1843. It also caused many abolitionists to rally behind Garrison's battle cry "No Union with Slaveholders." Mrs. Chapman expressed her approval of "No Union with Slaveholders" in an editorial in the *Standard,* July 4, 1844, signed with the initial, "C."

* * *

Sydney Howard Gay, who followed David Lee Child as editor of the *National Antislavery Standard,* with Mrs. Chapman and Edmund Quincy in Boston to advise and contribute articles, was a young man of about thirty, from one of the best families in New England, who so far had not been very active in the antislavery movement, but had had some editorial experience and wrote well. He had this important qualification. He was, as Edmund Quincy expressed it, "in perfect unity with the Boston clique."[10] He faced, as had previous editors, the precarious financial situation of the paper, and Mrs. Chapman did her best to encourage him, writing, "We are going to do all in our power to sustain the *Standard,* by putting the whole strength of the American Society on for six months. . . ."[11]

"I am sure," she continued, "there must be 5,000 in the U.S. who can be made to subscribe. I have not laboured for so many years to keep up the *Standard* without being fully aware of its importance . . . as the outward and visible sign of the movement. . . . The existence of the *Standard* is a proof to the eyes of the Nation that the highest morality does yet *live* in this Nation. . . . The *Liberator* is indispensable, but so is the *Standard,* especially now that the enemy actually dreads the *Standard* most. It does not take literary genius or skillful writers, or very knowing folks. . . . It needs only the steady eye, and the steadfast heart. . . ." She ended this letter, "Sandalled for immortality."

She corresponded with Gay frequently, not only sending him editorials and advice, but comments on fellow abolitionists. She was particularly concerned about those abolitionists who seemed to be straying from the fold. It was hard for her to understand how Mrs. Child who had "stood so firm and true for the Cause for so many years" could now be satisfied to turn into "a booksellers' hack."[12] When she thought of what Mrs. Child could be, she regretted seeing her follow in the path of Sarah J. Hale, Zeba Smith, and others writing for *Godey's Lady's Book.* "I should as soon have doubted a Quincy, Garrison, or Phillips, or any of the 'veterans,' " she wrote. She always hoped Mrs. Child would return again to the truly important work of the cause.

In addition to raising money for the *Standard,* Mrs. Chapman continued to contribute editorials and to translate French articles. Among her editorials was one on which she felt strongly, "Unitarianism and Slavery," for she herself was a Unitarian. She appreciated those Unitarians, like Samuel J. May, who stood wholeheartedly for the abolition of slavery, but criticized those, like William Ellery Channing, who, she felt, had been too tolerant of the sin of slavery. Yet, in spite of her frequent impatience and disappointment with Dr. Channing, she published in *The Liberty Bell* of 1843 an "Elegy on the Death of Dr. Channing" by James Russell Lowell.

Although she considered literary criticism not the function of the *Standard,* she nevertheless reviewed Margaret Fuller's *Woman in the 19th Century,* because "it merited attention." She asked Gay to proofread her review carefully, so that Miss Fuller might read it without the ludicrous mistakes which sometimes occur in the hurried composition of the paper. "The critics," she wrote Gay, "may say the book wants plan . . . is a mere cut from old histories . . . but such a cut could only be made by a rare heart. She ought to be at work with us. If there is anything in her (as there does seem to be by Jove!), she will be with us."[12] Although Margaret Fuller never affiliated with an antislavery organization, she did write an article for *The Liberty Bell* of 1846, showing her awareness of the evil of slavery and the need to ring out the Liberty Bell.

In her review of *Woman in the 19th Century,* Mrs. Chapman rated the book highly because it induced "a general feeling that a woman's duties like a man's, are to her country, her race, and her religion, as well as to her personal ties, and to her home." In Mrs. Chapman's opinion, "the last could never be well done where the first are left undone . . . This noble testimony . . . should be borne onward into general view for the sake of the antislavery cause and for the sake of all good and all truth."[13]

This gave Mrs. Chapman the opportunity to remind her readers how abolitionists had been maligned, assailed, betrayed, and deserted because they had stirred up the woman question. "Freedom begets freedom," she added, explaining that abolitionists were not to blame that the woman question was stirred in every heart that embraced the cause.

* * *

When the *Pennsylvania Freeman,* which had been discontinued for several years, resumed publication, Mrs. Chapman subscribed and wrote its editor, Miller McKim, that she hoped there would be nothing about the third party in it.

"Pennsylvania and Massachusetts," she added, "both owe i
to righteous principles to discriminate between pro-slaver
cheats and antislavery honest men. This is not a matter c
doctrine, but of practice of morality."[14]

She had very definite views on the third party, the Libert
party, which was attracting many old-time abolitionists. "Th
practical question is how is the Party led," she wrote Ga
"and how is the influence that honest men give it used again
our exertions. It was primed for that, it is used for that, i
accomplishes that. . . . I must treat the Liberty Party as I d
the Church; allow the honesty of its honest members, but i
treating it as a unit, deal with it as I do the Church, i.e., pu
it out of my way. . . . The old pro-slavery doctors of divinit
. . . are all voting the Liberty ticket, reading notices of Lil
erty consensus, and shutting Antislavery lecturers out c
their parishes. Let our watch word be 'down with the Libert
Party as at present constituted.' "[15]

She continued to be proud of the *Standard*, writing Ga
in 1846, "As the organ of the American Society, it is the onl
representative on Earth, the only one, of tolerance – unio
to do justice – respect for right. The world goes straight be
cause of it, as the great ship sails by the beacon light . . . I
is small and rough and scantily fed, but while it blazes, all
safe."[16] She felt it worthy of contributions from Harrie
Martineau, with whom she continued her friendship by corre
spondence. Harriet Martineau began writing for the *Standar*
in 1846 because she saw it as an opportunity to teach Ame
icans to distrust acting on impulse and to base their actior
on principle. She was appalled by the ignorance of Americar
in general, outside of abolitionist ranks. Her contributior
gave the paper a certain prestige but they also antagonize
many readers who resented her criticism, her dogmatism, he
patronizing air – as well as some of her views. In fact, sh

aroused such a storm of protest that after a few years she discontinued her articles.

Through all the ups and downs, Mrs. Chapman continued to give her best to the *Standard,* writing Abby Kelley, "I am hard at work. What I do makes no show, and I only tell you of it that you may not feel deserted and alone. But I am always encouraged to see how a few months after, comes up a harvest. . . . I average five columns a week for the *Standard;* so the rest of the days [go] to writing to stir up people's minds about the Fair. . . ."[17]

She was untiring in her efforts to make *The Liberty Bell* a high-grade annual of literary value as well as of propaganda value to the antislavery movement. According to Samuel J. May she accomplished this, as for twelve years, it rang out he clearest notes of personal, civil, and spiritual liberty. She was continually pleading with her antislavery friends to write a page for *The Liberty Bell,* among them Lucretia Mott, who eplied, "As to my poor self as an author, thou must by this ime be sensible that I could produce nothing worthy of *The Liberty Bell.*"[18] Eventually, however, she did contribute short article, "Diversities," in 1844, in which she made clear ier opposition to attempts to end slavery by the purchase of laves. To her this was a false gesture on the part of abolitionsts, benefiting slaveholders and enabling them to buy more laves. In 1845, she contributed, "What is Antislavery Work?" which continued her opposition to the purchase of slaves. ven though this seemed to be a charitable humane underaking, aiding abolition, she called it indirect support of the ystem of slavery.

Mrs. Chapman urged Abby Kelley to write a page for the 845 *Liberty Bell,* adding, "It will be a splendid *Bell,* but on't suit me without your note in it."[19] Abby did write, What is Real Antislavery Work?" in which she declared,

"We shall scorn and shudder at the idea of voting under
Constitution which pledges our support to a Governmen
founded on the plundered rights of millions, — which, instea
of weakening the Slave-power joins that power with its ow
strength." This "splendid *Bell,*" with an engraving of Wen
dell Phillips as its frontispiece, included his attack on th
Constitution, calling it a proslavery document, "a covenan
with death and an agreement with hell," which ought im
mediately to be annulled. "The experience of half a centur
. . ." he added, "is enough to convince us that Free an
Slave States cannot unite, on any conditions . . . withou
becoming partners in the guilt and responsible for the sin o
Slavery. We dare not prolong the experiment. There is n
course left for honest men, but to join the battle-cry o
the American Antislavery Society, 'No Union with Slav
holders.' "[20]

This was the policy adopted by the 1844 Convention o
the American Antislavery Society and it was outlined mor
fully in Garrison's *Address to the Friends of Freedom,* whic
was signed by Garrison, Phillips, and Maria Weston Cha
man, for the Executive Committee. There was no doubt tha
Abby Kelley and Mrs. Chapman were as militant on the di
union issue as Garrison.

* * *

Much had been happening on the national scene whic
was disturbing to abolitionists. The annexation of Texas i
1845 not only increased slave territory but strengthened th
slavery bloc in Congress. This was mitigated to a degree b
the acquisition of part of Oregon through a treaty with Grea
Britain. Then the Mexican War, in 1846, which ended wit
the conquest of California and New Mexico, reopened th
question of the extension of slavery and eventually led t

the organization of the Free Soil party from the ranks of the liberal Whigs and Democrats and the Liberty party.

During these years, more and more abolitionists turned to political action for the solution of the problem that was confronting the nation, and, to out-and-out Garrisonians like Mrs. Chapman, these abolitionists were not only disappointing, but were regarded as backsliders. One particular disappointment was Frederick Douglass, a fugitive slave whom Garrison had discovered at an antislavery meeting in Nantucket, where he spoke so well that he was at once employed as an agent of the Massachusetts Antislavery Society and became one of their most popular and effective speakers. In 1845 Douglass had published his autobiography. *A Narrative of My Life,* and it was reviewed by Mrs. Chapman in the *Standard.* His friends warned him it would be dangerous for him to remain in the United States, as his owner would probably claim him under the Fugitive Slave Law. They raised money to send him to England, where he was warmly received by abolitionists and liberals, who made it possible for him to purchase his freedom and to establish an antislavery paper when he returned to the United States. On his return he lectured with Garrison and Abby Kelley in New York and Ohio, and during this time he talked over political action with Garrison, and also told him of his desire to publish an antislavery paper. Garrison, of course, argued against political action, and discouraged the paper because he felt there were already more antislavery papers than could be adequately supported. He also pointed out to Douglass his real gift as a lecturer, which he felt would make more converts than one more antislavery paper. He did not criticize Douglass for buying his freedom, as did some abolitionists. In spite of Garrison's advice Douglass, wishing to prove that a Negro could manage and edit a paper, established the *North Star,* in 1847, in Rochester, New York, where it would not compete with the *Liberator*. Mrs. Chapman wished him and his *North Star* well in the *Liberator*, but added this warning, "may he never be seduced by party or sect to purchase popularity at the expense of fidelity, nor to increase the subscription to his paper by diminishing its antislavery power."[21] She warned further that he could not hope for support or respect for his paper from such opposites as the Liberty party and pure antislavery, which the Liberty party scoffed at as Garrisonianism. As she anticipated, Douglass soon supported political action.

In contrast to the disappointment caused by Douglass, was the interest in the antislavery cause expressed by the wealthy Boston merchant, Charles F. Hovey, who, disillusioned by political parties, called on Mrs. Chapman and talked with her, gave her fifty dollars for the fair, and, as Edmund Quincy expressed it, became "a thoroughgoing Garrisonian."[22] He soon was serving on the executive boards of the American and Massachusetts Antislavery Societies and gave them generous financial support. Theodore Parker was also showing his interest in the antislavery movement as well as other reforms and this was a satisfaction to Mrs. Chapman and other Unitarian abolitionists.

* * *

In spite of her involvement in all the activities of the antislavery movement, Mrs. Chapman now began to give some thought to the further education of her children. Remembering her years in London with her wealthy uncle, Joshua Bates, and all she had gained from them, she began to consider taking her children to Europe for several years. Hearing rumors of this, Edmund Quincy wrote Richard D. Webb that it would be "a terrible loss to us privately and to the cause generally." He questioned how the bazaars could be carried on without her and added, "It will be a serious loss in money to the Treasury."[23]

When her plans for Europe were definitely made, Garrison wrote her, "How to feel resigned to your separation from our little antislavery band, I hardly know," and added that he was confident that wherever she was, she would be "untiring to promote the sacred cause" in which she had so long and effectively labored. "We have few suggestive, creative, executive minds; and such is yours in an eminent degree . . . How joyfully I testify to the clearness of your vision in the darkest hours! . . . How immensely indebted I am to you for counsel, encouragement, commendation, and support."[24]

Then he asked, "How could the *Liberator* have been sustained . . . without your powerful cooperation? Where would have been the Boston Female Antislavery Society . . . ? How could the Massachusetts and American Antislavery Societies have put forth such exertions, independently of your own! The National Bazaar – what does it not owe to you! I know what others have done (I speak with special reference to the women in our cause) . . . but your position and influence have been preeminently valuable. . . . Accept my thanks, fervent but poor, for all you have done."

Mrs. Chapman, with her children and her sister Caroline, sailed for Europe on July 19, 1848, the very day the first Woman's Rights Convention, called by Lucretia Mott and Elizabeth Cady Stanton, was meeting in Seneca Falls, New York. This was a cause in which she believed and a convention to which she could have contributed much, but what she now regarded as her duty to her children took first place. She did not return to the United States until 1855.

"You can hardly imagine," Edmund Quincy wrote to Richard D. Webb, "what a difference the closing of Mrs.

Chapman's house makes to me . . . For I love not only the society of herself and family, but in a great degree her sisters too. But I have had the advantage of it for ten years, and that is a good slice of life."[25]

CHAPTER XIII

Abby Kelley

By this time Abby Kelley had found her place in the antislavery movement. After months of soul searching she had definitely decided in 1839 to choose the vocation of antislavery lecturer which Theodore Weld had advocated for her, after hearing her speak at the Antislavery Convention of American Women in Philadelphia in 1838.

Feeling ill-equipped for the task, she had been corresponding freely and frankly with Angelina Grimké Weld, who encouraged her, confessing her own and Sarah's feeling of inadequacy and their fears when they began lecturing. "As to the intellectual preparation for lecturing," Angelina wrote her, "I can only say that we both look back in amazement at the miserable pittance we began with."[1] Lecturing, she added, was like school teaching. In teaching you acquire knowledge as you teach, and so it was with lecturing. She assured Abby that it was no more necessary for her to pursue a course of study for lecturing against slavery than it would be to fit her for preaching the gospel. What was necessary was to have the heart right, and the point to settle was whether she was called to the work.

The question of the propriety of women on the lecture platform presented no problem to Abby, who had been brought up a Quaker and was accustomed to speak when the spirit moved. Yet she well knew what opposition the Grimkés' public speaking had aroused among the orthodox clergy and how they had opposed her own appointment to a committee of the American Antislavery Society. Henry C. Wright had encouraged her, as he had the Grimkés, writing, "I long to see more women in the field pleading the cause of Abolition and Non-Resistance. Who will go? I hope you will for one. I have no expectation that Sarah or Angelina will ever go forth again. They have retired, are, I fear, under an influence that has bound and fettered their souls. But the Lord will raise up others to go forth. . . . The Father of all Wisdom and Grace go with you. Seek direction of Him as a little child."[2]

This she did, and then one day when she was reading the Bible she came upon these words from I Corinthians, "Not many wise men . . . not many mighty, not many noble are called. But God hath chosen the weak things of the world to confound the things that are mighty . . . That no flesh should glory in his presence."

Turning to her mother, she said, "My way is clear, a new light has broken upon me. How true it is, as history records, that all great reforms have been carried forward by despised and weak means. The talent, the learning, the wealth, the Church and State are pledged to support slavery. I will go out among the honest-hearted, common people, into the highways and byways, and cry, 'Pity the poor slave.' "[3]

So she started out, going first to Connecticut, where she made the home of her oldest sister, Olive Newbury, in East Hampton, her headquarters. She made use of every possible opportunity to speak, and the few abolitionists in the vicinity opened the way for her. Occasionally she met kindness and interest, but when she attempted to hold a meeting in Hartford, all the clergy opposed it. Yet she was able to address a small group of women. In Torrington, she was invited to speak in the Methodist Church while the pastor was away. She stayed a week, holding meetings and arousing great inter-

Abby Kelley Foster

est. People of their own accord took up contributions for her. At this time she had only ten cents of her own left. She reorganized abolitionists into a state society, undoing the disruptive work of the New-Organization, which was stirring up the Connecticut clergy to oppose the activities of women.

In Salisbury, when she tried to speak in the Town Hall, the church bells began tolling, horns tooted, and tin pans were pounded so loudly that the meeting had to be dismissed. In another town she was given the village school house for her meeting. There was a candle on the desk, and several oil lamps in the schoolroom. The audience was respectful, but soon faces appeared at the windows and a rough man with a club strode in shouting, and smashed the lamps and candles with his club. Friends hurried her out, announcing there would be a meeting in the Methodist Church the next afternoon. "Less than twenty came," Abby reported, "and the same trouble-maker appeared with a gun and stalked up the aisle shouting, 'The first person that speaks for the nigger shall have the full charge of this gun!' " The meeting was adjourned to a friend's home where there was no disturbance, and the next day Abby went on her way "With faith for the future."[4]

A clergyman in one of the towns in which she next spoke preached a sermon against her, based on Revelation 2:20: "I have a few things against thee, because thou sufferest that woman Jezebel which calleth herself a prophetess, to teach and seduce my servants to commit fornication. . . ."[5] In another town, she had a hymn book hurled at her when she stood up to speak. Yet she continued her speaking, bravely enduring persecution, and at the same time making friends for the cause. She had no money for traveling expenses, but she found friends who would take her into their homes and drive her to the next town to speak. Best of all, she found she *could* speak, for her words came from the heart and people listened.

She wrote Garrison that in Connecticut she received aid not from the Friends and Unitarians, as she had expected, but from Baptists, Congregationalists, and Methodists, holding sixty-five meetings among them. At first she found there was strong prejudice against women's speaking in public. At a meeting of the Connecticut Antislavery Society, the Chairman asked her to be seated as he could not allow a woman to speak unless so ordered by a vote of the meeting. Abby, however, continued, and as the *Pennsylvania Freeman* reported, gave "one of the best speeches made during the day . . . brief, clear, and to the point."[6] In protest, the presiding officer walked out of the meeting, and several clergymen expressed themselves as against petticoat government. Soon the meeting was in an uproar, but Abby insisted that the Society's constitution gave women, as members, the right to speak and vote. "Like John Quincy Adams," she declared, "we refuse to submit to an unconstitutional rule."

She was doing so well in Connecticut that she was urged to come to western New York, and Mrs. Chapman begged her to speak at the annual meeting of the Boston Female Antislavery Society in 1840.

Coming back to Massachusetts after a year in Connecticut to address a public meeting of the Boston Female Antislavery Society, she wrote Garrison that "dear old Massachusetts . . . is still the State above all others."[7] To the antislavery women in Boston, she emphasized the fact that their country had declared as one of its first principles that no man should be deprived of his liberty without due process of law; then had forgotten these principles and "the world went on its round and no one seemed aware of the fact that one-sixth of th population were sitting under the shadow of slavery – groan ing in the fetters of the 'freest nation on earth'!"[8]

Reading a report of this "great speech," Esther Moore active in the Philadelphia Female Antislavery Society, wrot Garrison, "It stands unrivaled in my opinion. They have littl need to call upon men to address them while they can emplo so much talent and unborrowed eloquence. . . . I love Abb Kelley, tho' unseen. My heart responds to every word she ut ters. . . . I love too those noble women of Boston. . . . hope they may never let go their hold, but fight valiantly th holy cause for contending for equal rights, laying a goo foundation for coming generations to build upon. The eman cipation of woman from her degraded state is one of the im perative demands of the age."[9]

Abby also spoke to the Antislavery Convention in Spring field and in the opinion of Garrison "did wondrously." T Francis Jackson, he wrote, "Abby is taking to the field lik a lion."[10] The *National Antislavery Standard* reported, "Th presence and labors of Abby Kelley . . . were . . . of grea service to the Convention. The dignity of her appearance, he unassuming modesty, and the calmness and fidelity wit which she enunciated truth did much to disarm unrea sonable and vulgar opposition to the public efforts of he sex." Here she spoke of slavery as not only a Souther problem. "The mere existence of slavery in any sectio of our land," she declared, "is a danger to the liberties o the whole."[11]

Her reputation as an orator was fast being establishe not only in her own country, but by hearsay among abolition ists in Great Britain. Mary Howitt wrote her from Englan that she would like to meet "someone whom she so honore and loved,"[12] and from Ann Knight came these encouragin words, "Many times since thy noble exertions of lecturing to thy obdurate countrymen have I longed to send thee a greeting . . . to express my joy and sympathy with thy work of faith and labour of love." She praised as well Abby's insistence on woman's right to speak, adding "Do not, dear Abby, refrain from speaking when thou hast a remark to offer or a request to make in mixed gatherings."[13]

There was disapproval, however, from the Society of Friends at Uxbridge, Massachusetts, with which Abby was affiliated, and they disciplined her, not because of her speaking in public, but because she had joined an antislavery society and was working with abolitionists. When they disowned her, she withdrew from the Society of Friends, sending a letter explaining her position. Because this letter was not read at the meeting of discipline, she asked Garrison to publish it in the *Liberator*. She felt it her duty to "come out and be separate," because the Meeting had taken measures to prevent members "from uniting with persons of other denominations in the slaves' behalf"[14] and had closed the door of the meeting house to those who pleaded the cause of the slave.

* * *

Moving on to New York State, she made a great impression in Albany, where she stayed with cousins of James and Lucretia Mott, Abigail and Lydia Mott, whose home was a station on the Underground Railway. In Utica, where she spoke in the Court House on "The Church, the Main Bulwark of Slavery," the newspapers reported her eloquence, earnestness, sincerity, and zeal. In Seneca Falls, where both men and women jammed the hall to hear her, the press described her appearance as quite prepossessing, and added "Her eloquence, her good looks, her full mellow voice, and her evident sincerity make her hearers listen with interest."

Yet they questioned that she advanced the cause she tried to serve: "It is much to be regretted, that a lady with such advantages of person should not have found a more appropriate sphere of action, one better befitting her sex."[15]

Criticism of her continued because she, a woman, held public meetings, and most churches were closed to her. Yet she made many friends along the way, such as the McClintock family in Waterloo and Paulina Wright in Utica, who welcomed her to her home and kept her there for a few days of much needed rest. Traveling from place to place and speaking daily was taxing, but she saw much work to be done and the sad plight of the slave weighed on her mind. Often she traveled with Garrison, Frederick Douglass, and Charles Remond, holding meetings with them. She also organized women's sewing societies to make articles for the antislavery fairs held in Rochester and other western cities. In Rochester, she spoke in the Washington Street Church on the anniversary of emancipation in the West Indies, and the *Evening Post* reported that "she advocates the cause with great earnestness and ability."[16]

The Liberty party press in Utica, on the other hand, criticized her harshly in an editorial, so much so that the executive committee of the Central New York Antislavery Society adopted resolutions, expressing "most implicit confidence in the truthfulness, faithfulness, and devotion of Abby Kelley, who is acting as our agent with great self sacrifice . . . earnestly and constantly pleading the cause of the oppressed."[17]

The Liberty party was very active in western New York, and Abby sometimes felt that she converted many to the antislavery cause only to have them turn to political action and the Liberty party instead of to the American Antislavery Society. One of the founders and most active members of the Liberty party was Gerrit Smith of Peterboro, New York, wealthy landowner and philanthropist, a devoted abolitionist and friend of Garrison, who now saw political action as the only solution of the slavery question. An old friend of Abby Kelley, he urged her to come to his district to speak, to stay in his home, and offered to pay her $1,100 for two months of lecturing. Feeling that Gerrit Smith was trying to identify her with the Liberty party, she refused. He denied this and continued to urge her to come to Peterboro.[18]

During this time, she heard frequently from Mrs. Chapman, who wrote her frankly about differences among abolitionists and of her disappointment over the lukewarm editorial policy of the *National Antislavery Standard* which was prejudicing New England against it. In Abby Kelley, she found a radical come-outer and agitator, who would understand. She praised Abby's work, the subscriptions she was getting for the *Liberator* and the *Standard,* and the money she raised for the American Antislavery Society. She warned her however, that rumors, started by the Liberty party press, were reaching Massachusetts, claiming that she had gone over to the Liberty party and was denouncing Massachusetts abolitionists as autocrats, and she urged her to write for the *Standard* her stand on the Liberty party, contradicting these statements. "My darling child!" she added, "Come back to Massachusetts, this winter. It will be better for you and the cause in every way."[19] This letter reached Abby when she was too involved with lecture engagements to leave western New York.

* * *

By this time Abby had become well acquainted with two militant abolitionists, Stephen Foster and Parker Pillsbury, whom she met at antislavery conventions and on the lecture circuit. Both had prepared for the ministry, but gave it up to preach the gospel of freedom for the slave. They had started their antislavery lecturing in New Hampshire, their native state, where Stephen Foster made a point of carrying his message to the churches, which he regarded as the bulwark of slavery. Entering a church at the time of the service, he politely asked to speak, and continued pleading for the abolition of slavery until forcibly ejected. Often he was arrested for disorderly conduct. With the help of Parker Pillsbury, of Concord, he followed this practice throughout New Hampshire, stirring up a great deal of violence, so much that even Garrison and Wendell Phillips felt that their militancy was being carried too far. In 1843, Stephen Foster published a pamphlet, *The Brotherhood of Thieves; or a True Picture of the American Church and Clergy,* which was widely circulated and ran into twenty editions. To a come-outer such as Abby Kelley, this pamphlet and the militancy of these men had great appeal. She and Stephen Foster at once became firm friends and corresponded frequently. Soon this friendship ripened into love, and, as both were carrying out a strenuous lecture schedule, they became concerned about each other's health. Abby began checking on Stephen's diet and warning him to have more recreation. Expecting to meet him in New York in May, 1843, at the annual convention of the American Antislavery Society, she warned him not to let anyone know how they felt about each other, but to behave "as any good, orderly old bachelor should, never allowing a tell-tale to break out. . . . We can take a walk occasionally to talk over matters."[20]

She confided in him that she was troubled because Lydia Maria Child had left the *Standard* and David Lee Child would succeed her, adding "He is so strongly biased in favor of his party, that he cannot wish the paper impartial." In her opinion, Maria Weston Chapman was the person "to bear up our banner, boldly and gallantly. . . . I long to see our moral Napoleon at her true post. No person in the ranks is in my estimation so highy qualified to bring the antislavery society into one solid phalanx and direct their concentrated fire on the true point. . . . Everything almost to the American Society depends on the *Standard*'s editor. It has never yet been what I desire to see it. It may be, in Maria's hands."[21]

After the annual convention, when they returned to their lecturing in different parts of the country, they continued their frequent correspondence, and Stephen began to wonder whether Abby really wanted to share with him "the reproach and contempt which his course of life has incurred." Impatient with this, she replied, "As the thirsty traveler in the Sahara desert longs for the generous cool spring of the hill country, so does my heart pant to stand before the world the wife of Stephen S. Foster."[22]

After receiving this letter, he at last felt he was sure of her love, and began to question how much longer he ought to allow her to be strolling about the country. He wrote her "My conclusion is to limit the time."[23] Pleased with his ardor, she nevertheless made it clear that she could not be happy in domestic bliss, hearing "the wail of the Southern wife."[24]

From Seneca Falls, New York, she wrote Stephen that she had sold fifty copies of his *Brotherhood of Thieves,* and added, "Our outdoor meetings were as orderly as anyone could wish, and those in the house only a little disturbed one evening by one (rotten) egg. But I was severe, Stephen – most terribly severe, as severe as yourself, all but in manner." Later, however, she heard from her friend, Ansel Bascom, Seneca Falls' liberal Assemblyman, that people were expelled from their churches for listening to her make an exhibition of herself. "Your name," he added, "has become a terror to the Presbytery. . . . You are wanted here more than ever before. . . . I doubt if you can do as much good in any other part of America just now."[25]

She also described for Stephen her train journey to Rochester in a dark car, lighted only by a candle which Horace Greeley's brother had brought in. He protected her as well from pickpockets and porters who swarmed into the car at ten at night; and she reached her destination safely.[26]

* * *

Abby was very much disturbed at this time by David Lee Child's editorials in the *National Antislavery Standard* which seemed to her to encourage abolitionists not to sever all connections with political parties. Since Garrison did not criticize and even reprinted some of these editorials in the *Liberator,* she wrote him, "I am desirous of knowing where we stand. . . . Either the American Society and the Massachusetts Society must stand on the 'Come-outer' ground, or I must, as an individual, detach myself from them."[27] She explained that she had been getting subscribers for the antislavery papers on the ground that they upheld the "Come-outer" doctrine.

She also complained to Mrs. Chapman about Child's editorial policy. "My very soul," she wrote, "loathes his truckling course to the Whig party." This attitude, in her opinion, did as much harm as New-Organization. Then she added, "Had we only such a paper as you would have given us, we should be able to crush the nearest as well as the most distant foe."[28] As Stephen was leaving New York State for New England, she asked him to deliver this letter to Mrs. Chapman, as she wanted them to become better acquainted.

Later in November, she again wrote Garrison, asking, "Cannot something be done to bring Child up to the high-water mark? . . . I cannot think his sincerity in an error is any reason for his continuance in the Editorial Chair. He is doing the cause as much mischief as if he were not honest." Emphasizing the Liberty party influence in western New York, she pointed out that "there is an inclination among almost all abolitionists to go from us, for they have a strong belief that slavery can be abolished only by getting abolitionists in office."[29]

Early in 1844, she left New York State for Boston, because Mrs. Chapman had begged her to come to the Massachusetts Antislavery Convention, which would be extremely important, and where all things would be fully and freely talked out and plans for the year determined. "All will go right," added Mrs Chapman, "if friends take the pains the case merits. . . . Come — Come . . . You will defeat the enemy, strengthen and cheer the friends, and be better yourself perhaps — for seeing them as they will for seeing you. I want to talk with you about a vast number of things. We need to see each other."[30]

Abby too felt the need of getting a clear understanding of the abolitionists' position on various controversial matters and also to give her own views regarding the Liberty party. She wrote Stephen, "Union of effort is necessary and can be had. This belief sends me on this hateful journey. I dread traveling. I am sick of it." Hoping to see and talk with Garrison, she added, "He will stand erect though all else bend."[31]

She was not to be disappointed in Garrison who, at the time of the Convention, came out strongly for disunion and offered a resolution, "That the ballot box is not Antislavery, but a proslavery argument, so long as it is surrounded by the U.S. Constitution,[32] which forbids all approach to it except on condition that the voter shall surrender fugitive slaves, suppress Negro insurrections, and regard man-stealers as eligible for public office." Abby heartily agreed and was proud to hear Stephen protest against the Constitution at the Convention.

Encouraged by Garrison's stand for the dissolution of the Union, she returned to New York State, where she lectured three or four times a week. In the meantime, Stephen had a talk with Mrs. Chapman and still could not understand her. He thought her hypocritical. This disappointed Abby, who tried to explain to him that Mrs. Chapman was "full of the wisdom of this world" and incapable of understanding their kind of wisdom. She assured him that Mrs. Chapman did "value him as a man of integrity to the cause and of devotedness so deep that nothing can drive you to forsake it." She rejoiced that he had talked with Wendell Phillips and added, "I think him gifted with considerable spiritual discernment — having much grace in his heart — by nature a true nobleman. . . . There are so few who have sufficient spiritual discernment to appreciate a high moral (antislavery) movement."[33]

She felt it very important that those who love the cause get together in friendliness and talk things over. *The Antislavery Standard* still disappointed her, as did Child as editor, and she wrote Stephen, "Let us have an editor who, while he exposes the iniquitous new-organization schemes, will pour his fire heavily into the camp of the enemy . . . finding no time to make accusations as to which is the most and which is the least hostile, since all are hostile." She urged Stephen to express his opinions on this subject in the *Standard* and said she would call him lazy if he did not do so. In her opinion, it was most important that two people be placed in the *Standard* office in New York, who "will have editorial tact" and drive. She suggested Sydney Howard Gay, "a beautiful writer," and Maria Weston Chapman "to furnish rich editorials. Oh what a glorious *Standard* would we have then to bear up to the storm, for it would raise a storm. . . . The American Society has been at 'Child's play' long enough. It will, I hope, do man's work next year. . . . Let us all gather under the banner of dissolution and have for our watchword 'repeal.' "[34]

Then she broke the news to Stephen that she had decided to stay in the work two more years before marrying and begged him not to say a word against this, as it was final. She let him know, however, how much she yearned for their home. She urged him to remain in New England, and to carry himself like any good knight "who has labor and not love before him."[35] She suggested that they plan to meet in Utica occasionally, where, at the home of Paulina and Francis Wright, they would not need to be on guard about their love.

With a heavy heart, he replied, "It is yours to render me happy or miserable to an extent which you can hardly conceive." Then he expressed his concern over her continuous lecturing, which he felt was too great a strain, but she protested that her general health was "very fine, as fresh as a spring bird."[36]

* * *

Feeling that the Liberty party, rather than the American Antislavery Society, would profit from her further work in New York State, Abby started out for Ohio in June, 1844, by canal boat from Albany, finding canal boat travel "delightful," except for being alone and eating her "graham food in dumb silence." Her destination was New Lisbon, Ohio. Enthusiastic about this new country, she urged Stephen and Parker Pillsbury to come out, for the American Society had no good speakers there and the burden of the speaking fell on her. "They want you here," she wrote Stephen, "and have often asked if you could not be induced to come. The abolitionists here," she continued, "are planning to issue a paper, *The Antislavery Bugle,* whose motto will be No Union with Slaveholders. To get it underway Parker Pillsbury is needed and should be sent out by the American Society. I think," she added, "the American Society cannot employ funds to better account than to be raising a citadel to the west of the mountains this summer."[37]

The Antislavery Bugle was not established until 1845, and Abby, feeling she had done all she could in Ohio for the time being, returned to the East, stopping in Utica for a visit with Paulina Wright. Here she met Jane Hitchcock, who promised to travel with her. Jane was willing to do this because her brother was entering the Oneida Community and she did not want to go there with him. Stephen urged them both to come to New Hampshire to hold meetings, but Abby hesitated because she could ill afford the expense of travel and because it would be hard to interest people during the busy haying season. In August, however, she was there for a series of meetings to which she invited the popular Hutchinson Family Singers to sing their antislavery songs. "We are hoping to have Douglass . . . Remond . . . and occasionally Garrison and Phillips," she wrote them, "and if we can have the Hutchinsons along, we will not leave a stone unturned . . . they will move to music."[38]

The New Hampshire campaign proved to be very successful and also gave Abby a chance to see Stephen briefly. In November, she wrote him that "they had planted in the minds of the 'true,' the idea that 'the Liberty Party is the guardian of Slavery in the Church, and hence the first and greatest foe.' "[39] To Sydney Gay, she reported that New-Organization flourished in New Hampshire, but even so she was able to hold a meeting in the Congregational Church in Concord, where women were allowed to speak and where she pointed out that the Third Party, in voting under the U.S. Constitution, was as thoroughly sworn to the system of slavery as the Whigs and Democrats. She added that it was hypocritical to pretend to wish to destroy slavery "while cherishing and nourishing it in their churches . . . decking it out in the robes of Christianity."[40]

From New Hampshire, Abby, at the urging of Mrs. Chapman, went to Philadelphia for the Decade Meeting, which celebrated the anniversary of the Antislavery Convention of 1833. Prior to the meeting she raised $2,000 for the cause, but the meeting itself proved to be very disappointing, as it was dominated by a Liberty party group.

After leaving Philadelphia, she and Jane Hitchcock held meetings in eastern Pennsylvania. "The Pennsylvanians are hospitable and friendly beyond anything I ever before met with – real genuine, old-fashioned Quaker feeling," she wrote Stephen. "They carry us from place to place in their big wagons . . . and their hearthstones are so entirely like our own folks that I have not felt myself a stranger. . . . Enough has been collected so far to defray expenses and pay salaries. We are under the patronage of the American Society. It will be a gainer in numbers and influence." She praised the work of Jane Hitchcock, "I consider her one of our most efficient speakers . . . truly eloquent at times . . . extemporizing with great power."[41]

She urged Stephen to join them. She had found Pennsylvania a fertile field, and had been able to raise his and Douglass' expenses. "You are considered *the* man," she added, "and you must bring someone who will take." She told him she had already sold 500 copies of his *Brotherhood of Thieves* and that her meetings were packed. She assured him that they would not have to be together and so there would be no talk of their interest in each other.

His reply showed that he would prefer to go to New York and that he even contemplated buying a farm there. She protested, writing, "New York is one of the most barren fields in the country. . . . There is not material there for the non-voting position. They are eaten up with politics, and can see nothing but through the ballot box." Then she added, "Stephen dear, don't be offish . . . don't pout so, merely because I can't afford to marry till next winter. I want to have a long talk about many things."[42]

Stephen came to Pennsylvania, after all, and they had their long talk. She continued her work in Pennsylvania, reporting that her meetings were "large and deeply interesting" and the people were stirred. Soon she and Jane Hitchcock left for western New York en route to Ohio, where Abby thought a standard ought to be firmly planted.

CHAPTER XIV

Antislavery Evangelists

In Ohio, Abby Kelley and Jane Hitchcock held meetings almost daily, with long journeys in between – meetings so large that they had to be held in groves. It was a grueling schedule. "This great West," Abby wrote her sister, Olive Darling, "it is so tremendously big, and there is so much to be done in it, that I have scarcely had time to draw a long breath . . . This constant lecturing is enough to destroy the most vigorous constitution."[1] Encouraging letters of appreciation came from her colleagues in Boston, Eliza Follen writing, "The work you are doing seems to me a truly holy work."[2] Soon Stephen joined them, lifting the burden somewhat by sharing the lecturing.

Life in Ohio at this time was primitive, as it was everywhere on the western frontier. Houses were usually log cabins, often of only one room and a loft reached by a ladder. Transportation was difficult. Although they gladly faced frontier hardships for the sake of the slave, it often proved to be an endurance test. Abby found a great difference in the northern and southern sections of Ohio. Settlers from Pennsylvania, Virginia, Maryland, and Kentucky had come to southern Ohio, bringing "the badges of slavery with them," while in northern Ohio, settled by Yankees, there was some antislavery sentiment, introduced mostly by the Liberty party, and there was "enterprize, industry, and neat agricultural habits of New Englanders, with their intellectual shrewdness." Here she found people were more receptive to her message. They came in great numbers to her discussion lectures. She organized the Western Antislavery Society, affiliated with the American Society, and reported to her sister that hundreds had come out of the Liberty party and over to them. "So," she added, "we feel well paid for all our toil."[3]

The subject of her most popular lecture was "What is Real Antislavery Work?" This was published, in part, in the *Liberty Bell* in 1845. Real antislavery work, she said, "is to change the present proslavery heart of this nation." This could not be done, she pointed out, by merely expressing sympathy for the pitiful plight of the slave, or by distress over the separation of families, or by helping fugitives to Canada. It could be accomplished only by keeping the eye "steadily fixed on the polar star of principle." "Our work," she said, "is to inculcate these great truths – the right of man to Freedom, the atrocious sin of Slavery and the duty of ceasing to give it support, whether in Church or in State . . . We shall scorn and shudder at the idea of voting under a Constitution which pledges our support to a government founded on the plundered rights of millions – which instead of weakening the Slave-power joins that power with its own strength. And not only are we to cease from giving it support, we are to attack it wherever it may be found."[4]

She also encouraged the founding of the *Antislavery Bugle* in August, 1845, with Jane Hitchcock and Benjamin Jones as editors. This seemed more important than ever with the annexation of Texas well on its way. Within a few months, the *Bugle* had 700 subscribers.

Before the end of the year, Jane Hitchcock and Benjamin Jones were married, and Abby began to take time to make her own marriage plans. She wrote her sister in November that her intention and Stephen's had been to be married in the fall or early winter in western Pennsylvania in the home of friends, but there was so much work ahead that they had not yet set the day. They were married on December 21, 1845, in New Brighton, Pennsylvania, where they signed a handwritten marriage certificate which was witnessed by thirty-three of their friends, and which announced that Stephen S. Foster and Abby Kelley "had consummated a matrimonial connection in accordance with the divine law of marriage, by a public declaration of mutual affection and a covenant of perpetual love and fidelity," and they declared it their purpose to perform faithfully "all the relative duties of husband and wife."[5]

* * *

After their marriage, Abby and Stephen returned to Ohio to continue their antislavery work, making their headquarters in Salem, the home of Jane and Benjamin Jones. Abby was impressed with the importance of the Western field and in repeated letters called this to the attention of Mrs. Chapman. She praised the devoted self-sacrificing work of Jane Hitchcock Jones, who not only was helping her husband edit the *Antislavery Bugle* but was also lecturing at least twice a week. "In one town," she wrote, "there were eighty or ninety Liberty Party votes. This year only six, because of good work. . . . When the *Bugle* was started, I thought the West would not be able to sustain it. I am happily disappointed. The West will not only sustain it, but all its lecturers. . . . We think Ohio is to the West what Massachusetts is in point of influence to New England, and we trust our labors have a Massachusetts character, or at least have laid the foundation for such a character."[6]

Abby was not receiving a salary from the American Society for serving as their agent and lecturer, but raised enough money to pay her own meager expenses. "My life," she wrote Mrs. Chapman, "belongs to the cause. When I shall be compelled by circumstances to take a salary, I will frankly say so. . . ." Stephen, on the other hand, she added, needed a salary, as he felt it his duty to look out for a rainy day. She confessed that she had been so overworked in Ohio that she had decided to rest during the summer to regain her health and strength, but the Mexican War had interfered, making continuous work necessary. Even so she felt stronger, as did Stephen. "I am quite as vigorous, I think, as when I first entered the field, feeling equal to almost any task."[7]

They spent a few days in Oberlin, Ohio, where Stephen spoke at the College. His views were received with mixed feelings, except in the case of Lucy Stone, who was then a student there. Founded in 1833 for the purpose of educating ministers and missionaries for the Far West, Oberlin enrolled students without restrictions as to color or sex. Definitely antislavery in sentiment, it nevertheless followed the orthodox line, not the Garrisonian. Lucy, who had always admired Garrison, was surprised not to find a single *Liberator* there. Her interest in abolition had been growing ever since 1837 when she had heard Abby Kelley speak in her home town of Brookfield, Massachusetts. Lucy, then nineteen, was teaching to earn money for her tuition at Oberlin College, for while her father willingly financed her brother's education, he regarded woman's education as folly. This attitude and the degrading legal status of the farm women in the neighborhood roused rebellion in her and she resolved to learn Latin and Greek so that she could translate the Bible for herself to find out whether it actually taught men's superiority and their domination of women. She had enrolled at Oberlin in 1843, where she was regarded as one of the most radical students, advocating Garrisonian abolition and woman's rights.

Asked if she were not a New-Organization abolitionist, she replied, "I am not. . . . There seems to be no liberty about it. Its great object seems to be to crush Garrison and the women. While it pretends to endeavor to remove the yoke of bondage on account of color, it is actually summoning all its energies to rivet more firmly the chains that have always been upon the neck of woman. . . . I admire the calm and noble bearing of Abby Kelley . . . and cannot but wish there were more kindred spirits."[8]

Now in March, 1846, her path and Abby Kelley's crossed again. After hearing Stephen speak at the College and talking earnestly with Abby about abolition, woman's rights, and the Church, she wrote them, "I never felt sufficiently thankful that you came to Oberlin, for though you could not have the opportunity to present your views fully, yet you set a ball in motion, that is still rolling, and it will roll, for there are a few who are pushing it and who will continue to do so."[9] One of those pushing it was Lucy Stone, and she continued to do so through the years.

Abby had planted many seeds in Ohio which bore bountifully for the antislavery movement.

* * *

Abby and Stephen now returned to New England. While Abby visited Stephen's family in Canterbury, New Hampshire, and her sisters in Connecticut and Rhode Island, Stephen was lecturing in New Hampshire and in Worcester, and was looking for a home for them. A farmer at heart, he bought a farm of thirty-nine acres, in Tatneck, Massachusetts, about three miles from Worcester and not far from Abby's old home in Millbury. This proved to be a great disappointment to Abby, who heard the news when in Rhode Island. She wrote Stephen that "her air castles had all been demolished in one blow," for she had dreamed of a cottage at the end of a grassy lawn. Not only was she dissatisfied with the Tatneck neighborhood, but with the size of the farm, the poor soil, and the dilapidated buildings. She hoped he would not leave the antislavery cause to devote all his time to the farm. She suggested that he wait for her arrival to clean the house, for her capable sister-in-law would come with her and stay several weeks to help. Hearing he was tearing down some of the farm house, she asked, "Would it not be better to build a new house than to add to the old? I would rather have a very small house than part of a large one."[10] Then she reminded him that he had left her no money, making it necessary for her to borrow, and asked him to send her fifteen dollars.

After getting the farm somewhat habitable for Abby, Stephen returned to antislavery work in Ohio. Abby was unable to join him there as the birth of their baby was imminent. When their daughter Alla was born, Stephen was still in Ohio pleading the cause of the slave. Members of Abby's family came to the farm to be with her, and in August she wrote Stephen that the baby was doing fine and growing fast. She showed more concern about his health than about the farm problems which she had to face, and warned him not to overwork, adding, "How my heart yearns to help you. How pleasant it would be to see our old friends in Ohio. But my pleasure with our little one at home is much greater, only that her father is not here."[11] Expecting he would soon be in Oberlin, she sent her "overflowing love" to Lucy Stone, and reported that she had heard Lucretia Mott speak in Worcester, and had been told that Lucretia and James would soon be in Ohio. She urged Stephen to make use of Lucretia in his meetings in Ohio. Soon she heard from him that he,

Lucretia Mott, Garrison, and Frederick Douglass were speaking to audiences of 5,000, and realized gratefully that she had prepared the ground and planted the seed for these meetings. There was good news too of Lucy Stone, who was preparing to lecture for the cause and for the rights of women.

Stephen soon left Ohio for a glimpse of Abby and Alla, but returned shortly, and in September Abby was reporting to him that his father and mother were with her. She was fond of them and wrote Stephen, "I have often prayed that you and I may live as true a life and thereby secure as great happiness in old age . . ."[11]

When Stephen wrote her of his plan to work in New York State, hoping she would join him, her heart leaped up at the prospect, yet she dreaded the thought of leaving Alla.

Occasionally she thought of staying at home during the next winter to "lay in a stock of book knowledge" to fit her for greater usefulness. She made it clear, however, that she did not like the present arrangements of having two families living in the farm house. "I never want to keep house again," she added, "until I can live less mixed up . . . I have an increasing dislike of this mixture . . . We should all be better satisfied having our birds' nests separate."[12]

Stephen's next letter was written "in a dull blue mood." She too had been gloomy, longing to be with him. "The march of reform is so slow," she wrote him, "and there is so much folly and stupidity everywhere around us that we sicken and grow weary. . . . Then we ask ourselves what use are our efforts or the blood of martyrs?" She insisted, nevertheless, that their efforts were of use. "The world," she continued, "has made a wonderful advance through the ages and the scale of humanity is rising . . . If it were not so, I should still deem it our duty, not only to live well, but to live truly, and we could not do so, if, having the ability to use our voices for the utterance of truth, we should keep silence. The preaching of truth does do good."[13]

* * *

Because preaching the truth was so important to Abby, she now arranged to leave Alla occasionally to speak where she was most needed. Alla stayed happily with Stephen's sister, Caroline, in Canterbury, New Hampshire, on those occasions. In March, 1848, Abby was in Philadelphia with Sarah Pugh and Lucretia Mott, while Stephen was in Boston. In Philadelphia, she heard Lucy Stone speak, and on her way home, Lucy stopped over to visit Abby. They talked over Lucy's future and the plans she had had of lecturing for the Western Antislavery Society which did not materialize. When Lucy confessed that she did not know how to begin, Abby immediately wrote Mrs. Chapman recommending Lucy. At once she was employed as agent by the Massachusetts Antislavery Society, with expenses paid, and proved to be a great success as a lecturer. Her clear, sweet voice and her natural eloquence and fervent conviction swayed her audiences. Confident that antislavery lecturing was her duty, she continued, in spite of the disapproval of her mother who expected that she would disgrace the family and in spite of the pleas of her sister that she teach instead. "If in this hour of the world's need," she told them, "I should refuse to lend my aid, however small it may be, I should have no right to think myself a Christian, and I should forever despise Lucy Stone."[14]

Antislavery lecturing took courage and determination, for audiences were generally unfriendly to start with, and sometimes definitely hostile. Arriving in a town, Lucy often found that her lectures had not been announced, and when she herself posted notices of her meetings, boys tore them down. A

Universalist minister in one Massachusetts town patronizingly announced her lecture to his congregation in these words, "This evening at the Town Hall, a hen will attempt to crow." In another town, a hose was put through a window while she was speaking and icy water turned on her, but putting a shawl around her shoulders, she continued to speak. Occasionally, in Massachusetts, she lectured with Stephen Foster, who almost always stirred up violence. At one outdoor meeting the mob became so threatening, that Lucy, concerned for Stephen's safety, urged him to run. As he demurred, asking who would take care of her, a large man with a club strode up on the platform, and Lucy, looking up at him, replied calmly "This gentleman will take care of me."[15] He did, while the mob attacked Stephen, ripping his coat to pieces. Meanwhile, Lucy explained to her protector why antislavery work was important and won him over sufficiently to allow her to speak to the crowd from a tree stump, while he guarded her with his club. She was fearless and equal to any situation, like her colleague, Abby Kelley.

In almost every town she visited, Lucy, in addition to speaking on freedom for the slaves, made a point of calling attention to women's legal, moral, and economic disabilities. People came to hear her, curious about a woman who boldly spoke in public. An unfriendly press grossly misrepresented her, reporting that she smoked cigars and swore like a trooper. To their surprise, audiences found on the platform a small, refined young woman tastefully dressed in black satin, who spoke to them in a clear, well-modulated, ladylike voice. Hearing that Lucy brought woman's rights into many of her antislavery lectures, the general agent of the Massachusetts Antislavery Society, Samuel May, Jr., told her that though he agreed with her woman's rights sentiments, he felt they were out of place at an antislavery meeting. "Well, Mr. May," she replied, "I was a woman before I was an abolitionist. I must speak for the women."[16] She even suggested that she give up lecturing for the Antislavery Society to devote herself to woman's rights. The Antislavery Society however, could not allow such a valuable worker to leave them, and compromised, agreeing that woman's rights be handled in separate lectures.

Other women as well were thinking of their lack of legal rights, with the result that on July 19, 1848, the First Woman's Rights Convention in the world convened in Seneca Falls, New York, called by two of the women who had attended the World's Antislavery Convention in London, in 1840 – Lucretia Mott and Elizabeth Cady Stanton. There they had been so aroused by the refusal of the convention to seat the women who had been sent as delegates that they had vowed they would call a woman's rights convention when they returned to the United States. Eight years had passed but their purpose had not been forgotten. In the meantime Mrs. Stanton had moved to Seneca Falls, New York, from Boston, where her husband had been practicing law. Some of Lucretia Mott's Quaker friends lived near Seneca Falls and with their help and Mrs. Mott's, Mrs. Stanton organized a very successful convention which issued a protest against women's inferior legal, political, economic, and social status. This protest, their Declaration of Sentiments, patterned after the Declaration of Independence, stated boldly that men and women are created equal. Mrs. Stanton herself offered a daring resolution which was adopted and which read, "It is the duty of the women of this country to secure to themselves their sacred right to the elective franchise."

Both Lucy Stone and Abby Kelley were busy with lecture engagements in Massachusetts at the time of the First Woman's Rights Convention and did not take part. They may not even have been aware of it until the newspapers denounced it. Lucy, however, did hear of another woman's rights convention to be held in Salem, Ohio, in April, 1850, and sent an approving letter. Then in May, 1850, after a meeting of the Antislavery Society in Boston, nine women, including Lucy Stone and Abby Kelley, decided it was time that something be done for women as well as for Negroes. They issued a call for a National Woman's Rights Convention, to be held in Worcester, Massachusetts, in October, 1850, and among those signing the call were Lucy and Abby, Ann and Wendell Phillips, Helen and William Lloyd Garrison, and Abby's good friend Paulina Wright, now Mrs. Davis. It was Paulina Wright Davis who gave her time to organizing this National Woman's Rights Convention.

* * *

Early in 1850, Abby was called upon to raise money and to organize antislavery meetings in Massachusetts and eastern New York for George Thompson, who had returned to this country and was again receiving an unfriendly reception. Wendell Phillips, acknowledging $600 which she had collected for the Thompson meetings, wrote her "How can we ever value you enough? What a noble reception you have prepared for George! I congratulate you most sincerely on the triumph and success of your plans. . . . Take care of yourself, dear friend. The slave cannot spare you to heaven yet."[17]

She was now receiving a salary as agent of the American Society and this eased the financial burden of the family. Stephen was spending more and more of his time working on the farm and planting fruit trees — so much so that Abby warned him "not to invent excuses for retiring till victory is won."[18] Abby herself had never been more impressed with the importance of the work and the success of her meeting were the result of her dedication. From the sidelines, Stephe wrote that he had often told her she could accomplish mor without his aid and added that he felt he was not fit to be general agent or even a lecturing agent, and hoped she woul not urge him into the field.[19] He did, however, attend, as sh did, the May meeting of the American Antislavery Societ in New York which was attacked by the Rynders mob, an even he could not make himself heard above the tumult.

In June, Abby, on her way to Ohio, stopped over in Syracuse where Samuel J. May met her and drove her to his home He had arranged a meeting in City Hall which was such great success that he insisted she stop on her way back fo another meeting. She stayed in Ohio until late September holding successful meetings of 3,000 and more and gettin subscriptions for the *Liberator* and *Standard,* but she acknowledged to Stephen, "It is a great sacrifice for me to b away from Alla at this interesting period of her intellectual moral, and social development."[20]

Stephen, now speaking in Massachusetts, wrote her tha her meetings put his in the shade, and added, "I almost wis I had left all and accompanied you. But I suppose Massachusetts must be converted by somebody . . . and beside there is something in the productions of this barren soil tha I like better than anything that is produced by the fertil West."[21]

Abby returned East in time to attend the First Nationa Woman's Rights Convention, in Worcester, October 23, 1850 where she was reunited with Lucy Stone, who had had to giv up her antislavery lecturing for a time because of illness Many antislavery men and women took part in the convention. Lucretia Mott was there, and Frederick Douglass, Garrison, and Phillips. Elizabeth Cady Stanton was missin because of the illness of one of her children, but there was a new face, that of Ernestine Rose, an attractive, eloquent young woman from Poland who had been lecturing against slavery and for women's rights and had been petitioning the New York Legislature for property rights for married women. More than a thousand people crowded into the hall, showing respectful interest and a will to implement the resolutions adopted. One of these resolutions, adopted unanimously, read: "Resolved that the cause we advocate – the claim for woman of all her natural and civil rights – bids us remember the million and a half of slave women at the South, the most grossly wronged and foully outraged of all women; and in every effort for an improvement in our civilization, we will bear in our hearts the memory of the trampled womanhood of the plantation, and omit no effort to raise it to a share in the rights we claim for ourselves."[22] So spoke the abolitionist-feminist, who saw the whole picture of human rights and the relation between the woman's rights and antislavery movements.

Led by the New York *Herald,* the press ridiculed this convention as it had the one in Seneca Falls, calling it the Hen Convention and an "Awful Combination of Socialism, Abolitionism, and Infidelity." Only Horace Greeley's New York *Tribune* treated it with any seriousness and respect. It was the *Tribune*'s report, read in England by Harriet Taylor, the friend and later the wife of John Stuart Mill, which led to her article about it in the *Westminster Review,* widening its influence.

* * *

In spite of their interest in woman's rights, Abby and Lucy were soon back in the field, pleading for the slave. A great deal had been happening on the national scene which was of deep concern to abolitionists. Texas had been annexed in 1845, increasing slave territory; the Mexican War had added still more potential slave territory. An attempt by the Wilmot Proviso to insure that slavery should not exist in territory acquired from Mexico was defeated. During the Presidential campaign of 1848, the question of the extension of slavery was hotly debated. In 1849, the Territory of California adopted a constitution prohibiting slavery and petitioned Congress for admission to the Union as a free state. This opened debate in the Senate on the future of the territories. Trying to find a solution which would be satisfactory to both the North and the South, Henry Clay proposed that California be admitted as a free state, that a more effective Fugitive Slave Law be enacted, and that the slave trade, but not slavery, be abolished in the District of Columbia. Calhoun called this compromise a betrayal of the South, but Webster came to its rescue with his oratory, arousing the anger and disgust of abolitionists as he criticized what he called the "violence" of abolition agitation and the failure of Northerners to return fugitive slaves. After months of debate, the compromise, voted on in three separate measures, was adopted and signed by President Fillmore in 1850. The result was that California was admitted as a free state, the remainder of the disputed region was divided at the 37th parallel into two territories, New Mexico and Utah, without provision regarding slavery, and the claims of Texas to a portion of Mexico were to be satisfied by a payment of ten million dollars. In addition, a more drastic Fugitive Slave Law was enacted and slave traffic was prohibited in the District of Columbia.

The crisis had merely been postponed. To radical abolitionists like Abby Kelley and her colleagues, the situation was disheartening and their only answer was disunion — "No Union with Slaveholders."

CHAPTER XV

New Recruits

Early in 1851, Abby was in western New York organizing meetings for George Thompson, expecting Garrison to join them, but in April Garrison wrote her he would be unable to do so, because of illness, and he addressed her, "Most persevering, most meritorious of coadjustors."[1] He warned her not to overdo, adding, "Your devotion to the cause and self-sacrificing efforts in its behalf have no parallel. But you are exceeding the claims of duty, I fear, and putting in peril your valuable life, partly due to lack of discretion. All lecturing agents err in this – they speak from two to three hours." So absorbed was Abby in her subject that she found it hard to follow his advice. She had just decided to give more prominence in her lectures to the rule of the slave power to which the North was consenting under the Constitution. She felt she must awaken the North.

When she realized that Garrison might not be able to attend the meetings for George Thompson in western New York, she insisted that Stephen join them. This he did reluctantly because there was still so much work to be done on the farm. In Rochester, they met a promising recruit, Susan B. Anthony. Like Abby, she had been brought up a Quaker and had had early contact with antislavery sentiments. Now, in her young womanhood in Rochester, she associated with a group of antislavery Quakers, many of whom gathered at the Anthony farm on Sundays. Sometimes they brought with them Frederick Douglass, who then made his home in Rochester, or Garrison, or Phillips, if they happened to be in the neighborhood. The *Liberator* came regularly to the Anthony home. Because the Rochester Society of Friends continued to oppose antislavery activity, Susan and her father left it for the Unitarian Church.

Susan had of course heard of Abby Kelley's courageous work for the antislavery cause as one of its first women lecturers and agents. Meeting her and listening to her convincing words stimulated her interest in the cause, and she longed to follow Abby's example but questioned her ability to hold the attention of an audience. Sensing Susan's interest and hoping to enlist her as an active worker, Abby urged her to join them on a week's lecture tour. Accepting gladly, Susan was even more impressed by Abby's ability and her own inadequacy as a lecturer. With Abby and Stephen, she attended the convention of the American Antislavery Society, held that spring in Syracuse instead of in New York City where no meeting place was available to abolitionists, so strong was the feeling against them. Hearing George Thompson speak in Syracuse, Susan was so impressed that on her way home she stopped in Seneca Falls to hear him again, visiting her Temperance friend, Amelia Bloomer. Through Mrs. Bloomer, she met Elizabeth Cady Stanton, who had attended the World's Antislavery Convention in London with her husband.

These women of course discussed the antislavery movement. Mrs. Stanton's first contact with the antislavery cause had been in the home of her cousin, Gerrit Smith, an ardent abolitionist who lived in Peterboro, New York. Here she had come face to face with fugitive slaves who were being hidden and helped on their way to Canada. Here she heard earnest antislavery discussions and attended antislavery meetings

Lucy Stone

where she met her future husband, Henry B. Stanton, one of the most eloquent antislavery lecturers. After their marriage and the World's Antislavery Convention, they lived in Boston for a few years, where Mrs. Stanton made many good friends among the abolitionists, including the Garrisons, the Phillips, Whittier, and Frederick Douglass. Her interest in the antislavery cause continued through the years as did that of Susan B. Anthony, who became an agent for the American Antislavery Society in central New York in 1856.

Abolition, however, was not the only subject discussed by these women in Seneca Falls in 1851. They discussed as well the temperance movement in which women were beginning to take part, woman's rights, and dress reform, exemplified by the Bloomer costume, which Mrs. Stanton and Mrs. Bloomer were then wearing. The Bloomer costume, introduced by Mrs. Stanton's cousin, Elizabeth Smith Miller, was being publicized in Amelia Bloomer's temperance paper, *The Lily,* published in Seneca Falls, and as a result, became known as "The Bloomer." Abby Kelley, who was in Seneca Falls for George Thompson's lecture, was also introduced to the Bloomer costume, and like Mrs. Stanton, Susan B. Anthony, and Lucy Stone wore it for several years. To wear comfortable clothing which did not hinder physical activity seemed to them an important gesture for freedom.

When Lucy Stone began wearing the Bloomer costume on the lecture platform, some of the Boston abolitionists, including Anne Weston, protested and objected to inviting her to address an antislavery convention.[2] Wendell Phillips, as usual, came to the rescue, declaring, "If Lucy Stone cannot speak at that meeting, in any decent dress that she chooses, I will not speak either."[3] They needed Wendell Phillips, and accepted Lucy in the Bloomer costume.

Hearing Lucy Stone speak in Ohio, in 1853, in her

Bloomer costume, Frances Ellen Burr noted in her diary, "They . . . have a number of original and pleasing characters upon this platform, among them, Lucy Stone – hair short and rolled under like a man's, a tight fitting velvet waist and linen collar at the throat, bombazine skirt just reaching the knees, and trousers of the same."[4] The Bloomer costume made no difference in Lucy's success as a speaker. That summer in Ohio, she spoke to large, receptive audiences on the abolition of slavery, women's rights, and occasionally on temperance, and the *Liberator* reprinted accounts of her speeches from local papers, most of which were enthusiastic. As one paper commented, "The secret of Miss Stone's eloquence is she speaks from the heart. Her soul is in the subject. . . . She holds hearers in perfect captivity."[5] Even in Kentucky and St. Louis, where she spoke not for abolition but for woman's rights and temperance, she was well received in spite of her Bloomer costume. After a few years, however, Abby, Susan, and Elizabeth Stanton gave up wearing the Bloomer because of the attention they attracted on the streets and because they reluctantly came to believe it harmed the cause they were advocating. Lucy also finally capitulated, but not without protesting to Susan that to be compelled to travel in a long skirt dragging on wet, snowy, muddy streets "would cost her more in every respect than the short skirt ever did."[6]

* * *

Two more young women came into the antislavery picture about this time. Antoinette Brown, Lucy's classmate at Oberlin, had absorbed antislavery doctrine there, as well as woman's rights. As her long-range project was to enter the ministry, she studied theology at Oberlin, in spite of the opposition of the faculty. She could have been ordained there, but not wishing to embarrass the college, which was opposed to women's preaching, she waited to be ordained in her own denomination. In 1852 she was ordained in the Congregational Church of South Butler, New York — the first woman ever to be ordained and to enter the ministry. In the meantime, she preached wherever there was an opportunity and gave antislavery lectures. She could always be counted on to speak at antislavery and woman's rights conventions.

Sallie Holley, of Michigan, the daughter of Myron Holley, abolitionist and supporter of the Liberty party, had come to Oberlin the year Lucy Stone left. Attending an antislavery convention in Akron, Ohio, she was deeply moved by Abby Kelley's pleading for the slave woman, during which Abby asked her audience, "Who in this great assembly is willing to plead her cause?" During the intermission, Sallie Holley went up to Abby to volunteer, saying "I will plead the cause of the slave-woman."[7] Abby begged her to join her at once in the Ohio campaign, but Sallie asked for one more year to finish her course at Oberlin. Then she joined Abby, who gave her an assignment in the Ohio campaign — to hold conventions during the summer with Ohio abolitionists, together with Parker Pillsbury and Sojourner Truth, the remarkable Negro who led fugitive slaves to freedom. Traveling from place to place, they seldom were able to find a hall, church, or schoolhouse for their meetings and spoke where they could. Hearing an attractive young woman pleading earnestly for the slave, in shop or grove, people would stop to listen. In the fall, Abby asked Sallie Holley to come to New York State for meetings to be held in Syracuse and, to Sallie's surprise, told her that the antislavery society would pay her ten dollars a week and expenses. When Abby heard Sallie speak in Samuel J. May's church, she was so moved that she repeatedly had to wipe the tears from her eyes. Afterward, putting her hands on Sallie's shoulders, she said to her

"I have been prostrate before the Throne, all this evening, thanking God that, when I am so worn, weary, and feeble, He has raised up one who can and will speak so nobly, and winningly in this holy but hated and persecuted cause." Sallie Holley lectured for the cause in the West for ten years.

* * *

Harriet Beecher Stowe came into the limelight in 1852, not as an abolitionist converted by Abby Kelley and her colleagues, but as the author of *Uncle Tom's Cabin*. Their work, however, had prepared the way for the amazing success and influence of her book. During her girlhood in Connecticut, Harriet Beecher had not come into contact with antislavery sentiment. Her father, Lyman Beecher, had no sympathy with Garrison and his colleagues, feeling that colonization would solve the slavery problem. When Harriet was in her twenties, he was called to Lane Theological Seminary in Cincinnati to serve as president, and there slavery was forced on his attention by the antislavery debates introduced by a group of students, spurred on by Theodore Weld. Not only did these students decry colonization, but they advocated immediate emancipation, and they associated with Negroes, teaching them and trying to improve their lot. Almost the whole student body was eventually involved. Protests by the citizens of Cincinnati led the executive committee of the Seminary to rule against antislavery meetings, debates, and resolutions, and as a result three-fourths of the students, following the example of Theodore Weld, left the Seminary, many enrolling at Oberlin. This caused serious financial problems for the Seminary. There is no evidence that the debates made an impression on Harriet. She was, however, disturbed at the mob violence in Cincinnati in 1836, when the press of James G. Birney's antislavery paper, *The Philan-*

thropist, was destroyed. Although she had become antislavery in her sympathies, she was not an avowed abolitionist, nor was her husband, Calvin E. Stowe, professor of Biblical literature at Lane Seminary, whom she married in 1836. In fact, she had had no contact with abolitionists until she visited in a nearby town, where she met a member of the local Female Antislavery Society who presented her sister Catherine with a copy of the proceedings of the 1837 Antislavery Convention of American Women. Reading it, Harriet commented in a letter to her husband, who was in Europe at the time, "I should think them about as ultra as to measures as anything that has been attempted, though I am glad to see a better spirit than marks such proceedings generally."[8] Then she added, "It does seem to me there needs to be an intermediate society. If not, as light increases, all the excesses of the abolition party will not prevent humane and conscientious men from joining it. Pray what is there in Cincinnati to satisfy one whose mind is awakened on this subject? No one can have the system of slavery brought before him without an irrepressible desire to *do* something and what is there to be done?"

Her older sister, Catherine, was a very conservative influence as regards antislavery activity. Catherine's interest was education and the establishment of the Western Female Institute for the education of teachers. In her opinion, slavery was not a subject for women to discuss. She was appalled and distressed by the activities of the Grimké sisters from South Carolina, who were speaking against slavery in New York and New England, holding public meetings, and writing effective pamphlets on the subject. Through her Hartford Female Seminary, she had become acquainted with Angelina Grimké, and felt it her duty as an older woman to point out to her the error of her ways. In *An Essay On Slavery and Abolitionism, with Reference to the Duty of American Fe-*

males, published in 1837, she took issue with Angelina's anti-slavery activities. Angelina, convinced of the rightness of her course, answered Catherine Beecher in a series of letters in the *Liberator* which were published in book form in 1838, as *Letters to Catherine Beecher*. In these *Letters,* she forcefully stated her arguments against slavery and for woman's rights. There is no evidence that Harriet was particularly interested in this interchange of views. By this time she had three small children to care for and had little time to think of abolition problems. To help with the housework, she hired a young Negro girl from Kentucky who was regarded as free once she was in Ohio. However, after a few months, she came face to face with the operation of the fugitive slave law. The girl's master began searching for her, and Professor Stowe was obliged to drive her into the country where she would be safe. This experience Mrs. Stowe made use of in *Uncle Tom's Cabin*. She hired other women from the colored settlement in Cincinnati and heard from them some of the hardships of plantation life and the tragedy of families separated by slavery. She also taught some of their children to read and write.

Soon she began writing stories and character sketches again, sending them to magazines. A collection of these was published in 1842 by *Harper's* under the title of "The Mayflower." In 1845, she wrote a story about a fugitive slave for the *New York Evangelist,* called "Immediate Emancipation." These stories helped slightly to supplement the meager family income.

In 1849, the Stowes left Cincinnati for Brunswick, Maine, where Calvin Stowe had accepted the post of Professor of Natural and Revealed Religion at Bowdoin College. In the East, Harriet was confronted with more militant abolitionism. Aroused by the Compromise of 1850 and the stricter Fugitive Slave Law, her brother, Henry Ward Beecher, preaching in Brooklyn, denounced Webster for his part in these laws and auctioned off fugitive slaves in the Broadway Tabernacle and later in Plymouth Church to pay their ransoms. Her brother Edward, a Boston clergyman, was helping fugitive slaves escape to Canada. He was the ardent abolitionist of the family, who, when he was president of Illinois College, had helped Elijah Lovejoy move his antislavery press to Alton, but escaped Lovejoy's fate. Visiting in Edward's home, Harriet heard much antislavery discussion and her sister-in-law urged her to write on the subject, saying to her, "If I could use a pen as you can, I would write something to make this whole Nation feel what a cursed thing slavery is."[9] At the moment, this seemed impossible, for Harriet was worn out with moving and household cares. Then she heard about the fugitive slaves captured in Boston, where feeling ran so high among abolitionists that they formed a Vigilance Committee, while at the same time clergymen defended the seizure of fugitives on the ground that they were property and seizure was legal. This made her realize that she must do something. She had been sending articles to the *National Era* in Washington, edited by Gamaliel Bailey, who previously had edited Birney's antislavery paper, *The Philanthropist,* in Cincinnati. Now a letter came from Dr. Bailey with a check for $100, asking for the best antislavery story she could write. Realizing how slight her contact with slavery had been, she decided she needed more information on the subject and went to Boston to read what was available at antislavery headquarters. Here she found Theodore Weld's *American Slavery As It Is: Testimony of A Thousand Witnesses* and *The Narrative of the Life of Frederick Douglass.* Weld's *Slavery As It Is* made a tremendous impression with its eyewitness statements and newspaper clippings showing actual conditions under slavery. In fact, Angelina Grimké Weld in later years told her daughter that Mrs. Stowe had often said that "she had kept *Slavery As It Is* in her work basket by day and under her pillow by night until its facts crystallized into Uncle Tom."[10]

Mrs. Stowe now began to write with religious fervor, and let Dr. Bailey know that she was at work on a story which would be longer than any she had written — "a series of sketches which give the lights and shadows of that patriarchal institution, written either from observation, incidents which have occurred in the sphere of my personal knowledge, or in the knowledge of my friends." To this she added, "Up to this year I have felt that I had no particular call to meddle with this subject . . . But I feel now that the time is come when even a woman or a child who can speak a word for freedom and humanity is bound to speak."[11] Hearing from her that her story might extend through three or four numbers and would be ready in a few weeks, he sent her a check for $300. To her at the time, this seemed more than generous, but it proved to be all she was paid for the many installments of *Uncle Tom's Cabin* published in the *National Era.* In April, 1851, she sent the first pages to Dr. Bailey, who announced that in June a new story by Mrs. Stowe, *Uncle Tom's Cabin: or, The Man That was a Thing* would be published in the *National Era* in weekly installments. When the first installment appeared, May 8, 1851, the title had been changed to *Uncle Tom's Cabin: or Life Among the Lowly.* Book publication followed in March, 1852, under a contract with Jewell & Company of Boston. Almost immediately ten thousand copies were sold in this country and three hundred thousand within a year. The demand in foreign countries was tremendous. It was dramatized both here and in England. From London, George Thompson wrote, " 'Uncle Tom' is doing a great work here."[12]

It did "a great work" in this country as well, by arousing opposition to the Fugitive Slave Law and by bringing grim facts about slavery to the attention of many who had never thought seriously about it before. Without doubt, it was the great antislavery event of 1852.

Garrison, who had ignored *Uncle Tom* in the *National Era,* read it eagerly as a book and reviewed it enthusiastically in the *Liberator,* finding it "eminently serviceable in the tremendous conflict now waged for the immediate and entire suppression of slavery on American soil." He did mention in closing that it contained some objectionable sentiments respecting African colonization.[13] Wendell Phillips, praising Mrs. Stowe's great service to the cause, commented, "*Uncle Tom* would never have been written had not Garrison developed the facts; and never would have succeeded had he not created readers and purchasers. . . . Whether she knows anything of the real obstacles and difficulties of such a cause as ours, I cannot tell."[14] Whittier thanked her for her "immortal book,"[15] and Longfellow called it "one of the greatest triumphs recorded in literary history, to say nothing of the higher triumph of its moral effect."[16] Senator Seward regarded it as "the greatest book of the times," and Thomas Wentworth Higginson wrote, "To have written at once the most powerful contemporary fiction and the most efficient of antislavery tracts is a double triumph in literature and philanthropy, to which this country has heretofore seen no parallel."[17]

Uncle Tom, however, had its attackers as well, who claimed it was inaccurate and generalized extravagantly. An indignant South suppressed the book, claiming that Mrs. Stowe did not give a true picture of slavery, and Southerners sent her threatening letters. Orthodox clergymen did not approve of what she said about the Church.

In answer to her critics, Mrs. Stowe compiled *A Key to Uncle Tom's Cabin* in which she explained the characters she had used and related experiences of individual slaves to prove that the actuality was far worse than what she had recounted. She even criticized the churches, saying they could easily put an end to slavery if they wished to.

Uncle Tom's Cabin made such a profound impression in England, Scotland, and Ireland that a group of women there, headed by the Duchess of Sutherland, drew up *An Affectionate and Christian Address of Many Thousands of Women of Great Britain and Ireland to Their Sisters, the Women of the United States.* This was an appeal to women to wipe out the "crime" and "dishonour" of Negro slavery. Signed by five hundred thousand women and bound in black leather, it was sent to the author of *Uncle Tom's Cabin.*

In addition, Professor and Mrs. Stowe were invited by the New Ladies' Antislavery Society of Glasgow and the Glasgow New Association for the Abolition of Slavery to visit the British Isles at their expense. They sailed for Liverpool in April, 1853, with Mrs. Stowe's brother, Charles, to act as their secretary. Everywhere they received a warm welcome, and throughout her tour in the British Isles and on the Continent Mrs. Stowe, as the author of *Uncle Tom's Cabin,* was feted and lionized. In Paris, she had a happy visit with Maria Weston Chapman, who, separated from her beloved antislavery work in Boston while her children were being educated in Europe, still continued her work for the cause in every way possible.

When she sailed for Europe, Mrs. Stowe had received a letter from William Lloyd Garrison, and her reply, when she returned to this country opened a long, frank, friendly correspondence. "I am a constant reader of your paper," she wrote him, "and an admirer of much that is in it. I like its frankness, fearlessness, truthfulness, and independence. At the same time I regard with apprehension and sorrow much that is in it. Were it circulated only among intelligent, well-balanced minds able to discriminate between good and evil, I should not feel so much apprehension. . . . What I fear is, that it will take from poor Uncle Tom his Bible, and give him nothing in its place. . . . In this view, I cannot conscientiously do anything which might endorse your party and your paper without at the same time entering a protest against what I consider erroneous and hurtful. . . ."[18]

She had been invited to attend the celebration of the twentieth anniversary of the American Antislavery Society and refused. What troubled her was Garrison's attitude and that of his colleagues toward the Church and religion, which she felt lessened respect and reverence for the Bible. She asked him to call on her so that they could have a frank talk. This he did, and their conversations led to friendship, and respect, and working together for the common cause, each in his own way.

When, in 1854, the Kansas-Nebraska bill was pending in Congress, Mrs. Stowe was so concerned that she became a veritable militant, encouraging a group of clergymen to circulate and present to Congress a petition opposing the bill and she herself wrote *An Appeal to the Women of the Free States* for the *Independent*. "The question," she declared, "is not, shall we remonstrate with slavery on our own soil? but are we willing to receive slavery into the free States and Territories of the Union? Shall the whole power of these United States go into the hands of slavery? Shall every State in it be thrown open as a Slave State? This will be the final result and issue of the question which is now pending."[19]

She also had begun work on another book dealing with

slavery, *Dred, A Tale of the Great Dismal Swamp,* in which she used the Nat Turner rebellion as the main theme. She used much of the material which she had compiled for *A Key to Uncle Tom's Cabin*. Senator Sumner, hearing that she was at work on *Dred,* wrote her, "I feel it will act directly upon pending questions and help us in our struggle for Kansas, and also overthrow the slave-oligarchy in the coming Presidential election. We need your help at once in our struggle."[20]

Dred was published in 1856 when the Supreme Court was considering the case of the fugitive slave, Dred Scott, and Mrs. Stowe wrote her publisher that at this time when everyone was in an excited state, the title, Dred, was just right. *Dred* proved to be very popular in this country and in England and was a great financial success. The *Saturday Evening Post* serialized it after book publication. While some critics thought it did not have the vitality or fire of *Uncle Tom's Cabin,* Queen Victoria and Harriet Martineau preferred it to the first book. "Nothing I can say," wrote Harriet Martineau to Mrs. Stowe, "can give you any idea of the intensity of admiration with which I read it."[21] However, Abby Kelley's friend in Ohio, Elizabeth Hitchcock Jones, wrote Abby not to spend her time on it, because she knew the whole antislavery subject so well, and in other respects it was weak. "I do not know," she added, "how a woman who ever knew anything about the divine passion could have made such a surface work of such a matter. Nothing very deep has ever been awakened in her own heart, I am sure." Nevertheless she felt *Dred* would do good. She would say nothing against it except "among ourselves."[22]

Without doubt, both *Uncle Tom's Cabin* and *Dred* did a tremendous educational work in this country and Europe. They reached those in the North who had been apathetic toward abolition and thousands who would never have read an antislavery tract or papers like the *Liberator* or the *National Antislavery Standard.*

As a result, Harriet Beecher Stowe, who did not class herself as an abolitionist, who did not want to be a militant like the Grimké sisters or Abby Kelley, who did not want to meddle in political matters outside the sphere of women, did, through the publication of *Uncle Tom's Cabin* and *Dred,* have a marked effect upon the serious political questions that confronted the nation. In the opinion of William H. Seward, Lincoln would never have been President had there been no *Uncle Tom's Cabin.*[23]

CHAPTER XVI

Awakening the North

Resistance to the Fugitive Slave Law continued, and in response slave-owners hunted down fugitives who had lived on free soil for years. Vigilance committees of abolitionists in Boston, Syracuse, and elsewhere held protest meetings and attempted to rescue fugitives who were being returned to the South by the courts. Of great concern to abolitionists was the increasing power of the slavery bloc in Congress. In view of these disturbing developments, Abby Kelley could not stay quietly at home, much as she wanted to be with her young daughter. In 1853, she went with Stephen to Ohio and Michigan to lecture and to organize antislavery societies. Here they joined Garrison and Sallie Holley. All of them met surprising resistance. Often halls were closed to them. Nevertheless, they were able to hold an antislavery convention in Adrian, where a Michigan Antislavery Society was formed. In Michigan, the newly formed Free Soil party had great influence. It opposed the extension of slavery, but did not ask for its abolition, attracting many who were sympathetic to abolition but who felt that the slavery problem must be solved through a political party. As a result, abolitionists encountered in Michigan the same kind of opposition they had met in the past from the Liberty party in the East. "We little dreamed when we came here what we should have to encounter," Abby wrote Samuel J. May. "It never occurred to us that as a matter of course this conflict must be passed through everywhere before genuine antislavery could get a substantial footing."[1]

Abby continued her work in the West while the Kansas-Nebraska bill was being debated in Congress, but Stephen returned to the farm in April, 1854. Both were exhausted from their many speaking engagements, and Stephen hoped to regain his health by physical work on the farm. He also hoped to make the farm pay, for from the beginning it had proved to be a financial burden. He planned as well to improve it so that it would be fit to become their permanent home and would be more pleasing to Abby.

Abby returned from the West in time for the annual meeting of the American Antislavery Society in New York. Women were active at this meeting. Abby, Lucretia Mott, and Sarah Pugh of Philadelphia, Lydia Mott of Albany, and Amy Post of Rochester were elected to serve on the Business Committee. Lucretia Mott opposed a disunion resolution proposed by Garrison, which read, ". . . that the one grand vital issue to be made with the Slave Power is The Dissolution of the Existing American Union."[2] Her opposition was not against the idea of dissolution, but was based on the practical effect it would have on the Antislavery Society, for there were many members who still had financial interests in the South which dissolution of the Union would cut off. She pointed this out, and the resolution was defeated. She had had practical experience along these lines, as through the years she had unsuccessfully tried to persuade antislavery societies to take a stand on purchasing only free produce.

By the end of May, the Kansas-Nebraska Act had been passed, nullifying the Missouri Compromise and opening this western territory to settlement on the basis of popular sovereignty. Wendell Phillips expressed the opinion of all abolitionists when he wrote his English friend, Elizabeth Pease,

"The government has fallen into the hands of the Slave power completely. So far as national politics are concerned, we are beaten — there's no hope. . . . The future seems to unfold a vast slave empire . . . The sky was never so dark. Our Union, all confess, must sever finally on this question."[3]

On the Fourth of July, abolitionists, as was their custom, held a meeting of the Friends of Freedom at Framingham, Massachusetts, and this year, because of the Kansas-Nebraska Act, it was doubly important to them. Abby, Stephen, and Lucy Stone took part. Stephen called on everyone to resist the Fugitive Slave Law and warned against the Free Soil party because it recognized the Constitution, which upheld slavery. "Let the support of the Union be withdrawn from the slaveholder," declared Lucy Stone, "and the three million slaves will hew their way to freedom and their inalienable rights."[4] Garrison made a stirring speech, and holding up a copy of the Fugitive Slave Law put a lighted match to it and burned it while the audience watched approvingly. Then he burned the decision of Judge Loring in the Anthony Burns case. Finally, holding up a copy of the Constitution, he set fire to it, as he pronounced it the "source and parent of all the other atrocities, a 'covenant with death and agreement with hell.'" As all watched it burn, he vehemently declared, "So perish all compromises with tyranny. Let all the people say Amen," and the audience shouted Amen! Both Abby and Lucy heartily approved of this militant gesture.

Angelina Grimké Weld was so aroused by the Kansas-Nebraska Act that she sent an article to the *Liberator,* something she had not done for a long time. She praised Wendell Phillips and Theodore Parker for their attempts to rescue the fugitive slave, Anthony Burns. "The passage of the Nebraska Bill," she wrote, "though expected, nevertheless falls heavily upon every heart which beats for liberty. It seems to have aroused the slumbering North as no other slave enactment ever did before. I sincerely hope that the arrest of every fugitive may be contested even unto blood. Not another slave should ever be surrendered."[5]

* * *

Because Abby was so convinced of "the necessity of a thorough re-education of the public mind, as the only protection of our liberties,"[6] she continued her work for the cause in New England and New York, although completely exhausted physically. The vital, energetic antislavery evangelist of the 1840's had visibly aged, looking gaunt and worn. It troubled Stephen, who urged her to stay at home for a few months and take plenty of outdoor exercise. "I shall have strong hopes that you will ultimately regain much of your former vigor and elasticity. . . . What pleasure it would give me to see you once more the vigorous, animated, bounding creature that you were when first I became acquainted with you – so full of life and vivacity."[7]

Wendell Phillips, also concerned about Abby's health, implored her to stop working and to take a year's rest. "You have no right," he wrote her, "to waste yourself thus. With proper care your valuable life, experience, activity, energy and devotedness may be saved to us for many years. . . . My wife says tell her it is a duty she owes to the cause and the slave."[8]

Then he assured her that she need not worry about the farm or Stephen, as their friends would see that their needs were met. A few years before, the same friends had tried to send them to Jamaica for a few months to recuperate, expenses paid, but they had been unwilling to leave their antislavery work. This time Abby listened, and stayed at home on the farm for a year, while Stephen went on a speaking tour in Ohio and Pennsylvania, and later in New England. She spent a great deal of time working out-of-doors and reported progress to Stephen. She rejoiced in the companionship of Alla.

During this time, very gratifying news came in a letter to Stephen from Charles F. Hovey, the wealthy Boston dry goods merchant, who through the years had shown great interest in the antislavery cause and its active workers. "I say to you now,"[9] he wrote Stephen, "there is no one . . . in this or any other country in whom I feel more interest than yourself." Because of this he had made a will leaving $1,000 to him and to Abby and had decided to begin paying them six percent annual interest on it. He enclosed a check which was very welcome, as there never was quite enough money to meet their expenses.

Early in February, 1856, the *Liberator* reported, "The health of Mrs. Foster has been such as to withdraw her from the public service of the cause the greater part of the year. But while her health permitted, she conducted a brief but successful antislavery campaign in New Hampshire and also labored awhile in Rhode Island."

While Abby was taking her year off, Lucy Stone was married to Henry B. Blackwell of Cincinnati, the brother of Elizabeth Blackwell, the first woman physician in America. She had met him in Cincinnati while on her lecture tour. They were married by a fellow-abolitionist, Thomas Wentworth Higginson, who had established a Free Church in Worcester and who heartily approved of their Marriage-Protest against the unjust laws affecting married women. Together Lucy and Henry had drawn up the Protest and they read it at the ceremony. It was published in the Worcester *Spy* and later in the *Liberator,* causing considerable comment. True to her woman's rights principles, Lucy kept her own name, feeling that "a wife should no more take her husband's name than he should hers."[10]

After their marriage, Lucy and Henry returned to Ohio, and Lucy continued her antislavery and woman's rights lecturing. Less than a year later they had the good news that Antoinette Brown and Henry's brother, Samuel Blackwell, had been married in New York State.

* * *

The prophecy of Salmon P. Chase regarding the Kansas-Nebraska Act was being borne out in Kansas. During the debate in the Senate, he had declared, "It will light up a fire in the country which may consume those that kindle it."[11]

Proslavery settlers from Missouri were competing with the free-state settlers for control of Kansas. A New England Emigrant Aid Society had been formed to send out and finance settlers – not abolitionists, but men who wanted Kansas a free-labor state which they could develop with their own hard work. There was violence and there was bloodshed, as the town of Lawrence was sacked by proslavery men, and John Brown and his men retaliated with the massacre at Pottawatomie Creek.

During this bloody contest in Kansas, Senator Sumner made a vitriolic speech in the Senate, *The Crime Against Kansas,* calling by name offending Southern Senators. The next day, while he was sitting at his desk in the Senate, he was attacked with a cane by Preston Brooks of South Carolina and beaten into unconsciousness. Southern newspapers declared this was good discipline for Sumner and other abolitionists in the Senate. In the North, protest meetings were held. By his *Crime Against Kansas* speech Sumner redeemed himself in the eyes of Garrison and Abby and Stephen Foster, who had felt that he had not been serving the abolitionist cause in the Senate and had been dodging the issue of the Fugitive Slave Law.

The struggle in Kansas so aroused Sarah Grimké that she prophesied that "the lurid torch of slavery"[12] could only be quenched in blood. She hoped, however, that the end would come quickly before too many lives were lost. She believed that during her lifetime the slave would have his freedom, but she warned that the feelings of racial hate would take generations to heal.

Lydia Maria Child was also aroused by Kansas. She collected warm clothing from her friends to send to free-state settlers there. She wrote and circulated a poem, "Song for Free Soil Men," and wrote a short novel, *The Kansas Emigrants,* which Horace Greeley ran as a serial in the New York *Tribune.* In the Presidential campaign of 1856, she did her utmost for the election of the candidate of the new Republican party, the colorful hero and explorer of the Far West, John C. Frémont. "I would almost lay down my life," she declared, "to have him elected. There never has been such a crisis since we were a nation. If the slave-power is checked now, it will never regain its strength. If it is not checked, civil war is inevitable."[13]

A surprising number of heretofore nonvoting abolitionists were showing a definite interest in the Republican party because it opposed the extension of slavery. Abby and Stephen Foster and Susan B. Anthony were beginning to lean slightly toward the Republicans and Elizabeth Cady Stanton took her stand for Frémont. Even Garrison, who had heaped scorn on the Liberty and Free Soil parties, now, in a *Liberator* editorial, rated the Republican party as better than other rival parties in "virtuous character, human sentiment, and patriotic feeling" and added that its success would be a cheering sign of the times.

The defeat of Frémont and the election of conservative James Buchanan was very disappointing to them, and so alarmed Susan B. Anthony that she postponed her work for women's rights and dedicated herself to the antislavery cause. Remembering that a few years before the American Anti-slavery Society had asked her to be their agent in western New York, she now wrote Samuel May, Jr., "I shall be very glad if I am able to render even the most humble service to this cause. Heaven knows there is need of earnest, effective, radical workers." He replied, "We put all New York into your control."[14] For ten dollars a week and expenses, Susan B. Anthony now arranged for antislavery meetings and planned tours for a corps of speakers, including Abby and Stephen Foster, Parker Pillsbury, and two free Negroes, Charles Remond and his sister Sarah. Often their meetings met outright hostility, because Northern businessmen opposed abolitionists, whom they accused of stirring up trouble between the North and the South. As their meetings were long, often turning into debates between speakers and audience, the speakers lived under a strain and emotional pressure. As a result, they were not always easy to handle and were often dissatisfied with her arrangements for them.

Occasionally, to fill in, she took her turn at speaking, but always depreciated her efforts. "Antislavery prayers, resolutions, and speeches," she told her audiences, "avail nothing without action. . . . Our mission is to deepen sympathy and convert into right action. Our mission is to show that men and women of the North are slaveholders, those of the South slave-owners. The guilt rests on the North equally with the South. Therefore our work is to rouse the sleeping consciousness of the North."[15]

Traveling through New York State, arranging meetings for her corps of speakers, Susan saw many evidences of the good pioneering work Abby Kelley had done, which now made the way far easier and more productive for her. She wrote Abby and Stephen, "I . . . have been breathing the atmosphere of moral growth which seems to me the result of your early labors in the vineyard of Antislavery. Your spirits have hovered over me. . . . I can truly say my spirit has grown in grace, and that the experience of the past winter is worth more to me than all my Temperance and Woman's Rights labors – Though the latter were the school necessary to bring me into the Antislavery work."[16] However, in spite of her zeal, Susan could not make her antislavery meetings self-supporting and at the end of the first season faced a deficit of $1,000. This troubled her, but the American Antislavery Society, recognizing her value, wrote her, "We cheerfully pay your expenses and want to keep you at the head of the work." Recognizing her "business enterprise, practical sagacity, and platform ability."[17] they looked upon her as a good investment. In fact Samuel May, Jr. criticizing Stephen Foster's recent work for the Antislavery Society, held Susan up as the perfect example of an antislavery agent.

* * *

For abolitionists, the Dred Scott Decision, in March, 1857, was the next alarming development. In the case of Dred Scott, a fugitive slave, the Supreme Court held that the Constitution did not apply to Negroes, since they were citizens of no state when it was adopted, that therefore they had not the right of citizens to sue for freedom or to claim freedom in the territories, and that the Missouri Compromise had always been void since Congress did not have the right to enact a law which arbitrarily deprived citizens of their property. This decision glaringly reaffirmed for many abolitionists that the Constitution was truly a proslavery document, and that disunion was imperative. Susan B. Anthony, Lucy Stone, Abby Kelley, and Sallie Holley rededicated themselves to disunion.

At the convention of the American Antislavery Convention in New York in May, Lucy Stone declared that the attack on Sumner, the Fugitive Slave Law, and the Dred Scott Decision showed up the descendants of the fathers of 1776 as unworthy, and she urged women to explain to their children what was happening, to explain the meaning of the Dred Scott Decision, of the Personal Liberty bills, and the strife in Kansas. "Let no hour pass," she added, "without deepening in the minds of your little ones the impression of hatred of a system out of which come such scenes as those in Kansas."[18]

In October, 1857, Abby was in Cleveland, Ohio, preaching disunion. Abolitionists in Ohio had petitioned their legislature to take steps to withdraw from the Union and a Disunion Convention had been planned for Cleveland. Although it was called off because of the financial panic of 1857, Abby was on hand to deliver her disunion message. "Ours is a revolution," she declared, "not a reform. We contemplate the entire destruction of the present National Government and Union."[19]

Because American Antislavery Society finances were in such a critical condition, Abby was now asked to solicit funds and to get more subscribers for the *Liberator* and *Antislavery Standard*. It was discouraging work because of the business depression, and contributions to antislavery societies were fewer and smaller. One bright spot for Abby, while she was soliciting in New York City and Brooklyn, was meeting Henry Blackwell in the Antislavery Office in New York. He and Lucy had recently come East and were living in Orange, New Jersey. Henry insisted that Abby come to Orange with him to see Lucy. She found Lucy in a "neat little cottage, bright and happy as a bird," and as she commented to Stephen meaningfully, "only herself and Harry . . . a fine yard and garden . . . with abundant fruit trees growing."[20]

Abby and Stephen had also been passing through a financial depression, for Stephen was no longer receiving even the small salary of a regular antislavery agent, but was serving only as a volunteer. He had been critical of the way the Massachusetts Society was managed and there were differences between him and Samuel May, Jr. Therefore a letter from Wendell Phillips at this time, with a check for $100, was a godsend. The check was part of the money Phillips had collected from Abby's friends when she was taking a year off from antislavery work because of her health. With the check came a warning to Abby from Phillips urging her to continue to save herself. "You are too valuable capital to be hastily squandered," he wrote her. "The times ahead need you as much as the present. So take measures to continue to us, as long as may be, the skill, experience and devotedness which have grown with your years and which are so little likely to be replaced. . . ."[21]

* * *

Abby next moved on to Boston to solicit funds for the cause, staying in the home of Francis Jackson. Sometimes she collected only ten dollars a day. This troubled her, as antislavery agents were being dismissed because there were no funds to pay their pitifully small salaries.

Fortunately Maria Weston Chapman had returned from her seven years' stay in Europe and was again beginning to raise money for the cause with her popular annual antislavery bazaars and festivals and her own generous contributions. In his letter of welcome, Garrison wrote her, "We know that you have not only improved, but created opportunities to aid us on British and French soil, by speech, testimony, personal influence, the press, the preparation of circulars and tracts, a generous pecuniary contribution, multitudinous letters, and well-directed blows, struck at the right time and with irresistible force. . . . Welcome to a still further participation in a cause which, notwithstanding its grand advances, has yet to contend with Church and State, and all that is rich, strong, and powerful in the land!"[22]

Since her return from Europe, Mrs. Chapman was living happily in the old family home in Weymouth, and Abby spent a day with her there, writing Stephen, "We had a lot of talk on everything. She is the best person to lay plans for carrying on operations I ever knew. Without her help, I don't know as I could get a hundred dollars. . . . She knows what cord to touch in every heart. . . ."[23] At her suggestion, Abby called on James Russell Lowell and Henry Wadsworth Longfellow, and Lowell gave her fifty dollars.

"Maria is nearer us than Garrison on the Republican question," Abby confided to Stephen, "but she says she thinks it does no good to discuss it with Garrison. He will come right. She thinks the determination on your part and that of Pillsbury very wise and that I might profit by it."

* * *

Earlier that year, at the annual meeting of the Massachusetts Antislavery Society, Stephen had made a startling recommendation. He declared that the time had come when moral persuasion was not enough. It had done a great work, but the small audience at the convention had convinced him that it no longer was enough and was out of date. "Our people," he added, "believe in a government by force; but we are asking them to take an essentially nonresistant position which is wholly inadequate to the exigencies of the case. They wish to vote."[24] He called for a new antislavery party, a political party. Thomas Wentworth Higginson supported him, saying, "The moral position of this society is the highest and noblest possible, but their practical position does not take hold of the mind of the community." He did not know, he confessed, whether abolitionists ought to join the Republican party or, as Foster suggested, form an Antislavery party. The nonvoting abolitionists present were amazed at these suggestions and waited for directions from Garrison, who was obviously displeased and told them, "It is not my duty to contrive ways for men . . . determined to vote without regard to the moral character of their act to carry out their low ideas, and I shall do no such work."

Having taken a position against Garrison, both Abby and Stephen were out of favor. Because through the years they had been close friends of the Garrisons, Abby tried to smooth over Stephen's ruffled feelings, writing him, "I think that wisdom demands that we should bear much for the cause sake from those who have some great object at heart. . . . What if Garrison shall snap me up as if I were a puppy. . . . There are many ways in which we are to lay ourselves on the altar for Truth's sake. Union is strength and I will be united with all true souls so long as by self-forgetfulness, I can help the cause that needs more instead of less union." Then she told him that Garrison now stood alone on the Republican question and that all the executive committee were with them. "He can't stand alone long," she added. "Unconsciously he will slide into our position and not know he has changed a jot."[25]

In May, 1859, at the Convention of the New England Antislavery Society, Stephen again brought up this matter when he pointed out that although abolitionist sentiment was spreading, no new abolitionists were being made as in former years. He then proposed a resolution condemning the Republican party because its purpose was not to touch slavery where it existed. This, he declared made it "essentially and radically proslavery" in the eyes of every lover of liberty. In still another resolution, he questioned "the integrity of professed abolitionists who at this late day continue to give their countenance and support to such a party, knowing as every intelligent man must that to support a party that sustains slavery is to make himself a participant in its crimes."[26]

Abby supported these resolutions, asking those present to vote on the question, not on men or speeches. The resolution was carried by a small majority, but at the evening session, in a speech before a new audience, Garrison "cast disdain on those who advocated the resolution." There was a motion to reconsider and the original resolution was defeated. Once more Abby had evidence of Garrison's method of working and of his determination to keep control of the policies of antislavery societies. As she wrote Wendell Phillips later, "I have escaped from the priestly rule of the church, from the demagogism of politicians, from the tyranny of society. Heaven save me from any other dictatorship though it comes from the slave's best friend."[27]

In spite of Abby's good intentions to agree to disagree with Garrison and remain friends, Garrison goaded her a bit too far at the 1859 Convention. He not only referred to Abby's "cracked voice and graying hairs,"[28] but accused her of "obtaining money under false pretenses." In her solicitation of funds she had called on Republicans and received contributions from them, and Garrison made the most of this, intimating that she had not been honest with them. Abby was not present when Garrison made this accusation and could not speak for herself, but Stephen, Wendell Phillips, and others demanded a retraction, which Garrison would not make. After a few weeks, however, he wrote her, assuring her of his high respect for her character and of his affection for her, but he repeated his original charge and said he could not appoint her to act as financial agent of the American Antislavery Society.

Abby replied that since she now stood before her colleagues accused by him of "being fraudulent and obtaining money under false pretences," it would be futile for her to go West as she had planned, to aid the Western Antislavery Society in its extremity. "I am most effectively cut off from this work," she added. "Not only will the enemies, but the friends of the cause distrust me. . . ."[29]

Wendell Phillips, who was genuinely fond of Abby, did his best to clear up this misunderstanding, but with little success. Garrison continued to insist that his remarks had been misinterpreted and that he had nothing to retract. In fact, he wrote Abby that it would all have been forgotten if Stephen had not dragged the matter before the meeting and made "a long, highly injudicious speech on it." Then he assured her that he had neither impeached nor meant to impeach her personal integrity, and added, "I believe you to have always been actuated by the highest and finest motives, however lacking in judgement or consistency. Of all the women who have appeared on the historic stage, I have always regarded you as peerless – the moral Joan of Arc of the world . . . No one not of my family has been nearer or dearer to me than yourself."[30]

While this correspondence was continuing, Abby was elected to serve on the Board of Managers of the Massachusetts Antislavery Society. She refused to serve because, as she wrote them, one of the Board had accused her of being fraudulent and obtaining money under false pretenses, and her presence on the Board would be a source of irritation and distrust. The Board urged her to reconsider, and Wendell Phillips insisted that it was her duty to serve, but she could not be persuaded.

Discussing further with Phillips, Stephen's and her appraisal of the Republican party as essentially proslavery, she told him that many abolitionists agreed. "I am confident," she added, "that we shall ultimately stand together. If we are not brought together by a clearing up of our own moral vision, we shall be driven together by the developments of the Republican Party. There can be no middle ground – no ground of conservatism for us while slavery exists."[31]

CHAPTER XVII

Days of Decision

Abolitionists were watching the national scene with deep concern. Women were speaking out, and their speeches and letters were published in the *Liberator* and the *National Antislavery Standard*.

When Senator Seward spoke in Rochester, New York, of "an irrepressible conflict between opposing and enduring forces,"[1] he was expressing just what Susan B. Anthony believed. To her, this was a conflict between good and evil, between slavery and freedom. She was lobbying in the New York Legislature for a Personal Liberty Bill to protect slaves who were escaping from the South.

In the West, a young Republican, Abraham Lincoln from Illinois, debating with Stephen A. Douglas declared, "A house divided against itself cannot stand. . . . It will become all one thing or all the other."[2]

Elaborating on this theme in Ohio, Elizabeth Hitchock Jones was quoted in the *Liberator* as saying ". . . the time has now arrived when we must choose whether slavery shall tread out its last spark that slumbers on Liberty's Altar or whether American Freedom shall fulfill the promises of its birth."[3]

The contest between free-state and proslavery settlers in Kansas continued. Sharpe's rifles were being sent out to free-state settlers by the New England Emigrant Aid Society, and Abby Kelley, troubled by the bloodshed bound to follow, had written Garrison, whom she knew was as much of a nonresistant as she was, "I want those who have been thinking to establish freedom in Kansas by Sharpe's rifles to see that if one tithe of the indignation and money that has been expended against border ruffians in Kansas, had been used to create a just moral indignation against those around us who sustain these ruffians, Kansas would now be free. The mistake of the Free State party is that they have been striking at the tail of the serpent while they have let the head have full scope."[4]

John Brown had come to Boston in 1857 to raise funds to maintain a company of soldiers to fight for freedom in Kansas. Many of the abolitionists, including Wendell Phillips, were impressed by him, but Garrison, the pacifist and nonresistant, had nothing in common with him but a sense of mission. Brown attended the New England Antislavery Convention in 1859, where he remarked, "These men are all talk. What is needed is action."[5]

Action came in October, 1859, with John Brown's raid on Harpers Ferry, which he hoped would be a signal to the slaves to rise in rebellion. Instead, in two days he was taken prisoner by government troops and put in the Charlestown jail. Most abolitionists had great sympathy for John Brown, feeling he had saved Kansas for freedom. A few were suspected of being his accomplices, and hurriedly left the country. Susan B. Anthony, whose brother had settled in Kansas, near John Brown, was disappointed to find that Garrison in the *Liberator* called the raid on Harpers Ferry "a misguided, wild, apparently insane, though disinterested and well-intentioned effort by insurrection to emancipate the slaves of Virginia." She was glad that he added, "Let no one who glories in the Revolutionary struggle of 1776 deny the right of the slaves to imitate the example of our fathers."[6]

To most abolitionists John Brown was a hero and a martyr, for they felt his purpose was noble, just a step beyond the Underground Railroad and rescuing fugitive slaves. The majority of Northerners, however, regarded him as a menace, stirring up lawlessness, while Southerners, fearful of slave insurrections, called him a cold-blooded murderer. All saw before them the threat of civil war.

* * *

The raid on Harpers Ferry brought Lydia Maria Child hurrying back to active participation in the antislavery movement. Hearing that John Brown was wounded and in prison, she offered to nurse him, writing to him and to Governor Wise of Virginia. John Brown declined her offer, but asked her instead to help raise funds to aid his wife and young daughters and the families of the men who had been killed. This she did at once. Meanwhile her correspondence with Governor Wise was published in the New York *Tribune.* In these letters she pointed out that abolitionists had not been responsible for the raid, but that the high-handed encroachments of the slave-owners had incited it. "They sowed the wind in Kansas," she wrote, "and have reaped the whirlwind at Harpers Ferry."[7] Soon the wife of Senator Mason of Virginia, Margaretta Mason, took part in the correspondence, writing Mrs. Child, "No Southerner ought . . . to read a line of your composition, or to touch a magazine which bears your name in its list of contributors . . ." This sounded like old times, like the treatment Mrs. Child had received from Bostonians when she wrote *An Appeal in Favor of That Class of Americans Called Africans* in 1833. Her correspondence with Mrs. Mason continued, as she urged her to examine the subject dispassionately. Abolitionists, she told her, had been trying to reason with slaveholders through the press and in the halls of Congress for thirty years but their efforts had been met with violence and abuse. Then she added, "We, as a portion of the Union, involved in the expense, the degeneracy, the danger, and the disgrace of this iniquitous and fated system, have a right to speak about it, and a right to be heard also. . . . The despotic measures you take to silence investigation and shut out the light from your own white population prove how little reliance you have on the strength of your cause."

Mrs. Child had suggested to Horace Greeley that he publish her correspondence with Mrs. Mason in the *Tribune* because it would help the Republican party. It aroused tremendous interest, so much in fact that the American Antislavery Society published it as a pamphlet. Over 300,000 copies were sold.

During John Brown's trial, his friends did their utmost to save him, Wendell Phillips arranging for counsel and supplying legal advice. The jury declared Brown guilty of treason, of conspiring with the slaves to rebel, and of murder in the first degree. He was sentenced to die. Yet a few hoped he might still be saved. Higginson and others wanted to rescue him, but he forbade it. Still others wanted to kidnap Governor Wise of Virginia and hold him at sea as a hostage for John Brown.

On December 2, 1859, John Brown was hanged. Through the North protest meetings were held, church bells tolled, and people gathered to mourn and to pray. Lydia Maria Child spent the day mourning and praying with the Negroes in Boston. Abolitionists gathered at Tremont Temple in Boston where, before a tremendous audience, Garrison read John Brown's statement to the Court. For himself, Garrison said, he was a peace man. Even so, he added, it was no violation of his principles to "wish success to any slave insurrection in the South."[8] While he could not approve of John Brown's method, he approved of his aim. Among the other speakers at the Tremont Temple meeting was Ralph Waldo Emerson who spoke of "the new saint than whom none purer or more brave was ever led by love of man into conflict and death . . . who will make the gallows glorious."[9]

Susan B. Anthony arranged a similar meeting in Rochester, New York, to honor John Brown. At the big meeting in Philadelphia, Lucretia Mott and Mary Grew spoke, Lucretia Mott declaring that slavery was the great sin beclouding the light of America and that the consequences of this wrongdoing would undoubtedly be "The sword and bloodshed."[10] Lucy Stone, thinking over the disquieting events of the past weeks, wrote her mother, "Isn't it dreadful to think Old Brown could be hung – such a man! It seems as though the times of the martyrs had come again. Imagine we shall have bloodshed in Congress, and maybe the dissolution of the Union. . . . We are near a revolution, I think."[11]

All of the antislavery women were deeply troubled by the implications of the raid on Harpers Ferry. However, it put new life into Lydia Maria Child. She circulated petitions asking for mercy for two of John Brown's men. She sent her correspondence with Mrs. Mason to Harriet Martineau, Victor Hugo, Mazzini, and Queen Victoria, and sent letters to London newspapers and magazines explaining the John Brown tragedy. She wrote more antislavery pamphlets; *The Duty of Disobedience to the Fugitive Slave Act, The Patriarchal Institution,* and *The Right Way, the Safe Way, Proved by Emancipation in the West Indies and Elsewhere,* and mailed these pamphlets to people in the South whose addresses she had secured. Then Garrison asked her to edit the *Antislavery Almanac.* This was work she disliked, but she did it for the slave.

* * *

With the Presidential campaign of 1860 underway, abolitionists found none of the four candidates worthy of support. Lydia Maria Child was one of the few abolitionists to give her support to Lincoln, yet she did not give it with enthusiasm. The Republican party's value to the cause of freedom, in her opinion, was that it kept the discussion of slavery alive. Many abolitionists would have leaned toward the Republicans had not their candidate, Abraham Lincoln, approved of the enforcement of the Fugitive Slave Law and stated that he did not favor Negro citizenship. All they could do at this juncture was to continue to hold antislavery meetings and try to influence public opinion in the North. Susan B. Anthony was doing this in New York State. In her speeches, she called slavery the legalized, systematic robbery of the bodies and souls of nearly four million men, women, and children. She blamed the North for restricting the Negro's educational and economic opportunities. "Let the North," she urged, "prove to the South by her acts that she fully recognizes the humanity of the black man, that she respects his rights in all her educational, industrial, social, and political associations."[12] She was asking far more than the North was willing to give, but to her it was justice which she was obliged to demand.

Abby Kelley was back in Ohio, making speeches and getting many subscribers to the *Antislavery Bugle*. "The desire for lectures," she wrote Samuel May, Jr.,"is far beyond anticipation. The impression the truth has made is still greater." Then she added that, on the Fourth of July, all the leading men and officeholders – Republicans – sat in silence under the severest denunciations she had ever poured on an audience, and yet they contributed $25 to the Western Antislavery Society and subscribed to the *Bugle* and the *Antislavery Standard*. "I always get most when I am most severe," she commented. "Men respect conscience with courage enough to use it, and when they want slavery abolished, they have faith that the most conscientious and courageous will do it fastest."[13]

Shortly after the election of President Lincoln, South Carolina seceded from the Union, remembering Lincoln's statement that the Union must become all slave or all free. By February, 1861, six more states had followed her example, forming the Confederate States of America. This did not alarm abolitionists, who had long advocated disunion. What they feared was a compromise which would fasten slavery on the nation. Even Seward suggested a constitutional amendment guaranteeing noninterference with slavery in slave states for all time.

While the whole country marked time waiting for the inauguration of President Lincoln, abolitionists sent out their speakers, hoping to influence the North. Susan B. Anthony headed a group in western New York which included Elizabeth Cady Stanton, Samuel J. May, and the Fosters. They met resistance and animosity in every city from Buffalo to Albany. Mobs broke up their meetings and tore down Susan's banner, "No Union with Slaveholders." They continued their tour only because they felt it their duty to uphold the right of free speech.

It was the same in New England. Wendell Phillips was a special target in Boston, and, as he was to speak at the annual meeting of the Massachusetts Antislavery Society in Tremont Temple, there was great concern for his safety among his friends. Lydia Maria Child made a point of arriving at the meeting early and was relieved to find armed young men acting as a bodyguard for Phillips, for they could not count on police protection. Already the hall was crowded. Sallie Holley, who was in Boston at the time, described the meeting in a letter to an antislavery friend: "I think it was worth living a great many years to be present at the meeting in Tremont Temple . . . I may never live to witness another day as great as that was in courage, devotion, and fidelity to principle."

"The platform was crowded with the faithful and true – many a tried soldier in Freedom's long battle: Francis Jackson to preside, Edmund Quincy to aid, Mr. Phillips, like a conquering angel, with wit and wisdom . . . Mrs. Lydia Maria Child, as full of enthusiasm as she could express by flashing eye, glowing cheek, and waving handkerchief, as she sat by the organ . . . making everybody glad by her presence; Mrs. Maria Chapman, sitting with the calm dignity of a queen, her sister and daughter beside her. . . ."[14]

In his speech, Phillips hailed disunion, and commenting on the secession of South Carolina, said, "Build a bridge of gold and pay her toll over it." There was disturbance throughout his speech – hisses, stamping, and shouting – but Phillips as usual was able to hold the crowd in check. Finally, the police cleared the galleries for the afternoon session.

The evening meeting was called off, and Lydia Maria Child was relieved to learn that Phillips had reached home safely. These were difficult, anxious days for Phillips' wife, Ann, who since their return from England in the early 1840's had been an invalid, unable to leave her home. Nevertheless, her interest in the antislavery cause and her husband's part in it had continued. She kept herself fully informed and he turned to her constantly for counsel, for her judgment was keen and wise. Throughout their life together, she held up to him the advice she had given him at the World's Antislavery Convention in London in 1840, "Wendell, be brave as a lion."[15]

* * *

Lincoln's inaugural address was a great disappointment to most of the antislavery women, for he said, "I have no purpose directly or indirectly to interfere with the institution of slavery in the states where it exists. I believe I have no lawful right to do so, and I have no inclination to do so."[16] He made it clear that his purpose was to preserve the Union.

Now one startling event followed another. Fort Sumter, on an island in Charleston harbor held by Major Anderson and a small force, was bombarded by the Confederates and surrendered. This roused the war spirit, Lincoln called for volunteers, and soon war was in full swing. The antislavery women, amazed at the war spirit that surged through the North, looked for some indication that the war would be fought for the freedom of the Negro as well as for the preservation of the Union. Lydia Maria Child was disheartened when she heard that fugitive slaves seeking refuge at Fort Pickens were returned to their masters. Looking to Garrison, Phillips, and May for guidance in these critical days, the antislavery women heard Wendell Phillips declare for war before an enthusiastic audience of over four thousand in Boston. Garrison, the nonresistant, took his stand with the government. He saw in "this grand uprising of the manhood of the North"[17] a growing appreciation of liberty and free institutions and a willingness to defend them. He called upon abolitionists to stand by their principles, but asked them not to criticize Lincoln or the Republicans unnecessarily, not to divide the North, but to watch events and bide their time. He opposed those abolitionists who wanted to withhold support of the government until it took a definite stand for the Negro's freedom. He now removed from the front page of the *Liberator* the condemnatory superscription, "The United States Constitution is a covenant with death and an agreement with hell," and replaced it with "Proclaim Liberty throughout the Land, to all the inhabitants thereof."

The general preoccupation with war was trying to Quakers like Susan B. Anthony, Abby Kelley, Lucretia Mott, and others, who could not see war as the solution of any problem. Lucy Stone also felt that way, since this was not a war to free the slaves. All of these women marked time. There were no antislavery conventions, no speaking tours to carry the message of freedom. They were used to working for a principle, and other work seemed empty in comparison. Many women were busy with war work, forming Woman's Relief Associations and Ladies Aid Societies. Lucy Stone's sister-in-law, Dr. Elizabeth Blackwell, was training nurses whom Dorothy Dix was placing in service. In addition, there was aid to the Freedmen. While the antislavery women gave aid where needed, it seemed unimportant in comparison with the big issue, the abolition of slavery. They looked to Lincoln for some sign that emancipation of the slaves would come, only to be dismayed when he canceled Frémont's order freeing the slaves of rebels in Missouri.

This order, however, stimulated interest in emancipation and Emancipation Leagues were formed, taking the place in a measure of abolition societies. As Lydia Maria Child wrote Whittier, "The warmest of the Republicans and the most unprejudiced of the abolitionists are laying their heads together, with no more publicity than is necessary, to influence popular opinion through the press, and help turn the tide in the right direction.[18]

Now abolitionists found themselves in demand. No longer were halls and churches closed to them. They were asked to speak and write for the press. Mary Grew told of the respectful tributes in Philadelphia newspapers to men "whose names had hitherto been used as a cry wherewith to rally a mob.[19] However, abolitionists soon realized that this new interest did not come from any real concern for the rights of the Negro. Even Senator Sumner contended that emancipation should be supported as a military necessity rather than on the grounds of philanthropy. This military necessity argument distressed Lydia Maria Child, who wrote Gerrit Smith, "This entire absence of moral sense on the subject has disheartened me more than anything else. Even should they [the slaves] be emancipated merely as a 'war necessity,' everything must go wrong if there is no heart or conscience on the subject . . . It is evident that great moral work still needs to be done." Abby Kelley, as well, deplored the fact that politicians were willing to act against slavery only because of military necessity. On the other hand, Maria Weston Chapman, then working in New York in her son's brokerage office, was an advocate of the military necessity argument for emancipation.

Lincoln's message to Congress in December, 1861, was disappointing, as his only reference to emancipation was a recommendation to acquire territory to colonize slaves freed by the Confiscation Act. "The people head in the right direction," commented Lydia Maria Child, "but we are unfortunate in the men we have placed in power. Lincoln is narrow-minded, shortsighted, and obstinate."[20]

Petitioning for emancipation now began in earnest. Angelina Grimké Weld circulated a petition, headed *A Declaration of War on Slavery*. Susan B. Anthony, too, felt she must do something to influence public opinion. "I cannot feel easy in my conscience to be dumb in an hour like this," she wrote her good friend, Lydia Mott. So she carried her message to the small towns in western New York, where people were willing to listen because they were troubled by the defeats of the North. They were beginning to see that the problem of slavery had to be faced and Susan B. Anthony answered their questions.

"It is impossible longer to hold the African race in bondage," she told them, "or to reconstruct this Republic on the old slaveholding basis. . . . Hundreds of men who never thought of emancipation a year ago, talk it freely, and are ready to vote for it and fight for it."[21]

"Can the thousands of Northern soldiers," she asked, "who in their march through Rebel States have found faithful friends and generous allies in the slaves ever consent to hurl them back into the hell of slavery, either by word, or vote, or sword? No, no, there can be no reconstruction on the old basis. . . . Far less degrading and ruinous would be the recognition of the independence of the southern Confederacy."

To the questions of what to do with emancipated slaves, she replied, "Treat the Negroes just as you do the Irish, the Scotch, and the Germans. Educate them to all the blessings of our free institutions, to our schools and churches, to every department of industry, trade, and art."

* * *

Pressure for emancipation increased, and during the next few months Congress passed several antislavery measures, one prohibiting army officers from returning fugitive slaves, another for compensated emancipation of all the slaves in the District of Columbia, and still another, prohibiting slavery in all of the territories of the United States. Emancipation in the District of Columbia elicited this comment from Lydia Maria Child, "Well it is something to get slavery abolished in ten miles square, after thirty years of arguing, remonstrating, and petitioning. The effect it will produce is of more importance than the act itself. I am inclined to think that 'old Abe' means about right, only he has a hidebound soul."[22]

The New York *Tribune* had been pressing for emancipation, and now Horace Greeley issued his *Prayer of Twenty Million,* to which Lincoln replied publicly, saying "My paramount object in this struggle is to save the Union, and is not either to save or to destroy slavery. If I could save the Union by freeing any slave, I would do it, and if I could save it by freeing all the slaves I would do it, and if I could save it by freeing some and leaving others alone I would also do that."[23]

In September, 1862, President Lincoln promised freedom, on January 1, 1863, to all slaves in the rebellious states and, as promised, he issued the Emancipation Proclamation on New Year's Day, 1863. Jubilee meetings were held throughout the North and among the abolitionists there was great rejoicing. Yet the abolitionists realized that while the Proclamation was a step in the right direction, it left slavery in the Border States untouched. Slavery still remained, and had to be dealt with. More propaganda was needed for emancipation, and women came forward.

Feeling that more needed to be done to inform the North on the important issues of the war, and that the women of the country must be aroused to demand that this be a war for freedom, Susan B. Anthony conferred with Mrs. Stanton, then living in New York City. Mrs. Stanton, she knew, could always be counted on for sound, forward-looking suggestions. Both felt that women must do more in this crisis than serve as angels of mercy, as valuable and well-organized as this phase of their work had become. Women must be aroused to think about the basic issues of the war and take part in molding public opinion. So far, no decisive Northern victory had inspired confidence. The low morale of the North, the flagrant profiteering, and the insidious propaganda of the Copperheads had to be faced and met and women could help. Women had a big stake in this war with their sons and husbands enlisted in the Army. Men were forming Union Leagues and Loyal Leagues. Why not organize a Women's Loyal League? They talked their ideas over with New York abolitionists, and with Horace Greeley, Theodore Tilton, Henry Ward Beecher, and Robert Dale Owen, the head of the Freedman's Inquiry Commission. All agreed that the Emancipation Proclamation needed to be implemented by an amendment to the Constitution, a Thirteenth Amendment, freeing the slaves. Women could help. They would circulate petitions for a Thirteenth Amendment. Mrs. Stanton then drafted a challenging *Appeal to the Women of the Republic* which she sent out in March, 1863, with a notice of a meeting in New York in May at the Church of the Puritans for the purpose of planning accelerated work in this crisis.

Women responded beyond their highest expectations, coming from many states and filling the church to overflowing. Most of the faithful antislavery women were on hand — Angelina Grimké Weld, Lucy Stone, Antoinette Brown Blackwell, Ernestine Rose, and the popular Hutchinson Singers. Abby Kelley did not come because, as she wrote Susan B. Anthony, she could not in any way commit herself "to the idea of loyalty to the present government."[24] She believed that if the Administration had done its duty, the rebellion would have been put down long ago, and she regarded it, with its supporters, responsible for the terrible waste of treasure and blood thus far, and for that which is to follow. "It needs" she added "strong rebuke instead of unqualified sympathy and support."

Susan B. Anthony opened the meeting with a challenge to women to recognize the real cause of the war. "There is great fear expressed on all sides," she said, "lest this war shall be a war for the Negro. I am willing that it shall be. . . . Shame on us if we do not make it a war to establish the Negro in freedom."[25]

Lucy Stone was elected president, then one by one the women expressed their opinions. Susan B. Anthony proposed a resolution declaring that there could never be a true peace until the civil and political rights of all citizens were established, including Negroes and women. The inclusion of women was questioned by a few. Speaking to the resolution Lucy Stone declared, "If the right of one single human being is to be discarded by us, we fail in our loyalty to the country. . . . We come today to say to those who are administering our Government and fighting our battles, 'While you are going through this valley of humiliation, do not forget that you must be true alike to the women and Negroes.' We can never be truly loyal if we leave them out."

Angelina Grimké Weld added her support to the resolution, saying, "I rejoice exceedingly that the resolution should combine us with the Negro. I feel that we have been with him, that the iron has entered our souls. . . . Woman is full grown today, whether man knows it or not, equal to her rights and equal to the responsibilities of the hour. I want to be identified with the Negro, for until he gets his rights, we shall never have ours."[26]

The resolution was adopted by a large majority. Then Susan B. Anthony, analyzing the issues of the war, reproached Lincoln for suppressing the fact that slavery was the real cause of the war and for waiting for two long years before freeing the slaves in the rebel states. "Every hour's delay, every life sacrificed up to the proclamation that called the slave to freedom and arms," she declared, "was nothing less than downright murder by the government . . . I therefore hail the day when the government shall recognize that it is a war for freedom."[27]

The Women's National Loyal League was then organized, with Mrs. Stanton as president and Susan B. Anthony, secretary, and adopted this resolution, "We loyal women of the Nation, assembled in convention this 14th day of May, 1863, hereby pledge ourselves one to another in a Loyal League to give support to the government in so far as it makes a war for freedom." The League sent a copy of this resolution to President Lincoln, thanking him for the Emancipation Proclamation. Their own immediate task, they decided, was to circulate petitions asking Congress to emancipate "all persons of African descent held in involuntary servitude."

To publicize its work, the League held a large evening meeting at Cooper Institute with speeches by Antoinette Brown Blackwell and Ernestine Rose, and also by Mrs. Stanton, who left the audience with this challenge, "Women have their share in the responsibilities of this hour; in the reconstruction of the government. The battles now being fought on Southern soil, will be fought again in the capital at Washington, when we shall need farseeing statesmen to base the new union on justice, liberty, and equality. Ours is the work of educating the people to make this demand."[28]

Now the humdrum work of circulating petitions began. Susan B. Anthony and Mrs. Stanton opened an office for the Women's Loyal League at Cooper Institute, and here they and their colleagues handled the work of sending out petitions. With each petition went this battle cry, "Women you cannot vote or fight for your country. Your only way to be a power in the government is through the exercise of this one, sacred, constitutional right of petition, and we ask you to use it to the utmost. . . ."

At first the signed petitions came back slowly. Surprising questions were asked, such as, "Is not the work already done? Has not the President proclaimed freedom? Is he not doing the work as fast as he can?"[29] Gradually people began to understand. Republican and antislavery papers endorsed the work of the Women's National Loyal League. The Hovey Trust Fund helped them pay their office expenses and some of the postage. All signing the petitions were asked to contribute a penny to help with expenses and in this way $3,000 was slowly raised. Henry Ward Beecher took up a collection for the League at Plymouth Church, Gerrit Smith sent them a generous contribution, and Wendell Phillips, Frederick Douglass, Horace Greeley, and George William Curtis spoke for them at Cooper Institute, turning over to them the admission fees. In time, Senator Sumner, realizing the value of the petitions in arousing public opinion for a Thirteenth Amendment, saved them the postage by sending their petitions out under his frank. By the end of 1863 they had 100,000 signatures. Assured by Senator Sumner of their great value, they raised the number of signatures in the next few months to 400,000. During the summer of 1863, their work was interrupted by draft riots in New York City during which abolitionists and Negroes were singled out for attack. This made these women realize more than ever the need for the educational work they had undertaken.

The Thirteenth Amendment was introduced in the Senate in January of 1864. In February, the first of the Women's Loyal League petitions were presented to the Senate, making an impressive showing as they were carried into the Senate by two imposing Negroes. More installments followed. When in April, the Thirteenth Amendment passed the Senate and prospects for it in the House were promising, the Women's National Loyal League disbanded, assured that they had played an effective role in creating sentiment for the Amendment, which was adopted December, 1865, and which read: "Neither slavery nor involuntary servitude, except as a punishment for crime, whereof the party shall have been duly convicted, shall exist within the United States or any place subject to their jurisdiction."

CHAPTER XVIII

Looking Toward the Future

Meanwhile, in December, 1863, the American Antislavery Society had held its Third Decade Meeting in Philadelphia to commemorate its founding and to rededicate itself to "the entire and speedy extinction of slavery in every part of the country."[1] There was rejoicing over the President's Emancipation Proclamation which had freed the slaves in the rebel states, but at the same time there was recognition of the work still to be done. While, through the years, differences had developed in the Society over policies, personalities, the support of political parties, and Presidential candidates, all still held to their main object – the complete abolition of slavery.

The antislavery women were on hand for this meeting and expressed their opinions. Lucretia Mott rejoiced over the progress made and over the young people who had joined the ranks. "It may not be necessary," she said, "to continue operations in precisely the same way. But it will be necessary to multiply our periodicals, and scatter them, as we have done heretofore with good effect."[2] Many, she added, who had previously opposed the work of the antislavery society, now acknowledged they were wrong. "Let us welcome them, hail them in their coming and gladly receive them."

Sarah Grimké, Angelina Grimké, and Theodore Weld, unable to be present, sent words of greeting and a warning that "the fittest celebration of the past is to gird ourselves anew for the present and the future."

Maria Weston Chapman was not with them, and Samuel J. May explained her absence. "She thinks," he said, "that our work as an associated body is at an end; and it is not for us to condemn her for that opinion. . . . If she withdraws from us before we think our work is done, let us remember how much earlier than most of us she enlisted in its ranks: how early her clear foresight saw the danger, how eloquent were her pen and her voice . . . how clear was her faith; how brave was her heart." He reminded them how unflinchingly she had faced the Boston mob in 1835, and added, "We can have no blame for such a servant as that."[3]

Susan B. Anthony then told her colleagues what she saw as the important work ahead. She recalled how she, when new in the antislavery movement, had felt that work with fugitive slaves was very important, but she soon learned that fugitive slaves would be aided by common philanthropy and benevolence and that radical abolitionists must give their attention and efforts to the removal of the reason for the existence of fugitive slaves. Just so today, she was convinced, the abolitionists, who for thirty years had worked for the freedom of the slave, "must now go on with their fundamental work of removing the laws which allow the existence of slavery, leaving to others the care of the freedmen and the sick and wounded on the battlefield."[4]

Lucy Stone expressed her gratitude to the men and women who had founded the American Antislavery Society in 1833. "I thank God for them," she declared, "and I concur in the ground they take that much remains to be done. Prejudice against the Negro is to be overcome; for slavery is let down deeper in the hearts of the people of this country than they themselves know. . . . I cannot help feeling that there is a great deal of proslavery sentiment yet to be rooted out. We all need to work for it."[5]

Abby Kelley warned her colleagues that although there had been a great change in public sentiment because of the work of the American Antislavery Society, they must not be too confident. She reminded them of the mobs that abolitionists had faced in Boston in 1860 and 1861 and in western New York and Pennsylvania, mobs that were determined to wipe out free speech. She believed that this spirit still smoldered. "It is only by labor, incessant labor, in season and out of season," she declared, "that we can create such a public sentiment as we need." She warned that many men and women who had worked long and devotedly in the antislavery societies now felt that their work was over. "Let us not be too confident," she added. "Do not let us dwell too much on what has been done. . . . Nothing is done while anything remains to be done, so far as the death of American slavery is concerned. . . . So far as the accomplishment of the overthrow of slavery is concerned, were success to attend the Federal arms today, I feel confident that slavery would linger . . . and I am willing therefore to wait . . . if need be in order to insure its destruction."[6]

* * *

Abolitionists, both men and women, differed over the reelection of Abraham Lincoln. Many did not trust him to handle the Negro question adequately. Even Garrison and Phillips were at odds on this subject, Garrison endorsing Lincoln in the *Liberator* and Phillips campaigning vigorously for Frémont until he withdrew as a candidate. They continued to disagree over what those critical days demanded of abolitionists. Most of the antislavery women, with the exception of Lydia Maria Child, opposed the reelection of Lincoln, and when he was reelected she commented, "With all his deficiencies, it must be admitted that he has grown continually. . . . It was great good luck to have the people elect a man who was willing to grow."[7]

In January, 1865, Garrison proposed that the Massachusetts Antislavery Society be dissolved after the Thirteenth Amendment had been adopted, believing as he did that there then would be no more work for abolitionists. The Thirteenth Amendment had been passed by the Senate in 1864, was passed by the House on January 31, 1865, and was ratified by the states in December, 1865. Garrison then discontinued the *Liberator*.

In May, he had tried unsuccessfully to persuade the American Antislavery Society to disband. By this time Lee had surrendered, Lincoln had been assassinated, and Andrew Jackson had succeeded him as President. Garrison's proposal to dissolve the Society was vigorously opposed by Wendell Phillips, Parker Pillsbury, the Fosters, Frederick Douglass, James and Lucretia Mott, and others, with the result that Garrison retired from the Society, Wendell Phillips was elected President, and the *National Antislavery Standard*, with Parker Pillsbury as editor, was continued. Most of the active antislavery women agreed with Phillips that the Society and its paper were still needed. Their work as they saw it was to win full citizenship rights for the Negro. This seemed increasingly important with Andrew Jackson at the helm. Lucretia Mott pointed out the serious conditions existing in the South among Negroes in spite of the legal abolition of slavery and urged the continued existence of the Antislavery Society to keep its members on the watch and to keep their interest alive in the great cause. Abby Kelley, Elizabeth Cady Stanton, and Susan B. Anthony likewise saw much work still ahead, and began campaigning for political and civil rights for the Negro.

Women had learned a great deal in the antislavery movement. Working for an ideal, the freedom of Negro slaves, they had been ready to defy tradition by speaking at antislavery meetings and by holding antislavery conventions. So out of tune was this with the general conception of woman's place in society and with what the Church taught regarding the role of women, that at first even some of the men in antislavery societies had questioned their activities and opposed them. In fact, a few even left the American Antislavery Society because they disagreed on this issue. This attitude made it plain to the antislavery women that their own status under law and custom was much like that of the Negro slave, and they had begun to work for women's rights as well as for Negro rights. Angelina and Sarah Grimké were among the first to recognize the need of this. Elizabeth Cady Stanton and Lucretia Mott were influenced by the World's Antislavery Convention to call the First Woman's Rights Convention in Seneca Falls, New York, in 1848. The First National Woman's Rights Convention in Worcester, Massachusetts, in 1850, was called by antislavery men and women, thus showing plainly the antislavery origins of the woman's rights movement. In fact, up to the Civil War, woman's rights conventions were held annually in conjunction with the May meetings in New York of the American Antislavery Society, whose members usually took part. During these years, some progress was made in improving the property rights of married women.

With the war over and reconstruction in the South underway, people began thinking about and discussing the rights of citizens and the Constitution. Amendments to the Constitution were being proposed, rebel states were being readmitted to the Union with new constitutions, state constitutions in the North were being revised and western territories were seeking statehood. In the opinion of Susan B. Anthony,

Elizabeth Cady Stanton, and Lucy Stone, the time was ripe to demand equal rights for all – for Negroes and for women.

It was becoming obvious that a Fourteenth Amendment was necessary to extend civil rights and suffrage to Negroes, and Susan B. Anthony, speaking in Kansas in 1865, warned that slavery could "readily be re-enthroned under the new guise of Negro disfranchisement," and added that "unless the Negro was given the vote, rebels would be put in office and a new code of laws apprenticing Negroes would be formed, establishing a new form of slavery."[8]

The Fourteenth Amendment, which it was thought would extend civil rights and suffrage to Negroes, read: "All persons born or naturalized in the United States and subject to the jurisdiction thereof, are citizens of the United States and of the State wherein they reside. No State shall make or enforce any law which shall abridge the privileges or immunities of citizens of the United States; nor shall any State deprive any person of life, liberty, or property, without due process of law; nor deny to any person within its jurisdiction the equal protection of the laws."

Reading it over hopefully, Mrs. Stanton and Susan B. Anthony discovered to their dismay that the word "male" had been written into the second section as a qualification for voters. At once they sounded an alarm among their antislavery colleagues and petitioned Congress to enfranchise women either before or at the same time as Negroes. Expecting support as a matter of course from the men with whom they had worked in the antislavery movement, they were astonished to hear Wendell Phillips say that he did not want to mix Negro and woman suffrage. To him the Negro came first. Women could wait. This was the Negro's hour. This slogan was repeated so constantly that people in general, and even some women, actually believed that it was more important to enfranchise thousands of illiterate Negroes than to confer the inherent right of citizenship upon educated, intelligent women, granddaughters of the founders of the Republic. Mrs. Stanton, Susan B. Anthony, and Lucy Stone pleaded with Senator Sumner to leave the word "male" out of the Fourteenth Amendment, but with no success. He told them he had written and rewritten the resolution, trying to avoid the word, but he and other Republicans had come to the conclusion that the only way they could confer suffrage on Negroes without granting it to women was to write "male" into the Amendment. They were convinced that Negro suffrage was all the strain the Republican party could bear. Mrs. Stanton and Susan B. Anthony were not fooled by this sophistry. They realized that Republican politicians saw in the Negro vote in the South the means of keeping their party in power for a long time. In comparison, the women of the North were unimportant.

Meanwhile, Susan B. Anthony, Mrs. Stanton, Lucy Stone, and others continued to send petitions with many signatures to Congress, asking for woman suffrage. These petitions in 1866 were the first demands ever made for Congressional action on woman suffrage. Senator Sumner, for whom women had rolled up petitions for the Thirteenth Amendment, now presented, under protest as most inopportune, a woman suffrage petition, headed by the name of his good friend, Lydia Maria Child.

The Fourteenth Amendment, with the word "male" in its second section as a qualification for voters, was passed by Congress in 1866, but was not ratified until 1868.

* * *

After the ratification of the Fourteenth Amendment, Republicans began to realize that it would not enfranchise

Negroes. Actually it did not even guarantee them civil rights, for the Supreme Court had previously ruled in the Dred Scott Decision that Negroes were not citizens. To enfranchise Negroes, the Fifteenth Amendment was then proposed. Seeing this as an exceptional opportunity to enfranchise women as well, Susan B. Anthony, Elizabeth Cady Stanton, and Lucy Stone did their best to convince Republicans that it should be worded to include women by adding the word "sex" to the phrase, "race, color, or previous condition of servitude."

Again, the politicians opposed them, and again the leading men of the antislavery movement urged women to step aside for the Negro and press their claims later. In this crisis, Lucy Stone wrote John Greenleaf Whittier, "You know Phillips takes the ground that this is the Negro's hour, and that women, if not criminal, are at least not wise to urge their own claims. Now, so sure am I that he is mistaken and that the only name given, by which the country can be saved is woman, that I want to ask you . . . to use your influence to induce him to reconsider the position he has taken."[9]

Among the leading men in the antislavery movement only Parker Pillsbury, Samuel J. May, James Mott, and Robert Purvis, the cultured, wealthy Philadelphia Negro, were willing to support women in their demand for woman suffrage at that time. Frederick Douglass and the Fosters deserted them, regarding the Negro as all-important. Many of the antislavery women were persuaded to be unselfish and to step aside for the Negro. Less than a dozen remained steadfast for woman suffrage as well as Negro suffrage – Susan B. Anthony, Elizabeth Cady Stanton, Lucretia Mott, Martha C. Wright, Ernestine Rose, and, for a time, Lucy Stone.

In February, 1869, both the Senate and House of Representatives passed and sent to the states for ratification the Fifteenth Amendment, enfranchising male Negroes and ignoring women, although women had been asking for the vote for twenty-one years, since 1848. The Fifteenth Amendment was ratified in 1870 and read: "The right of citizens of the United States to vote shall not be denied or abridged by the United States or by any State on account of race, color, or previous condition of servitude."

Disappointed, but undaunted, women now pressed for a Sixteenth Amendment, granting suffrage to women. Continuing their campaign, they built up strong woman suffrage organizations, but it took fifty more years before women were enfranchised throughout the United States by the Nineteenth Amendment, in 1920. In the meantime, they had tried several times through legal appeals to establish their right to vote, claiming this right as "persons" under the Fourteenth Amendment and as "citizens" under the Fifteenth Amendment, but the Supreme Court had ruled against them.

* * *

During these later years, the Negro's civil rights and voting rights have again become burning issues. Integration of Negroes in the public schools has been enforced by a Supreme Court decision based on the Fourteenth Amendment, but to enforce civil and voting rights for the Negro, it was found necessary to implement the Fourteenth and Fifteenth Amendments by means of the Civil Rights Act. Through all this, many women, with their eyes on the American ideal of equal rights for all, have given their support to the Negro's struggle for human rights. A few alert women were able to get the word, sex, included in the no-job-discrimination provision of the Civil Rights Act, with the result that job discrimination on the ground of race, color, religion, national origin, and sex is now prohibited by law.

This is not only the Negro's hour, it is also woman's hour.

Negroes and women continue to press toward the goal of complete citizenship. Angelina Grimké Weld saw clearly in 1863 that the Negro's rights and woman's rights were inseparable in the larger struggle for human rights.

The experience of the Negro indicates clearly that women, too, need to implement the Fourteenth Amendment in order to make applicable to them the Amendment's guarantee of the "equal protection of the laws." Through the years, repeated Supreme Court decisions, as late as 1961, have held that women do not rate the "equal protection of the laws" because they were not regarded as legal "persons" when the Constitution and the Fourteenth Amendment were adopted. This means that women have no legal protection against discrimination. To remedy this, an Equal Rights for Women Amendment is now before Congress. It reads: "Equality of rights under the law shall not be denied or abridged by the United States or by any State on account of sex." This Amendment was first introduced forty-four years ago, and has been reintroduced in every session of Congress. It is of vital importance because it would remove from the law all surviving evidences of the common-law doctrine of the subordinate position of women and would establish the principle of the equality of the sexes as a fundamental part of the legal system of our country.

May the women of today finish the work for Negroes and women which the intrepid antislavery women began!

NOTES

CHAPTER I *Voices Crying in the Wilderness*

1. Elizabeth Margaret Chandler, *Poetical Works* (Philadelphia, 1836), p. 136.
2. Thomas E. Drake, *Quaker and Slavery in America* (New Haven, 1950), pp. 13, 72.
3. Dwight S. Dumond, *Antislavery, The Crusade for Freedom in America* (Ann Arbor, Michigan, 1961), pp. 29, 30, 49.
4. John J. Chapman, *William Lloyd Garrison* (New York, 1913), p. 9.
5. Benjamin Lundy, *Memoirs of the Life and Character of Elizabeth Margaret Chandler* (Philadelphia, 1836), pp. 22–24.
6. Elizabeth Margaret Chandler, *Essays, Philanthropic and Moral* (Philadelphia, 1836), pp. 9, 46.
7. Russel B. Nye, *William Lloyd Garrison* (Boston, 1955), p. 28.
8. Letters of June 20, 1832. Margaret Chandler Papers, Michigan Historical Collections, University of Michigan.
9. *Ibid.,* February 12, 1832.
10. *Ibid.,* March 25, 1831.
11. Wendell P. and Francis J. Garrison, *William Lloyd Garrison* (New York, 1885–1889), I, 304.
12. Chandler Papers, Michigan Historical Collection, March 30, 1832.
13. *Genius of Universal Emancipation* (Washington, D.C., September, 1833), p. 174.
14. Lundy, *Memoirs of the Life and Character of Elizabeth Margaret Chandler,* p. 39.
15. *The Liberator* (Boston, December 2, 1853), p. 190.
16. Chandler Papers, Michigan Historical Collections, May 4, 1835.
17. *Ibid.,* August 8, 1835.
18. *Genius of Universal Emancipation,* December, 1836.

19. Maria Weston Chapman, *Right and Wrong in Massachusetts.* Report of Boston Female Antislavery Society, 1836, p. 77.
20. William Lloyd Garrison Papers, Boston Public Library.

CHAPTER II *William Lloyd Garrison Calls Out the Women*

1. Wendell P. and Francis J. Garrison, *William Lloyd Garrison* (New York, 1885–1889), I, 305.
2. *The Liberator* (Boston, 1832), 2:183.
3. W. P. and F. J. Garrison, *William Lloyd Garrison,* II, 49.
4. *Ibid.,* I, 225.
5. Maria Weston Chapman, *Right and Wrong in Boston.* Report of Boston Female Antislavery Society, 1839, pp. 4–5.
6. Samuel J. May, *Some Recollections of Our Antislavery Conflict* (Boston, 1869), p. 37.
7. Lydia Maria Child, *Letters from New York* (New York, 1846), II, 255.
8. John White Chadwick, *A Life for Liberty* (New York, 1899), pp. 175–176.
9. John Albree (ed.), *Whittier Correspondence from the Oak Knoll Collections,* 1830–1892 (Salem, Mass., 1911), p. 146.
10. *The Liberator,* May 25, 1833.
11. William Lloyd Garrison Papers, Boston Public Library, January 12, 1833.
12. *The Liberator,* March 2, 1833.
13. Wendell Phillips Garrison, *Century Magazine,* September, 1885, pp. 782–783.
14. Garrison Papers, Boston Public Library, March 18, 1833.
15. Edwin W. and Miriam R. Small, *Prudence Crandall, Champion of Negro Education* (Brunswick, Maine, 1944), p. 317.
16. Cornell University Library. April 17, 1833.
17. W. P. Garrison, *Century Magazine,* September, 1885, p. 785.
18. Samuel J. May, *Some Recollections of Our Antislavery Conflict,* p. 55.

19. Dwight S. Dumond, *Antislavery, The Crusade for Freedom in America* (Ann Arbor, Michigan, 1961), p. 212.
20. W. P. and J. F. Garrison, *William Lloyd Garrison,* I, 432.
21. Portrait given by S. J. May, to Cornell University.
22. Samuel J. May Papers, Cornell University Library, Letter to Miller McKim, September 25, 1834.
23. Samuel J. May, *Some Recollections of Our Antislavery Conflict,* p. 7.
24. George B. Thayer, *Pedal and Path* (Hartford, 1888), pp. 528–529.
25. Connecticut College Library, Prudence Crandall Papers, November 3, 1885.
26. W. and M. Small, *Prudence Crandall,* p. 528.

CHAPTER III *Women Take Hold*

1. Anna Davis Hallowell, *James and Lucretia Mott* (Boston, 1884), pp. 115–116.
2. Samuel J. May, *Some Recollections of Our Antislavery Conflict* (Boston, 1869), p. 852.
3. *Proceedings of the American Antislavery Society at its Third Decade Meeting* (New York, 1864), p. 41.
4. W. P. and F. J. Garrison, *William Lloyd Garrison* (New York, 1885–1889), I, 413.
5. Anna Davis Hallowell, *James and Lucretia Mott* (Boston, 1884), p. 121.
6. *Letters of Lydia Maria Child* (Boston, 1883), p. 15.
7. Maria Weston Chapman, *Right and Wrong in Boston, 1836* (Boston, 1836), p. 14.
8. *Ibid.,* p. 28.
9. *Ibid.,* pp. 33–34.
10. *Ibid.,* p. 38.
11. Weston Papers, Boston Public Library.
12. Harriet Martineau, *The Martyr Age* (Boston, 1839), p. 54.
13. Maria Weston Chapman, *Right and Wrong in Boston, 1836.* (Boston, 1836), p. 49.

14. W. P. and F. J. Garrison, *William Lloyd Garrison* (New York 1885–1889), I, 422.
15. L. B. Chace Wyman and A. C. Wyman, *Elizabeth Buffum Chace, 1806–99, Her Life and Its Environment* (Boston, 1914) p. 136.
16. W. P. and F. J. Garrison, *William Lloyd Garrison* (New York 1885–1889), I, 433.
17. *Ibid.*, I, 423.
18. Harriet Martineau, *Autobiography* (London, 1877), II, 39–41
19. *Ibid.*, p. 32.
20. Maria Weston Chapman, *Right and Wrong in Boston, 183*[illegible] (Boston, 1836), p. 94.
21. Harriet Martineau, *Autobiography* (London, 1877), II, 39–41
22. ——— *Retrospect of Western Travel* (London, 1887), II, 218
23. W. P. and F. J. Garrison, *William Lloyd Garrison* (New York 1885–1889), II, 98–99.

CHAPTER IV *"A Parcel of Silly Women"*

1. John W. Chadwick, *William Ellery Channing* (Boston, 1903) p. 275.
2. W. P. and F. J. Garrison, *William Lloyd Garrison* (New York 1885–1889), II, 65.
3. *Ibid.*, p. 55.
4. *Ibid.*, p. 91n.
5. *Ibid.*, p. 90.
6. Maria Weston Chapman, *Right and Wrong in Boston* (Boston 1836), p. 30.
7. *Ibid.*, p. 36.
8. W. P. and F. J. Garrison, *William Lloyd Garrison* (New York 1885–1889), II, 76.
9. Russel B. Nye, *William Lloyd Garrison* (Boston, 1955), pp 103–104.
10. W. P. and F. J. Garrison, *William Lloyd Garrison* (New York 1885–1889), II, 96–97n.
11. L. B. C. Wyman and A. Wyman, *Elizabeth Buffum Chace*

1806–99, Her Life and Its Environment (Boston, 1914), I, 56–58.

12. Maria Weston Chapman, *Right and Wrong in Boston* (Boston, 1836), pp. 50–62.
13. *Ibid.*, pp. 64–70.
14. *Ibid.*, p. 116.
15. Weston Papers, January 22, 1836, Boston Public Library.
16. *Ibid.*, October 17, 1836, Boston Public Library.
17. *Ann Phillips: A Memorial Sketch* (Boston, 1886), p. 5.
18. Weston Papers, December 13, 1836, Boston Public Library.
19. Harriet Martineau, *The Martyr Age* (Boston, 1839), p. 70.
20. Irving H. Bartlett, *Wendell Phillips* (Boston, 1961), p. 48.
21. Oscar Sherwin, *Prophet of Liberty* (New York, 1958), p. 67.
22. Chapman Papers, December 30, 1837, Boston Public Library.
23. *Ibid.*, December 1, 1839.
24. November 25, 1837, Abby Kelley Foster Papers, American Antiquarian Society, Worcester, Mass.
25. January 26, 1885, Abby Kelley Foster Papers, Worcester Historical Society.
26. *Ibid.*, December 10, 1837.

CHAPTER V *Voices from the South*

1. Catherine H. Birney, *The Grimké Sisters* (Boston, 1885), p. 18.
2. *Ibid.*, p. 123.
3. *Liberator*, September 9, 1835.
4. Catherine H. Birney, *The Grimké Sisters* (Boston, 1885), p. 138.
5. *Ibid.*, p. 146.
6. *Ibid.*, p. 148.
7. *Ibid.*, p. 155.
8. *Ibid.*, p. 159.
9. *Ibid.*, p. 162.
10. G. H. Barnes and D. L. Dumond, *Weld-Grimké Letters* (New York, 1934), p. 363.

11. Catherine H. Birney, *The Grimké Sisters* (Boston, 1885), p. 166.
12. *Ibid.*, p. 165.

CHAPTER VI *The First Antislavery Convention of American Women*

1. September 9, 1836, Maria Weston Chapman Papers, Boston Public Library.
2. *Ibid.*, April 17, 1837, Weston Papers, Boston Public Library.
3. *Proceedings First Antislavery Convention of American Women* (New York, 1837).
4. G. H. Barnes and D. L. Dumond, *Weld-Grimké Letters* (New York, 1934), p. 396.
5. Samuel J. May, *Some Recollections of Our Antislavery Conflict* (Boston, 1869), pp. 234–235.
6. July 30, 1837, Garrison Papers, Boston Public Library.
7. Catherine H. Birney, *The Grimké Sisters* (Boston, 1885), p. 198.
8. G. H. Barnes and D. L. Dumond, *Weld-Grimké Letters* (New York, 1934), p. 413.
9. *Ibid.*, p. 416.
10. *Ibid.*, p. 418.
11. Catherine H. Birney, *The Grimké Sisters* (Boston, 1885), p. 183.

CHAPTER VII *The Pastoral Letter*

1. Maria Weston Chapman, *Right and Wrong in Boston* (Boston, 1837), pp. 46–47.
2. Whitman Bennett, *Whittier, Bard of Freedom* (Chapel Hill, 1941), p. 109.
3. Elizabeth Cady Stanton and Susan B. Anthony, *History of Woman Suffrage* (New York, 1881), I, 82–83.
4. Maria Weston Chapman, *Right and Wrong in Boston* (Boston, 1837), pp. 74–75.
5. G. H. Barnes and D. L. Dumond, *Weld-Grimké Letters* (New York, 1934), I, 415.

6. Otelia Cromwell, *Lucretia Mott* (Cambridge, Mass., 1958), p. 145.
7. Catherine H. Birney, *The Grimké Sisters* (Boston, 1885), p. 190.
8. Oliver Johnson, *William Lloyd Garrison and His Times* (Boston, 1879), p. 259.
9. Catherine H. Birney, *The Grimké Sisters* (Boston, 1885), pp. 193–194.
10. G. H. Barnes and D. L. Dumond, *Weld-Grimké Letters* (New York, 1934), I, 439, 441.
11. Catherine H. Birney, *The Grimké Sisters* (New York, 1885), p. 224.
12. G. H. Barnes and D. L. Dumond, *Weld-Grimké Letters* (New York, 1934), I, 483.
13. *Ibid.*, I, 500.
14. *Ibid.*, I, 424, 426–427.
15. Catherine H. Birney, *The Grimké Sisters* (New York, 1885), pp. 212–213.
16. G. H. Barnes and D. L. Dumond, *Weld-Grimké Letters* (New York, 1934), I, 428–430.
17. Catherine H. Birney, *The Grimké Sisters* (New York, 1885), pp. 225–226.
18. G. H. Barnes and D. L. Dumond, *Weld-Grimké Letters* (New York, 1934), II, 520.
19. *Ibid.*, II, 532–535.
20. *Ibid.*, II, 537–538.

CHAPTER VIII *Angelina Grimké Overrides the Woman Question*

1. Catherine H. Birney, *The Grimké Sisters* (Boston, 1885), pp. 227–228.
2. G. H. Barnes and D. L. Dumond, *Weld-Grimké Letters* (New York, 1934), II, 564.
3. *Liberator*, March 9, 1838, p. 35, Birney, p. 228.
4. G. H. Barnes and D. L. Dumond, *Weld-Grimké Letters* (New York, 1934), II, 573–574.

5. *Ibid.*, II, 605.
6. *Ibid.*, II, 612.
7. E. C. Stanton and S. B. Anthony, *History of Woman Suffrage* (New York, 1881), I, 399.
8. G. H. Barnes and D. L. Dumond, *Weld-Grimké Letters* (New York, 1934), p. 611.
9. *Ibid.*, II, 610, 628.
10. *Ibid.*, II, 637.
11. *Ibid.*, II, 647, 649.
12. *Ibid.*, II, 657, 661.
13. May 10, 1835, Abby Kelley Foster Papers, American Antiquarian Society, Worcester, Mass.
14. Catherine H. Birney, *The Grimké Sisters* (Boston, 1885), pp. 232–233.
15. To Elizabeth Pease, August 30, 1838, Maria Weston Chapman Papers, Boston Public Library.
16. G. H. Barnes and D. L. Dumond, *Weld-Grimké Letters* (New York, 1954), II, 678–679.
17. Lawrence Lader, *The Bold Brahmins* (New York, 1961), p. 59.
18. Catherine H. Birney, *The Grimké Sisters* (Boston, 1885), pp. 237–241.
19. *History of Pennsylvania Hall* (Philadelphia, 1838), p. 126.
20. W. P. and F. J. Garrison, *William Lloyd Garrison* (New York, 1885–1889), II, 215.
21. *Antislavery Convention of American Women, Report of a Delegate* (Boston, 1838).
22. To Elizabeth Pease, August 30, 1838, Maria Weston Chapman Papers, Boston Public Library.
23. *Antislavery Convention of American Women, Report of a Delegate* (Boston, 1838).
24. June 7, 1838, Maria Weston Chapman Papers, Boston Public Library.
25. *Antislavery Convention of American Women, Report of a Delegate* (Boston, 1838).

26. Anna Davis Hallowell, *James and Lucretia Mott* (Boston, 1884), p. 136.
27. G. H. Barnes and D. L. Dumond, *Weld-Grimké Letters* (New York, 1934), II, 747.

CHAPTER IX *The Doors Open for Women*

1. Oliver Johnson, *William Lloyd Garrison and His Times* (Boston, 1879), p. 271.
2. W. P. and F. J. Garrison, *William Lloyd Garrison* (New York, 1885–1889), p. 221.
3. July 15, 1838, Weston Papers, Boston Public Library.
4. *Liberator,* 8:154.
5. 1839, Maria Weston Chapman Papers, Boston Public Library.
6. *Ibid.,* May 15, 1839.
7. April 14, 1839, Abby Kelley Foster Papers, American Antiquarian Society, Worcester, Mass.
8. *Ibid.,* February 25, 1839.
9. Maria Weston Chapman, *Right and Wrong in Boston* (Boston, 1839), pp. 100–109.
10. *Ibid.,* p. 117.
11. *Liberator,* Extra, May 15, 1840.
12. Walter M. Merrill, *Against the Wind, A Biography of William Lloyd Garrison* (Cambridge, Mass., 1963), p. 156.
13. *Liberator,* May 17, 1839, p. 79.
14. March 18, 1839, Abby Kelley Foster Papers, American Antiquarian Society, Worcester, Mass.
15. March 16, 1840, Maria Weston Chapman Papers, Boston Public Library.
16. Russel B. Nye, *William Lloyd Garrison* (Boston, 1955), p. 126.
17. *Ibid.,* p. 127.
18. December 15, 1839, William Lloyd Garrison Papers, Boston Public Library.
19. *Ibid.,* December 30, 1839.
20. *Liberator,* March 6, 1840.
21. *New England Quarterly,* June, 1964, p. 252.

22. Albert Mordell, *Quaker Militant* (Boston, 1933), p. 115.
23. G. H. Barnes and D. L. Dumond, *Weld-Grimké Letters* (New York, 1934), II, 842.
24. *Ibid.*, pp. 836, 938.

CHAPTER X *The World's Antislavery Convention*

1. Garrison Papers, Boston Public Library.
2. *Liberator*, May 22, 1940.
3. Catherine H. Birney, *The Grimké Sisters* (Boston, 1885), p. 252.
4. G. H. Barnes and D. L. Dumond, *Weld-Grimké Letters* (New York, 1934), p. 842.
5. May 13, 1840, November 4, 1840, Weston Letters, Boston Public Library.
6. Frederick B. Tolles, Editor, *Slavery and the Woman Question* (Haverford, Pa., 1952), pp. 14, 22–23, 25.
7. Mary Grew, Diary, 1840, p. 27, Alma Lutz Collection, Schlesinger Library, Radcliffe College.
8. Otelia Cromwell, *Lucretia Mott* (Cambridge, Mass., 1958), p. 79.
9. Theodore Stanton and Harriot Stanton Blatch, Editors, *Elizabeth Cady Stanton as Revealed in Her Letters, Diary, and Reminiscences* (New York, 1922), I, 75.
10. Frederick B. Tolles, Editor, *Slavery and the Woman Question* (Haverford, Pa., 1952), p. 41.
11. *Ibid.*, p. 29.
12. E. C. Stanton and S. B. Anthony, *History of Woman Suffrage* (New York, 1881), I, 60.
13. *Eminent Women of the Age* (Hartford, Conn., 1869), p. 369.
14. Lorenzo Sears, *Wendell Phillips* (New York, 1909), p. 81.
15. E. C. Stanton and S. B. Anthony, *History of Woman Suffrage* (New York, 1881), I, 55–58.
16. Theodore Stanton and Harriot Stanton Blatch, Editors, *Elizabeth Cady Stanton as Revealed in Her Letters, Diary and Reminiscences* (New York, 1922), I, 77.

17. W. P. and F. J. Garrison, *William Lloyd Garrison* (New York, 1885–1889), II, 361.
18. *Ibid.,* II, 374, Note p. 376.
19. Mary Grew, Diary, 1840, Alma Lutz Collection, Schlesinger Library, Radcliffe College.
20. Frederick B. Tolles, Editor, *Slavery and the Woman Question* (Haverford, Pa., 1952), p. 47.
21. W. P. and F. J. Garrison, *William Lloyd Garrison* (New York, 1885–1889), II, 388.
22. Anna Davis Hallowell, *James and Lucretia Mott* (Boston, 1884), p. 189.
23. Frederick B. Tolles, Editor, *Slavery and the Woman Question,* p. 79.
24. W. P. and F. J. Garrison, *William Lloyd Garrison* (New York, 1885–1889), II, 378.
25. G. H. Barnes and D. L. Dumond, *Weld-Grimké Letters* (New York, 1934), II, 847.
26. December 14, 1840, Garrison Papers, Boston Public Library.
27. July 29, 1840, Maria Weston Chapman Papers, Boston Public Library.
28. *Ibid.*
29. *Ibid.*
30. Theodore Stanton and Harriot Stanton Blatch, Editors, *Elizabeth Cady Stanton as Revealed in Her Letters, Diary and Reminiscences* (New York, 1922), p. 77.

CHAPTER XI *Women to the Rescue*

1. January 29, 1843, Quincy-Webb Letters, Boston Public Library.
2. June 11, 1841, *National Antislavery Standard.*
3. *Ibid.,* August 10 and July 15, 1841.
4. *Ibid.,* June 24, 1841.
5. *Liberator,* October 29, 1841.
6. July 8, 1841, Weston Papers, Boston Public Library.
7. Margaret Farrand Thorp, *Female Persuasion* (New Haven, Conn., 1949), p. 254.

8. Lydia and David Child Papers, Boston Public Library.
9. August 25, 1841, Weston Papers, Boston Public Library.
10. November 11, 1841, *National Antislavery Standard.*
11. Ethel K. Ware, *Lydia Maria Child and Antislavery,* Bulletin of the Boston Public Library, October 1951, p. 267.
12. Lydia Maria Child, *Letters from New York* (New York, 1846), Introduction.
13. James Russell Lowell, *Fables for Critics* (Boston, 1891).
14. Margaret Farrand Thorp, *Female Persuasion* (New Haven, Conn., 1941), p. 239.
15. 1841, Lydia and David Child Letters, Boston Public Library.
16. *Ibid.*
17. W. P. and F. J. Garrison, *William Lloyd Garrison* (New York, 1885–1889), III, 53.
18. 1841, Lydia and David Child Letters, Boston Public Library.
19. *Ibid.*
20. *National Antislavery Standard,* June 4, 1842.
21. *Liberator,* April 29, 1842.
22. Lydia and David Child Letters, Boston Public Library.
23. Texas had declared its independence from Mexico in 1836.
24. July 22, 1843, Abby Kelley Foster Papers, American Antiquarian Society, Worcester, Mass.
25. 1843, Lydia and David Child Letters, Boston Public Library.
26. September 14, 1845, Abby Kelley Foster Papers, American Antiquarian Society, Worcester, Mass.
27. October 22, 1843, Gay Collection, Columbia University Library.
28. *National Antislavery Standard,* December 9, 1843.

CHAPTER XII *Garrison's Lieutenant*

1. Thomas Wentworth Higginson, *Letters and Journals* (Boston, 1921), pp. 9–10.
2. W. P. and F. J. Garrison, *William Lloyd Garrison* (New York, 1885–1889), III, 178–182.

3. *Bulletin of Friends Historical Association* (Haverford, Pa.), Vol. 35, No. 2, pp. 68–75.
4. 1842, Maria Weston Chapman Papers, Boston Public Library.
5. January 29, 1843, Quincy-Webb Letters, Boston Public Library.
6. *Ibid.*
7. *Liberator,* July 9, 1843.
8. Oscar Sherwin, *Prophet of Liberty* (New York, 1955), p. 136.
9. *Ibid.,* p. 138.
10. September 14, 1844, Quincy-Webb Letters. Boston Public Library.
11. Gay Papers, Columbia University Library.
12. *Ibid.*
13. March 20, 1845, *National Antislavery Standard.*
14. February 10, 1844, Cornell University Library, Ithaca, N.Y.
15. October 22, 1843, Gay Papers, Columbia University Library.
16. *Ibid.,* February, 1846.
17. September 14, 1845, Abby Kelley Foster Papers, American Antiquarian Society, Worcester, Mass.
18. Maria Weston Chapman Papers, Boston Public Library.
19. September 14, 1845, Abby Kelley Foster Papers, American Antiquarian Society, Worcester, Mass.
20. *Liberty Bell* (Boston, 1845).
21. W. P. and F. J. Garrison, *William Lloyd Garrison* (New York, 1885–1889), III, p. 211.
22. *Ibid.,* pp. 220–221.
23. March 9, 1848, Quincy-Webb Letters, Boston Public Library.
24. W. P. and F. J. Garrison, *William Lloyd Garrison* (New York, 1885–1889), III, 229.
25. March 9, 1848, Quincy-Webb Letters, Boston Public Library.

CHAPTER XIII *Abby Kelley*

1. February 24, 1838, Abby Kelley Foster Papers, Worcester Historical Society.

2. February 25, 1839, Abby Kelley Foster Papers, American Antiquarian Society, Worcester, Mass.
3. *Ibid.,* to Alla, 1885.
4. *Ibid.*
5. *Ibid.,* 1885.
6. June 11, 1840, *National Antislavery Standard,* New York.
7. *Liberator,* April 11, 1840, Boston.
8. November 19, 1840, *National Antislavery Standard,* New York.
9. Garrison Papers, Boston Public Library.
10. W. P. and F. J. Garrison, *William Lloyd Garrison* (New York, 1885–1889), II, 419.
11. October 15, 1840, *National Antislavery Standard,* New York.
12. Abby Kelley Foster Papers, Worcester Historical Society.
13. August 7, 1841, Abby Kelley Foster Papers, American Antiquarian Society, Worcester, Mass.
14. *Liberator,* September 30, 1841, Boston.
15. *Liberator,* November 16, 1842 and September 23, 1843.
16. October 30, 1843, Abby Kelley Foster Papers, American Antiquarian Society, Worcester, Mass.
17. *Ibid.,* November 30, 1843.
18. *Ibid.,* August 24, 27, 30, 1843.
19. *Ibid.,* October 12, 1843.
20. *Ibid.,* 1843.
21. *Ibid.,* March 28, 1843.
22. *Ibid.,* August 30, 1843.
23. *Ibid.,* August 10, 1843.
24. *Ibid.,* August 13, 1843.
25. *Ibid.,* February 16, 1844.
26. *Ibid.,* September 4, 1843.
27. September 1, 1843, Garrison Papers, Boston Public Library.
28. Maria Weston Chapman Papers, Boston Public Library, November 2, 1843.
29. November 5, 1843, Garrison Papers, Boston Public Library.

30. January 11, 1844, Abby Kelley Foster Papers, American Antiquarian Society, Worcester, Mass.
31. *Ibid.,* September 4, 1843.
32. W. P. and F. J. Garrison, *William Lloyd Garrison* (New York, 1885–1889), III, 96.
33. November 25, 1843, Abby Kelley Foster Papers, American Antiquarian Society, Worcester, Mass.
34. *Ibid.,* April 22, 1844.
35. *Ibid.,* March 18, 1844.
36. *Ibid.,* April 22, 1844.
37. June 9, 1844, Abby Kelley Foster Papers, Worcester Historical Society.
38. August, 1844, Arthur and Elizabeth Schlesinger Library, Radcliffe College, Cambridge, Mass.
39. November 13, 1844, Abby Kelley Foster Papers, American Antiquarian Society, Worcester, Mass.
40. *Ibid.,* December 19, 1844.
41. *Ibid.,* February 2, 1845.
42. April 11, 1843.

CHAPTER XIV *Antislavery Evangelists*

1. March 11, 1845, Abby Kelley Foster Papers, Worcester Historical Society.
2. March 12, 1845, Abby Kelley Foster Papers, American Antiquarian Society, Worcester, Mass.
3. November 3, 1845, Abby Kelley Foster Papers, Worcester Historical Society.
4. *Liberty Bell* (Boston, 1845), pp. 207–208.
5. 1845, Abby Kelley Foster Papers, Worcester Historical Society.
6. February 18, 1846, Maria Weston Chapman Letters, Boston Public Library.
7. *Ibid.,* September 21, 1846.
8. Alice Stone Blackwell, *Lucy Stone* (Boston, 1930), pp. 38–39.
9. March 25, 1846, Abby Kelley Foster Papers, American Antiquarian Society, Worcester, Mass.

10. *Ibid.,* February 2 and 7, 1847.
11. *Ibid.,* August 18, 1847.
12. *Ibid.,* September 9, 1847.
13. *Ibid.,* September 28, 1847.
14. Elinor Rice Hays, *Morning Star* (New York, 1961), p. 66.
15. *Ibid.,* pp. 72.
16. Alice Stone Blackwell, *Lucy Stone* (Boston, 1930), p. 90.
17. 1850, Abby Kelley Foster Papers, American Antiquarian Society, Worcester, Mass.
18. *Ibid.,* April 15, 1850.
19. *Ibid.,* August 11, 1850.
20. *Ibid.,* August 11, 1850.
21. *Ibid.,* September 11, 1850.
22. Yuri Suhl, *Ernestine Rose* (New York, 1959), p. 112.

CHAPTER XV *New Recruits*

1. March 11, 1851, Abby Kelley Foster Papers, American Antiquarian Society, Worcester, Mass.
2. John White Chadwick, *A Life for Liberty* (New York, 1899), p. 114.
3. Alice Stone Blackwell, *Lucy Stone* (Boston, 1930), p. 104.
4. E. C. Stanton and S. B. Anthony, *History of Woman Suffrage,* III, 335.
5. Elinor Rice Hays, *Morning Star* (New York, 1961), p. 111.
6. Alice Stone Blackwell, *Lucy Stone* (Boston, 1930), p. 109.
7. John White Chadwick, *A Life for Liberty* (New York, 1899), pp. 60–65.
8. Charles E. Stowe, *The Life of Harriet Beecher Stowe* (Boston, 1891), pp. 87–93.
9. Catherine Gilbertson, *Harriet Beecher Stowe* (New York, 1937), p. 138.
10. Gilbert H. Barnes, *The Antislavery Impulse* (New York, 1933), p. 231.
11. Forest Wilson, *Crusader in Crinoline* (New York, 1941), pp. 259–260.

12. W. P. and F. J. Garrison, *William Lloyd Garrison* (New York, 1885–1889), III, 362.
13. *Ibid.*, p. 360.
14. *Ibid.*, p. 363.
15. Catherine Gilbertson, *Harriet Beecher Stowe* (New York, 1937), p. 166.
16. Forrest Wilson, *Crusader in Crinoline* (New York, 1941), p. 283.
17. Catherine Gilbertson, *Harriet Beecher Stowe* (New York, 1937), pp. 166–167.
18. W. P. and F. J. Garrison, *William Lloyd Garrison* (New York, 1885–1889), III, 396.
19. Forrest Wilson, *Crusader in Crinoline* (New York, 1941), p. 402.
20. *Ibid.*, p. 409.
21. Catherine Gilbertson, *Harriet Beecher Stowe* (New York, 1937), p. 179.
22. November 4, 1856, Abby Kelley Foster Papers, American Antiquarian Society, Worcester, Mass.
23. Forrest Wilson, *Crusader in Crinoline* (New York, 1941), p. 190.

CHAPTER XVI *Awakening the North*

1. W. P. and F. J. Garrison, *William Lloyd Garrison* (New York, 1885–1889), III, 393.
2. Otelia Cromwell, *Lucretia Mott* (Cambridge, Mass., 1958), p. 161.
3. W. P. and F. J. Garrison, *William Lloyd Garrison* (New York, 1885–1889), III, 411.
4. *Liberator*, July 7, 1854.
5. *Ibid.*
6. *Ibid.*, June 5, 1854.
7. September 27, 1855, Abby Kelley Foster Papers, American Antiquarian Society, Worcester, Mass.

8. May 31, 1855, Abby Kelley Foster Papers, Worcester Historical Society.
9. *Ibid.,* August 8, 1855.
10. Elinor Rice Hays, *Morning Star* (New York, 1961), p. 131.
11. Homer C. Hackett and A. M. Schlesinger, *Land of the Free* (New York, 1944), p. 291.
12. Benjamin P. Thomas, *Theodore Weld* (Brunswick, N.J., 1950), p. 236. Sarah Grimké and Angelina and Theodore Weld had moved in 1852 to Raritan, New Jersey, where Marcus Spring, a wealthy abolitionist had established a community, Raritan Union, in which Theodore Weld established a coeducational boarding school, Eagleswood, with Angelina and Sarah as assistant teachers. When the Union disbanded in 1856, Weld continued his school. Among its students were the sons of James A. Birney, Henry B. Stanton, and Gerrit Smith.
13. Milton Meltzer, *Tongue of Flame* (New York, 1965), pp. 126–128.
14. Ida Husted Harper, *The Life and Work of Susan B. Anthony* (Indianapolis, 1899), I, 148.
15. Susan B. Anthony Papers, Library of Congress.
16. April 20, 1857, Abby Kelley Foster Papers, American Antiquarian Society, Worcester, Mass.
17. Ida Husted Harper, *The Life and Work of Susan B. Anthony,* I, 154.
18. *Liberator,* May 22, 1858.
19. November 21, 1857, *National Antislavery Standard.*
20. July 16, 1857, Abby Kelley Foster Papers, Worcester Historical Society.
21. *Ibid.,* May 19. 1857.
22. W. P. and F. J. Garrison, *William Lloyd Garrison* (New York, 1885–1889), III, 432–433.
23. August 7, 1858, Abby Kelley Foster Papers, American Antiquarian Society, Worcester, Mass.
24. John L. Thomas, *The Liberator* (Boston, 1963), p. 395.

25. December 14, 1858, Abby Kelley Foster Papers, American Antiquarian Society, Worcester, Mass.
26. *Liberator,* June 3, 1859.
27. June 21, 1859, Abby Kelley Foster Papers, American Antiquarian Society, Worcester, Mass.
28. John L. Thomas, *The Liberator* (Boston, 1963), p. 390.
29. August 22, 1859, Abby Kelley Foster Papers, American Antiquarian Society, Worcester, Mass.
30. *Ibid.,* July 25, 1859.
31. *Ibid.,* June 21, 1859.

CHAPTER XVII *Days of Decision*

1. Charles and Mary Beard, *The Rise of American Civilization* (New York, 1927), II, 9.
2. H. C. Hockett and A. M. Schlesinger, *Land of the Free* (New York, 1944), p. 297.
3. *Liberator,* June 1, 1859.
4. December 15, 1955. Garrison Papers, Boston Public Library.
5. W. P. and F. J. Garrison, *William Lloyd Garrison* (New York, 1885–1889), III, 488.
6. *Ibid.,* p. 486.
7. Milton Meltzer, *Tongue of Flame* (New York, 1963), pp. 141–144.
8. Russel B. Nye, *William Lloyd Garrison* (Boston, 1955), p. 167.
9. Alma Lutz, *Susan B. Anthony* (Boston, 1959), pp. 65–66.
10. Otelia Cromwell, *Lucretia Mott* (Cambridge, Mass., 1958), p. 169.
11. Elinor Rice Hays, *Morning Star* (New York, 1961), p. 167.
12. Susan B. Anthony Papers, Library of Congress.
13. November, 1860, Garrison Papers, Boston Public Library.
14. John White Chadwick, *A Life for Liberty* (New York, 1899), p. 177.
15. Lorenzo Sears, *Wendell Phillips* (New York, 1909), p. 81.

16. Carl Sandburg, *Abraham Lincoln, The War Years* (New York, 1939), I, 125.
17. W. P. and F. J. Garrison, *William Lloyd Garrison* (New York, 1885–1889), IV, 30.
18. September 10, 1861, Child-Whittier Correspondence, Library of Congress.
19. James M. McPherson, *The Struggle for Equality* (Princeton, N.J., 1964), p. 89.
20. January 21, 1862, Child-Whittier Correspondence, Library of Congress.
21. Susan B. Anthony Papers, Library of Congress.
22. James M. McPherson, *The Struggle for Equality* (Princeton, N.J., 1964), p. 97.
23. *Ibid.*, p. 116.
24. E. C. Stanton and S. B. Anthony, *History of Woman Suffrage* (New York, 1882), II, 877.
25. *Ibid.*, II, 57.
26. *Ibid.*, II, 60.
27. *Ibid.*
28. *Ibid.*, II, 78.
29. *Proceedings, American Antislavery Society, Third Decade Meeting* (New York, 1864), p. 74.

CHAPTER XVIII *Looking Toward the Future*

1. *Proceedings, American Antislavery Society, Third Decade Meeting* (New York, 1864), p. 3.
2. *Ibid.*, p. 66.
3. *Ibid.*, pp. 67–68.
4. *Ibid.*, pp. 73–74.
5. *Ibid.*, p. 83.
6. *Ibid.*, pp. 72–73.
7. Milton Meltzer, *Tongue of Flame* (New York, 1965), p. 171.
8. Alma Lutz, *Susan B. Anthony* (Boston, 1959), p. 113.
9. John Albree (ed.), *Whittier Correspondence from the Oak-knoll Collections* (Salem, Mass., 1911), p. 158.

BIBLIOGRAPHY

MANUSCRIPT COLLECTIONS

American Antiquarian Society, Worcester, Mass.
  Abby Kelley Foster Papers
Arthur and Elizabeth Schlesinger Library, Radcliffe College, Cambridge, Mass.
  Lydia Maria Child Papers
  Alice Gray Loring Papers
  Mary Grew Diary, 1840
Boston Public Library, Manuscript Division
  Maria Weston Chapman Papers
  Lydia Maria Child Papers
  William Lloyd Garrison Papers
  Samuel J. May Papers
  Quincy-Webb Letters
  Weston Papers
Clements Library, Ann Arbor, Michigan
  Angelina Grimké Weld Papers
  Sarah Grimké Papers
  Theodore Weld Papers
Columbia University Library, New York
  Sydney Howard Gay Papers
Connecticut College Library, New London, Conn.
  Prudence Crandall Papers
Cornell University Library, Ithaca, New York
  Lydia Maria Child Papers
  Samuel J. May Papers
  Gerrit Smith Papers
Huntington Library, San Marino, California
  Susan B. Anthony Papers
Library of Congress, Manuscript Division, Washington, D.C.

Susan B. Anthony Papers
Elizabeth Cady Stanton Papers
Suffrage Archives (Edna M. Stantial)
Child-Whittier Correspondence
Michigan Historical Collections, University of Michigan, Ann Arbor, Mich.
Roy D. Chapin Papers
Chandler Papers
Benjamin Lundy Letters
Smith College Library, Northampton, Mass., Sophia Smith Collection
Garrison Family Papers
Syracuse University Library, Syracuse, New York
Angelina and Sarah Grimké Letters
Samuel J. May Letters
Lucretia Mott Letters
Lucy Stone Letters
Worcester Historical Society, Worcester, Mass.
Abby Kelley Foster Papers
Vassar College Library, Poughkeepsie, New York
Elizabeth Cady Stanton Papers

NEWSPAPERS AND MAGAZINES

Antislavery Bugle, New Lisbon and Salem, Ohio
Bulletin of Friends Historical Association, Haverford, Pa.
Boston *Transcript*
The Casket, Philadelphia
The Emancipator, New York
Genius of Universal Emancipation, Washington, D.C.
The Liberator, Boston, Mass.
The National Antislavery Standard, New York
New England Quarterly, Brunswick, Maine
New York *Tribune*

Bibliography

General Reference Works

Adams, Alice Dana. *The Neglected Period of Antislavery in America, 1808–1831*. Boston, Ginn & Co., 1908.

Albree, John, Editor. *Whittier Correspondence from the Oak Knoll Collections, 1830–1892*. Salem, Mass., 1911.

American Antislavery Society Annual Reports. New York, 1834–1861.

American Antislavery Society, Proceedings of Its Third Decade, Dec. 3, and 4th, 1863. New York, American Antislavery Society, 1864.

American Antislavery Society, Seventh Annual Report with the Proceedings of the Anniversary Meeting held in the City of New York. American Antislavery Society, 1840.

Antislavery Almanac. Boston, Mass. Webster & Southard, 1836.

Antislavery Convention, Assembled at Philadelphia, Dec. 4, 5, 6, 1833, Proceedings of. New York, Dorr and Butterfield, 1833.

Antislavery Convention of American Women, Held in Philadelphia, Proceedings of. New York, William S. Dorr, 1837.

Antislavery Convention of American Women, Held in Philadelphia, Proceedings of. Philadelphia, Merrihew & Grew, 1838.

Antislavery Convention of American Women, Proceedings of. Philadelphia, Merrihew and Thompson, 1839.

Antislavery Convention of American Women. Report of by a Delegate. Boston, Isaac Knapp, 1838.

Aves, Thomas. *Case of the Slave-Child, Med*. Report of Arguments of Counsel, and of the Opinion of the Court in the Case of Commonwealth vs. Aves. Tried and Determined in the Supreme Judicial Court of Massachusetts. Boston, I. Knapp, 1836.

Baer, Helene G. *The Heart Is Like Heaven, The Life of Lydia Maria Child*. Philadelphia, University of Pennsylvania Press, 1964.

Barnes, Gilbert H. *The Antislavery Impulse*. New York, D. Appleton-Century, 1933.

Barnes, Gilbert H. and Dumond, Dwight L., Editors. *Letters of Theodore Dwight Weld, Angelina Grimké Weld and Sarah Grimké, 1822–1844*. New York, D. Appleton-Century, 1934.

Bartlett, Irving H. *Wendell Phillips, Brahmin Radical*. Boston, Beacon Press, 1961.

Beard, Charles A. and Mary. *Rise of American Civilization*. 2 vol. New York, The Macmillan Co., 1927.

Beecher, Catherine E. *An Essay on Slavery and Abolitionism with Reference to the Duty of American Females*. Boston, Perkins and Marvin, 1837.

Billington, Ray Allen, Editor. *The Journal of Charlotte Forten*. New York, Dryden Press, 1953.

Bennett, Whitman. *Whittier, Bard of Freedom*. Chapel Hill, University of North Carolina Press, 1941.

Birney, William. *James G. Birney and His Times*. New York, D. Appleton-Century, 1890.

Birney, Catherine H. *The Grimké Sisters, Sarah and Angelina Grimké*. Boston, Lee and Sheperd. 1885.

Blackwell, Alice Stone. *Lucy Stone*. Boston, Little Brown & Co., 1930.

Brink, Carol. *Harps in the Wind, The Story of the Singing Hutchinsons*. New York, The Macmillan Company, 1947.

Buckmaster, Henrietta. *Let My People Go*. New York, Harper & Brothers, 1941.

Centennial History of the Town of Millbury. Millbury, Mass., 1915.

Chadwick, John White. *A Life for Liberty, Antislavery and Other Letters of Sallie Holley*. New York, G. P. Putnam's Sons, 1899.

——— *William Ellery Channing*. Boston, Houghton Mifflin Co., 1903.

Chandler, Elizabeth Margaret. *Essays, Philanthropic and Moral, Principally Relating to the Abortion of Slavery in America*. Philadelphia, L. Howell, 1836.

——— *The Poetical Works of Elizabeth Margaret Chandler with a Memoir of Her Life and Character by Benjamin Lundy.* Philadelphia, Lemuel Howell, 1836.

Chapman, John Jay. *Memoirs and Milestones.* New York, Moffat, Yard & Co., 1915.

——— *William Lloyd Garrison.* New York, Moffat, Yard & Co., 1913.

Chapman, Maria Weston, Editor. *Liberty Bell.* Boston, 1843, 1845, 1846, 1848.

——— *Right and Wrong in Massachusetts.* Boston, Report of Boston Female Antislavery Society, 1835, 1836, 1837, 1839.

——— *Songs of the Free and Hymns of Christian Freedom.* Boston, Isaac Knapp, 1836.

——— *Ten Years of Experience.* Boston, Oliver Johnson, 1842.

Channing, William Ellery. *Slavery.* Boston, Munroe & Co., 1836.

Child, Alfred Thurston, Jr. *Prudence Crandall and the Canterbury Experiment.* Swarthmore, Pa. Bulletin of Friends Historical Association, 1933.

Child, Lydia Maria. *An Appeal in Favor of That Class of Americans Called Africans.* Boston, Allen and Ticknor, 1833.

——— *Antislavery Catechism.* Newburyport, Charles Whipple, 1836.

——— *Correspondence between Lydia Maria Child and Gov. Wise and Mrs. Mason of Virginia.* Boston, American Antislavery Society, 1860.

——— *The Evils of Slavery and the Cure of Slavery.* Newburyport, Charles Whipple, 1836.

——— *Isaac Hopper, A True Life.* Boston, Houghton Mifflin Co., 1883.

——— *Letters from New York.* 2 vol. New York, Charles S. Francis & Co., 1843, 1846.

——— Letters of Lydia Maria Child. Boston, Houghton Mifflin Co., 1883.

——— *The Oasis.* Boston, Benjamin Bacon, 1834.

——— *The Patriarchal Institution.* New York, American Antislavery Society, 1860.

——— *The Right Way, the Safe Way*. New York, 1860.

Clarke, James Freeman. *Antislavery Days*. New York, Lovell & Co., 1883.

Coombs, Zelotes W. *Stephen Symonds and Abby Kelley Foster*. Worcester Historical Society Publication, April 1934.

Crandall, Prudence. *Report of the Trial of, Before the County Court for Windham County, Charging Her With Teaching Colored Persons Not Inhabitants of This State*. Brooklyn, Conn., Unionist Press, 1833.

Report of the Arguments of Counsel in the Case of Prudence Crandall Before Court of Errors, Brooklyn, Conn. Boston, Garrison & Knapp, 1834.

Cromwell, Otelia. *Lucretia Mott*. Cambridge, Mass., Harvard University Press, 1958.

Debate at the Lane Seminary. Boston, Garrison & Knapp, 1834.

Dillon, Morton L. *Elizabeth Chandler and the Spread of Antislavery Sentiment in Michigan*. In *Michigan History*. Vol. 39, No. 4, Dec. 1955.

Douglass, Frederick. *My Bondage and My Freedom*. New York, Miller, Orton & Mulligan, 1855.

——— *Narrative of the Life of Frederick Douglass As American Slave*. Boston, Antislavery Office, 1843.

——— *The Life and Times of Frederick Douglass*. Hartford, Conn., Park Publishing Co., 1881.

Drake, Thomas E. *Quakers and Slavery in America*. New Haven, Conn., Yale University Press, 1950.

Duberman, Martin. *The Antislavery Vanguard*. Princeton, N.J., Princeton University Press, 1963.

Dumond, Dwight Lowell. *Antislavery, The Crusade for Freedom in America*. Ann Arbor, Michigan. University of Michigan Press, 1961.

——— *A Bibliography of Antislavery in America*. Ann Arbor, Michigan. University of Michigan Press, 1961.

Earle, Thomas. *The Life, Travels and Opinions of Benjamin Lundy*. Philadelphia, William D. Parrish, 1847.

Eminent Women of the Age. Hartford, Conn., S. M. Betts & Company, 1869.

Fladeland, Betty. *James Gillespie Birney, Slaveholder to Abolitionist*. Ithaca, New York, Cornell University Press, 1955.

Fauwcett, Dame Millicent. *Some Eminent Women of Our Time*. London, Macmillan Co.

Filler, Louis. *The Crusade Against Slavery, 1830–1860*. New York, Harper & Brothers, 1960.

Foster, Stephen S. *The Brotherhood of Thieves; or A True Picture of the American Church and Slavery*. New London, Conn., W. Bolles, 1843.

Franklin, John Hope. *The Emancipation Proclamation*. Garden City, New York, Doubleday & Company, Inc., 1963.

Foner, Philip S. *The Life and Writings of Frederick Douglass*. New York International Publishers, 1950.

Furnas, J. C. *The Road to Harper's Ferry*. New York, Wm. Sloane Associates, 1959.

Garrison, Wendell Phillips. *Connecticut in the Middle Ages*. In *Century Magazine*, New York, Vol. XXX, No. 5. Sept. 1885.

Garrison, Wendell P. and Francis J. *William Lloyd Garrison*. 4 vol. New York, The Century Company, 1885–1889.

Garrison, William Lloyd. *Helen Eliza Garrison, A Memorial*. Cambridge, Riverside Press, 1876.

Gilbertson, Catherine. *Harriet Beecher Stowe*. New York, D. Appleton-Century Company, 1937.

Gill, John. *Tide Without Turning, Elijah P. Lovejoy and Freedom of the Press*. Boston, Starr King Press, 1958.

Grimké, Angelina E. *An Appeal to the Christian Women of the South*. New York, American Antislavery Society, 1836.

——— *An Appeal to the Women of the Nominally Free States*. Boston, Isaac Knapp, 1838.

——— *Letters to Catherine E. Beecher*. Boston, Isaac Knapp, 1838.

Grimké, Sarah M. *An Epistle to the Clergy of the Southern States*. New York, 1836.

——— *Letters on the Equality of the Sexes and the Condition of Women.* Boston, Isaac Knapp, 1838.

Hallowell, Anna Davis. *James and Lucretia Mott, Life and Letters.* Boston, Houghton Mifflin and Company, 1884.

Hare, Lloyd M. *Lucretia Mott.* New York, American Historical Society, 1937.

Harlow, Ralph V. *Gerrit Smith, Philanthropist and Reformer.* New York, Henry Holt and Company, 1939.

Harveson, Mae Elizabeth. *Catherine Esther Beecher, Pioneer Educator.* Philadelphia, 1932.

Harper, Ida Husted, *The Life and Work of Susan B. Anthony.* Vol. 1–2, Indianapolis, Bowen-Merrill Company, 1899, Hollenbeck Press, 1908.

Haviland, Laura S. *A Woman's Life Work.* Grand Rapids, Mich., S. B. Shaw, 1881.

Hays, Elinor Rice. *Morning Star, A Biography of Lucy Stone.* New York, Harcourt, Brace and World, Inc., 1961.

Heyrick, Mrs. Elizabeth. *A Brief Sketch of the Life of.* Leicester, England, 1862.

Higginson, Mary Thacher, Editor. *Letters and Journals of Thomas Wentworth Higginson.* Boston, Houghton Mifflin Company, 1921.

——— *Contemporaries.* Boston, Houghton Mifflin Company, 1899.

——— *Cheerful Yesterdays.* Boston, Houghton Mifflin Company, 1898.

History of Weymouth, Massachusetts. 4 vol. Boston, Weymouth Historical Society, 1923.

Hackett, Homer C. and Schlesinger, Arthur M. *Land of the Free.* New York, The Macmillan Co., 1944.

James, Janet Wilson. *The Early Antislavery Propaganda. Bulletin of the Boston Public Library.* Nov.–Dec. 1944, February 1945.

Johnson, Oliver. *William Lloyd Garrison and His Times.* Boston,

B. R. Russell & Co., 1879.

Kimball, John C. *Connecticut Canterbury Tale, Its Heroine, Prudence Crandall, and Its Moral for Today*. Hartford, Conn., 1889.

Korngold, Ralph. *Two Friends of Man*. Boston, Little Brown & Co., 1950.

Lader, Lawrence. *The Bold Brahmins, New England's War against Slavery*. New York, E. P. Dutton, 1961.

Larned, Ellen D. *History of Windham County, Connecticut*. 2 vol. Worcester, 1874.

Lincoln, William. *History of Worcester, Massachusetts*. Worcester, 1862.

Lovell, Malcolm R., Editor. *Two Quaker Sisters*. New York, Liveright Publishing Corporation, 1937.

Lowell, James Russell. *Fables for Critics*. Boston, 1891.

Lundy, Benjamin, Editor. *The Poetical Works of Elizabeth Margaret Chandler With a Memoir of Her Life and Character*. Philadelphia, Lemuel Howell, 1836.

Lutz, Alma. *Created Equal, A Biography of Elizabeth Cady Stanton*. New York, John Day, 1940.

——— *Susan B. Anthony*. Boston, Beacon Press, 1959.

Macy, Jesse. *The Antislavery Crusade*. New Haven, Conn., Yale University Press, 1919.

Martineau, Harriet. *Autobiography*. 3 vol. London, Smith, Elder & Co., 1877.

——— *Society in America*. 2 vol. New York, Saunders and Otley, 1837.

——— *The Martyr Age in the United States*. Reprinted from the *London and Westminster Review*. Boston, 1839.

——— *Retrospect of Western Travel*. London, Smith, Elder & Co., 1887.

——— *Views on Slavery and Emancipation*. Reprinted from *Society in America*. New York, 1837.

May, Samuel J. *Letters to Andrew Judson, Esq., and Others in Canterbury, Remonstrating with Them on Their Unjustifiable Procedures Relative to Miss Crandall and Her School for Colored Females.* Brooklyn, Conn., Advertiser Press, 1883.

——— *Some Recollections of Our Antislavery Conflict.* Boston, Fields, Osgood & Co., 1869.

Merrill, Walter M. *Against the Wind, A Biography of Wm. Lloyd Garrison.* Cambridge, Mass. Harvard University Press, 1963.

Meltzer, Milton. *Tongue of Flame, The Life of Lydia Maria Child.* New York, Thomas Y. Crowell Company, 1965.

Mordell, Albert. *Quaker Militant, John Greenleaf Whittier.* Boston, Houghton Mifflin Company, 1933.

Munsterburg, Margaret. *The Weston Sisters and the "Boston Mob."* Boston Public Library Quarterly, October, 1957, January 1958.

McPherson, James M. *The Struggle for Equality, Abolitionists and the Negro in the Civil War and Reconstruction.* Princeton, N.J., Princeton University Press, 1964.

New England Antislavery Society, First Annual Report, Jan. 9, 1833. Boston, Garrison and Knapp, 1833.

New England Antislavery Society, Second Annual Report. Boston, Garrison & Knapp, 1834.

New England Antislavery Convention, 1837, Proceedings of the Fourth. Boston, Isaac Knapp, 1837.

Newhall, James R. *History of Lynn.* Nichols Press, Lynn, Mass., 1897.

Nye, Russel B. *Fettered Freedom.* East Lansing, Michigan State College Press, 1949.

——— *William Lloyd Garrison.* Boston, Little Brown & Co., 1955.

O'Connor, Lillian. *Pioneer Women Orators.* New York, Columbia University Press, 1954.

Parrington, Vernon L. *Main Currents in American Thought.* 3 vol. New York, Harcourt Brace and Company, 1930.

Pennsylvania Hall, History of, Which Was Destroyed by a Mob, on the 17th of May, 1838. Philadelphia, Merrihew & Gunn, 1838.

Philadelphia Female Antislavery Society, Reports of 1838–1841, 1843–1847.

Phillips, Ann. *A Memorial Sketch.* Boston, 1886.

Phillips, Wendell. *The Constitution, A Proslavery Compact.* New York, American Antislavery Society, 1856.

Pillsbury, Parker. *Acts of the Antislavery Apostles.* Concord, New Hampshire, 1883.

Powell, Aaron M. *Reminiscences.* New York, 1899.

Pugh, Sarah. *Memorial of.* Philadelphia, 1888.

Robinson, William S. *"Warrenton" Pen Portraits.* Boston, Mrs. S. W. Robinson, 1877.

Sandburg, Carl. *Abraham Lincoln, The War Years.* New York, Harcourt, Brace & Co., 1939.

Sears, Lorenzo. *Wendell Phillips, Orator and Agitator.* New York, 1909.

Sherwin, Oscar. *Prophet of Liberty, The Life and Times of Wendell Phillips.* New York, Bookman Associates, 1958.

Siebert, Wilbur H. *Underground Railroad from Slavery to Freedom.* New York, The Macmillan Co., 1899.

Sillen, Samuel. *Women Against Slavery.* New York, Masses & Mainstream, 1955.

Small, Edwin W. and Miriam R. *Prudence Crandall, Champion of Negro Education.* Brunswick, Maine, 1944.

Stacy, George W., Compiler. Antislavery Hymns. Hopedale, Mass., Community Press, 1844.

Stanton, E. C., Anthony, S. B. and Gage, M. J., Editors. *History of Woman Suffrage.* Vols. I and II. New York, Fowler and Wells, 1881, 1882.

Stanton, Henry B. *Remarks of Henry B. Stanton in the Representatives Hall of the House of Representatives of Massachusetts.* Boston, Isaac Knapp, 1837.

Stanton, Theodore and Blatch, Harriet Stanton, Editors. *Elizabeth Cady Stanton as Revealed in Her Letters, Diary, and Reminiscences.* New York, 1922.

Stoddart, Anna M. *Elizabeth Pease Nichol.* New York, E. P. Dutton Co. 1899.

Stowe, Charles Edward. *The Life of Harriet Beecher Stowe.* Boston, Houghton Mifflin Co., 1891.

Stowe, Harriet Beecher. *A Key to Uncle Tom's Cabin, Presenting the Original Facts and Documents Upon Which the Story Is Founded.* Boston, John P. Jewett & Co., 1853.

Stowe, Harriet Beecher, *Uncle Tom's Cabin.* Boston, J. P. Jewett & Co., 1852.

Strother, Horatio. *The Underground Railroad in Connecticut.* Middletown, Conn., Wesleyan University Press, 1962.

Suhl, Yuri. *Ernestine Rose.* New York, Reynal & Company, 1959.

Thayer, George B. *Pedal and Path,* Hartford, Conn., 1888.

Thomas, Allen Clapp. *The Attitudes of the Society of Friends toward Slavery in the Seventeenth and Eighteenth Centuries, Particularly in Relation to Its Own Members.* New York, American Society of Church History, 1897.

Thomas, Benjamin P. *Theodore Weld.* New Brunswick, N.J., Rutgers University Press, 1950.

Thomas, John L. *The Liberator, William Lloyd Garrison.* Boston, Little Brown and Company, 1963.

Tolles, Frederick B., Editor. *Slavery and "The Woman Question," Lucretia Mott's Diary of Her Visit to Great Britain to Attend the World's Antislavery Convention of 1840.* Haverford, Pa., Friends Historical Association, 1952.

Thorp, Margaret Farrand. *Female Persuasion, Six Strong Minded Women.* New Haven, Yale University Press, 1949.

Tyler, Alice F. *Freedom's Ferment.* Minneapolis, University of Minnesota Press, 1944.

Wade, Mason, Editor. *The Writings of Margaret Fuller.* New York, The Viking Press, 1941.

Wagenknecht, Edward. *Harriet Beecher Stowe, The Known and the Unknown*. New York, Oxford University Press, 1965.

Ware, Ethel K. *Lydia Maria Child and Antislavery. Bulletin of the Boston Public Library,* October 1951.

Webb, R. K. *Harriet Martineau*. New York, Columbia University Press, 1960.

Weld, Angelina Grimké. *In Memory of* Boston, George H. Ellis, 1880.

Weld, Theodore. *American Slavery As It Is*. New York, American Antislavery Society, 1839.

Wheatley, Vera. *The Life and Work of Harriet Martineau*. London, Secker & Warburg, 1957.

Whittier, John Greenleaf. *The Antislavery Convention of 1833*. Boston, Directors of the Old South, 1874.

——— *Poems Written During the Progress of the Abolition Question in the United States*. Boston, Isaac Knapp, 1837.

Wilson, Forrest. *Crusader in Crinoline, The Life of Harriet Beecher Stowe*. New York, Lippincott, 1941.

Wolf, Hazel C. *The Martyr Complex in the Abolition Movement*. Madison, Wisconsin. University of Wisconsin Press, 1952.

Worcester Historical Society Publications. New Series. Vol. I, No. 7, April 1934.

Wyman, Lillie Buffum Chace. *American Chivalry*. Boston, W. B. Clarke Company, 1913.

Wyman, Lillie Buffum Chace and Wyman, Arthur Crawford. *Elizabeth Buffum Chace, 1806–1899, Her Life and Environment*. Boston, W. B. Clarke Company, 1914.

Yates, Elizabeth. *Prudence Crandall, Woman of Courage*. New York, Aladdin Books, 1955.

INDEX